Y0-BYV-484

NEVER A BURNT BRIDGE

SYLVIA SUN MINNICK

Foreword by:
Linda Sun Crowder, Ph.D.

SMC Press
Stockton, California

Copyright © 2013 by Sylvia Sun Minnick
All Rights Reserved
No portion or photos may be used without the permission of the author

Cover Design: Cheryl Chang Design
Honolulu, Hawaii
Layout and Formatting: Wellman Chin
Published by: SMC Press
Stockton, California
2nd Printing - 2014

Library of Congress Control No: 2013909884

ISBN No: 978-0615-82748-3
0615827489

This book is dedicated to

Richard S. Minnick
And
Ethel Chew Chang

My late husband, Richard Minnick, had asked that I write about my life. One day about a decade ago I was in Auntie E's living room spending a rare quiet time with her. She mentioned that it was time to write as most of the people have passed. She meant my parents and her generation. I took that not as permission but an encouragement to fulfill an enormous promise to capture her family as well as mine.

In periods of introspection I developed a deep love and appreciation for people – people who touched my life, those who lifted me with their words, their comforting ways, their encouragement and, most of all, for standing with me during good as well as tragic times. They were God's gift to me - the living angels and guides. Without them there is no dedication.

ACKNOWLEDGEMENT

It was actually in 2002 when I first picked up the pen and began the first line of this journal. For the past ten years I periodically jotted down remembrances, brief flashes of time, space and people. Before then I felt overwhelmed with obligations, chores, and even wanting fun time. I reasoned writing was a matter of waiting – waiting until I had nothing else better to do. When one phase of activity wound down another began and I was again thrown into more challenges. Now that I have come to the senior stage of life, there is an urgent push to complete this project fearing my years may be limited or senior moments become a permanent disease. It is time to cite pain, pleasure, disappointments, and gratefulness. My intention is not to offend but I opined when pain, be it physical or mental, was inflicted. I smile when I think of the good years, the completion of rewarding projects. Writing has been a wonderful catharsis. It helped release buckets of tears. I've come to realize my life was not wonderful, it could have been better but why dwell on what didn't happen. Contentment comes with focusing on how much worse it could have been.

As I wrote I needed more information, validation, and people to fill in the gaps. To Dr. Chen Liem thank you for the medical information, Gail Kulhavy for filling in the Sesquicentennial years, the late Bill Strobridge for finding information on Bangkok in the early years, Jason Hill recalling moments at Sacred Falls and to Irene Borelli and Wellman Chin for recalling our junior high days.

The manuscript circulated through a dozen literary friends hailing from different walks of life, region, and culture. Some saw me as the semicolon queen; a great many belonged to the "comma club", and a few sprinkled dashes with flair. To Del and Betty McComb, James Shebl, Bob Shellenberger, Don Geiger, John Jung, Claudia Jeung, Nick Bartel, Linda Sun Crowder, cousin Diana Wong and Mike Fitzgerald – thank you, thank you for long and grueling hours deciphering my thoughts and finding better words for my corrupted English. I can still see Shebl's sideline scratches of "don't go there" or "play nice." And I did.

Without a doubt graphics enhance all manuscripts. Nick Bartel created my journey's map. He was truly a layman at work. Allan Low, Claudia Jeung, Roger and Lydia Kim, and Richard Kim searched their cache of photos to fill in my school years as did John Jung's photo of the old Lowell. I am grateful to Shirley Cloyd of Johnson City, Tennessee and Bob Cloyd of Huntsville, Alabama for the picture of the East Tennessee clan. Most importantly my brother, Philip, came to my rescue with my parents' photo albums. These helped rounded out my childhood years.

My husband, Wellman, has been a real partner in this venture. My computer has a mind of its own and the project would have been sent to oblivion if it were not for Wellman's hours upon hours at the computer formatting, checking and correcting for technical consistency.

To you all this, book is as much yours as it is mine. Thank you.

Sylvia M.

TABLE OF CONTENTS

Chapter		Page No.
	Foreword	ix
1	Birth, War, and Abandonment	1
2	Suns in Manila	12
3	A Bangkok Palace	26
4	A California Legacy	38
5	Powell Street Living	52
6	Silver and Gold	68
7	Moving On	87
8	Dreams and Realities	93
9	On My Own	108
10	Warmth in an Old House	118
11	A Period of Grieving	132
12	The Many Roads of *Samfow*	146
13	Community Activism	156
14	The Power of Politics	165
15	Footprints	185
16	A Mother's Day Tragedy	203
17	A Door Closes	218
	Epilogue	227
	Appendices	231

FOREWORD

Many Chinese women have written books about their lives. Some express what it means to be Chinese living in different cultures or historical contexts—Maxine Hong Kingston and Amy Tan come to mind; others reveal personal struggles with hyphenated identities (Gish Jen, et al); and many more hauntingly recall enduring suffering and deprivation to not only emerge from it but to eventually bear descendants (Cheng Nien, Jung Chang, et al). They are all women's stories of survival and of finding personal significance as females of Chinese descent. So what is special about this Chinese + female equation?

To begin, traditional Chinese culture is Confucian—a social philosophy that asserts that a harmonious society is one with a hierarchy of authority headed by males who are to be obeyed by subordinate males and females. In a Confucian ordered society, "a woman first obeys her father, then her husband, and then her son." It is a highly structured patriarchal society—a man's world where males have the authority and a family's lineage is reckoned through its male descendants. Males are the only ones that matter when it comes to establishing a social identity of significance.

Sylvia Sun's memoirs testify to what it meant to be yet the *third* unwanted daughter of Confucian oriented parents who valued sons; and who as members of the Chinese diplomatic corps, led lives demanding duty and protocol. Both from 'good' prominent families, the Suns were attractive, sophisticated and well-educated—the 'beautiful people' of their day. Yet their prestigious positions, glamorous public personas and respectable backgrounds contrasted sharply with their brutish mistreatment of their youngest daughter—only their youngest daughter. The two older girls were treated well and enjoyed a more normal family life indulged by their parents. Sylvia alone was the object of her father's wrathful resentments which went unopposed by her dutifully passive mother. Indifferent, dismissive and often physically abusive, these mystifyingly aberrant parents defined who Sylvia would become—someone very unique.

It was in 1941, the middle of World War II, that Sylvia Sun was born in Malaysia when the Japanese invaded this British protectorate.

During this turbulent period of world history, Sylvia was saved by family friends—good people who risked their own welfare to care for her when her own parents essentially abandoned her to her fate. While their decision seems appalling (would they have done the same if she had been a boy?), it instated a strong sense of 'fate' in Sylvia given that she was not expected to survive let alone thrive. Yet perhaps the bizarre tragedies that befell her were fate's payback for having survived, and the price to be paid for having thrived to achieve outstanding accomplishments with periods of personal happiness.

Each culture has its own discourse of fate and systematic methods of prophecy, whether they be astrological calculations, or the use of tarot cards, bones, faces or palms for fortune telling. The Chinese not only assign a zodiac animal symbol for the year of one's year of birth, they also assign one of the Chinese elements (fire, wood, metal, earth and water) to the four critical times of birth: the hour, day, month and year. Together, these eight factors ("*ba tze*") of time and element explain why we are the way we are (temperament, personality), and what will befall us (fortunate or unlucky in love, money, success, etc.). Today, modern minds factor in the biological and social influences that construct our identity and destiny. But do the 'nature and nurture' arguments conflict with that of our *ba tze* or alter it?

If you are a person who is a product of East and West, all of the above determine who you are. In Sylvia's case, she inherited her intellect, short stature and beauty from her ancestral genes; and arguably, her outgoing personality and plucky character were crafted from coping with fearful circumstances along with receiving the nurture of loving, positive role models. From this upbringing of extremes grew a feisty, outspoken person of initiative, intense drive and devotion to duty coupled with humor, compassion, and an accommodating social flair. Sylvia's respect for the inevitability of fate and how she interprets it derives from her Chinese culture as well as from the cross-cultural fortune tellers she frequented, and has been uncannily validated by the events that have occurred to her and her family. As such, fate and fortune remain genuine concerns for her.

Was it my fate that I met Sylvia? It was certainly due to her initiative that I got to know her. Learning about my anthropological research on Chinese mortuary practices in San Francisco Chinatown, she contacted me and we met for lunch in Honolulu while I was there on a business trip. This was in the 1990s when I was a flight attendant flying the Los Angeles-Honolulu route while working on my Ph.D. at the University of Hawai'i's Manoa campus. Death rituals fascinate many people but for the Chinese it has bad luck associations and Sylvia was curious as to why a Chinese person would study it in conjunction with Chinese American identity. Since she had grown up in San Francisco Chinatown, Sylvia was interested in which people we might know in which people we might know in common, what funeral traditions we had observed and could compare, and in sharing anecdotes about America's first and oldest Chinatown.

As soon as I met Sylvia, I liked her. She is an upbeat, positive go-getter; a people-person who laughs easily, which amazed me as I learned about the hardships and tragedies of her life. How could anyone endure the heartbreaks she had and still be so life affirming and happy-go-lucky? I quickly developed a profound respect for her—there was definitely more to this diminutive woman than meets the eye! Her life lessons gave me a perspective as to the possibilities that can arise from given disadvantages, the strength that can emerge from pain, inequity and despair, the courage to love deeply in a healthy way, and to still be excited about life. We laughed and chatted animatedly as we shared stories of our lives, our love of history and food, and what it meant to be a Chinese American woman today—all this over lobster with black bean and garlic sauce, which became our trademark order at subsequent luncheons. I think she liked me when I suggested having lobster for lunch (more typically a dinner item for a Chinese meal), and when she expressed surprise, I quipped, "why not?"

A topic that we still revisit is Sylvia's father and why he reacted to her the way he did. Was it a matter of 'saving face' because she survived when she wasn't expected to? Was it because she was a disappointment as a third daughter? It is a mystery that prompts a cultural anthropologist to search for comparisons rooted in culture. One similar life story comes to mind that in many ways parallels

Sylvia's—that of Adeline Yen Mah's (the author of *Fallen Leaves* and *Chinese Cinderella*). Both were the youngest daughter of prominent, wealthy Chinese families, both were subjected to cruelty and disdain, both were raised in Asia but came to America where they pursued professional careers, both had failed first marriages but successful second ones, both continually sought their parents' approval, and both dutifully took care of their aging parents.

But despite some obvious differences (for one, Sylvia did not have a step-mother), a single cultural feature stands out that may explain why both were deemed unworthy and mistreated: the Chinese concept of fate. Both of the girls' births were associated with bad luck—Adeline's birth resulted in the death of her mother, and Sylvia's birth was timed with the Japanese invasion of Malaysia that forced her family to separate and flee. Add the 'girl' component to these unlucky birth events and the stamp of misfortune was imprinted indelibly on these youngest daughters.

Fate and female: two compelling factors that can determine the outcome of a Confucian Chinese family! Since Sylvia and Adeline were born only a few years apart (1941 and 1937 respectively), their families, modern, educated and Westernized with a position in society, shared similarities typical of that pre-World War II era: cosmopolitan & sophisticated yet maintaining key traditional Chinese values. In their families, the father was the unquestioned patriarch, sons were considered "big happiness" while daughters were "small happiness;" "saving face" was crucial, and fate as part of the conventional wisdom was not to be tempted or ignored.

That these two "small happiness" harbingers of ill-fate flourished instead of flagged during their childhoods may have fueled their parents' anger and resentment towards them as symbols of defiance towards their (the parents') attempts to thwart bad luck by beating it/them down. As the girls came into their own as accomplished adults, perhaps their parents' fear of them as bad luck faded and was replaced by guilt or reluctant acceptance—this is not certain, but some of their actions later in life seem to reflect this.

In addition to providing a lens through which to gain insight into a distinguished Chinese family and the personal journey of its unwanted daughter, this memoir enriches our understanding of the diversity of those who participated in the Chinese American saga.

While many Chinese American lives have been drawn from the harsh and bitter experiences of their immigrant ancestors, others have emerged from early immigrant successes. Like Sylvia's ancestors who were prominent scholars and professionals in China and whose descendants quickly became successful businessmen as first generation immigrants in America, their narratives are a departure that augments those of the majority of Chinese immigrants.

The Asian American literature is now rich with the histories and contributions of the impoverished 19th c. Chinese immigrants whose hard labor developed the infrastructure of the American West while suffering racist victimization. While this body of literature has filled the long neglected gap in American history, yet to be fully examined are those first generation immigrants who ventured abroad already established or who rapidly became financial successes. These include the merchant princes who organized the transport of the nineteenth century Chinese immigrants and who formed and led the family clan associations which structured American Chinatowns, and the entrepreneurs who early on started canneries, shoe factories and dollar stores, among others. They facilitated the acculturation of their countrymen by providing them with assistance, jobs, and liaisons with the larger society, and became models of the American dream. These success stories, like those of Sylvia's family, serve to provide a rare glimpse into a relatively little known area of Chinese American history and contributes another dimension to it.

As she was searching to find a suitable title for this book, I asked Sylvia what image she thought best described her. "Bridge" quickly came to her mind. "Bridge" has a personal meaning to her, being that it defines who she is. Committed to never burning bridges with anyone (even with her parents), she firmly believes that maintaining ties has been a key to her survival. It has certainly been an element of her success both professionally and personally. Rightfully, it is a point of pride with her. Everyone she has encountered has become a part of her; and to burn any bridge would diminish the life she has crafted for herself.

In herself, Sylvia also sees a bridging of East and West, of the World War II past to the Al Qaeda terrorism of the present, of the old folk wisdom of using bitter melon to prevent malaria to the cyber technology of using twitter to communicate. Journeying with Sylvia through her memoirs with her as a bridge, the past is not lost to us.

Rather, the past continues to be a working force in the present, to be woven later into the complexity of a future that will probably apply technology to transform ancient knowledge into user-friendly products (bitter melon extract in a pill for malaria?), and that generates multicultural, hyphenated identities and practices.

Sylvia's memoirs are a reminder that we are all complex beings with multiple identities and the power to heal ourselves while making a difference to others. Most importantly, like her, we are all bridges for transitioning our life's knowledge and experiences as a lasting legacy.

Linda Sun Crowder, Ph.D.

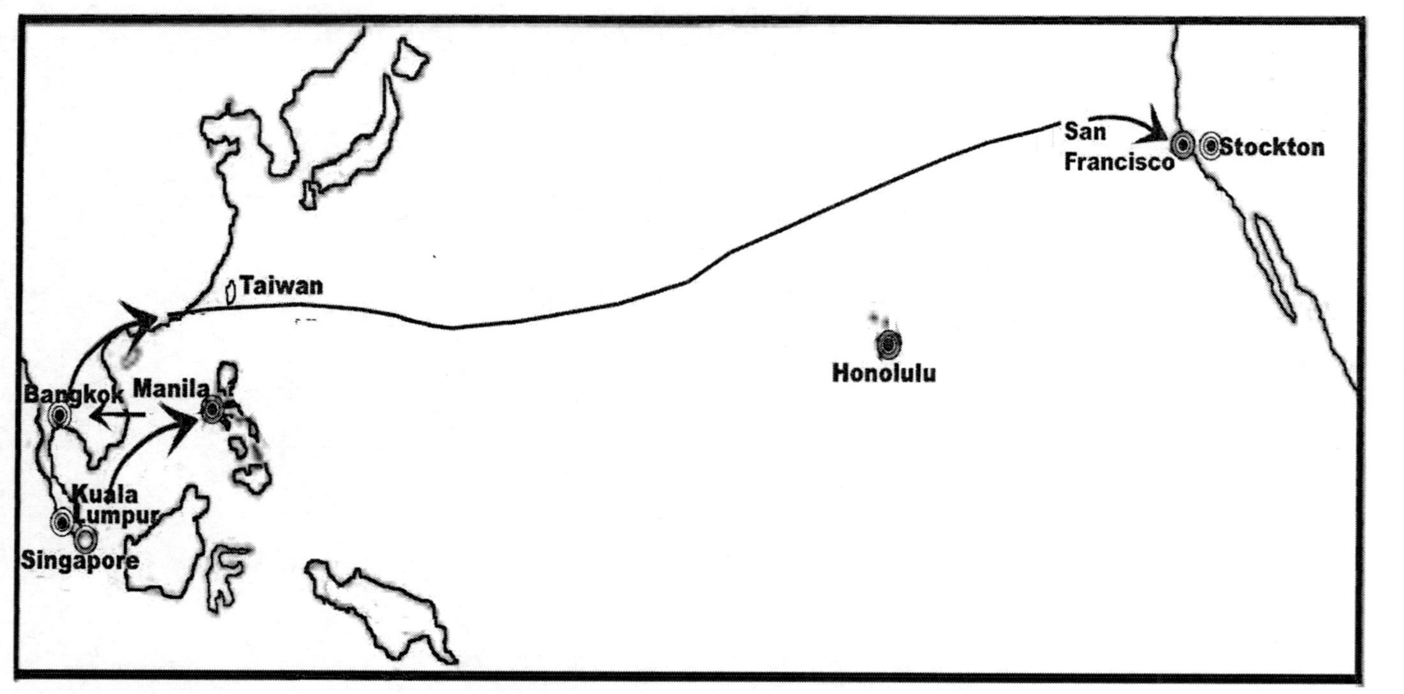
San Francisco
Stockton
Taiwan
Honolulu
Bangkok
Manila
Kuala Lumpur
Singapore

Chapter 1

Birth, War and Abandonment

According to the Chinese calendar I was born on the first day of the fourth month in the year of the Golden Serpent. In the western calendar it was April 26, 1941. My entrance was less than meaningful considering the traumatic events in the world at that time with Hitler and his anti-Semitic army settling in Poland and goose-stepping into Czechoslovakia. That was on the far side of the globe. Closer to home the Japanese Imperial Army had already slaughtered thousands of people in Nanking, Shanghai and other parts of China as they moved southward preparing to launch further conquests into Southeast Asia. Talk about one jittery world, no wonder my being a girl was less than propitious - particularly since I was the THIRD female born to a young aspiring Chinese diplomat and his wife. They already had two daughters, the youngest barely 13 months old when I appeared on the scene. I am sure everything would have been different were I a boy. In Chinese society the male is very important; he carries on the family name. What is a girl but a person who has to be clothed and fed until she is married, then her obligation is no longer to her parents but to that of her husband's.

Nevertheless, I was born at home between 9AM and 11AM at No. 9 Freeman Lane (the street was renamed Jalan U Thant), Kuala Lumpur, Malaya. My parents registered my birth at the Selangor Police Station three weeks later. My early life circumstances suggest that I was born cursed. And I carried this inner sadness for three decades, all along collecting evidence to bear out my intuition.

My father was assigned as the Vice Consul to the Chinese Consulate at Kuala Lumpur, capitol of The Federated Malaya States in the middle of the Malay Peninsula. Politically, the country was divided into three divisions: the Strait Settlements consisting of Singapore, Malacca and Penang; the Federated Malaya States consisting of Selangor, Perak, Pahang and Negri Sembilan, and the Unfederated Malay States consisting of Johore, Trengganu, Kelantan, Perlis and Kedah.

Kuala Lumpur was clean, dotted with mosques, government buildings and parks. The entire population of the city was 140,000 of which 120,000 were Chinese. In the Federated Malay States, there were one million Chinese. If one was to count the total Chinese in the entire country (including Singapore), that population numbered two and a half million.

Franklin D. Roosevelt declared December 7, 1941 "a date that would live in infamy." How right he was, but he was only speaking about the Japanese attack on Pearl Harbor. He was not referring to their simultaneous bombing of Hong Kong, Burma and Singapore and a raid at Kota Batu, an important airfield at the northeastern tip of the Malay Peninsula. The following excerpts from my father's memoirs: *Recollection of a Floating Life* recalls in greater details the immediacy of the situation:

The British authorities, caught by surprise, had attempted to suppress the news. No information was disclosed then, and even when the war was in progress very little information was available.

As the Japanese invasion began, the headquarters at Singapore issued daily communiqués in very short and terse terms. These communiqués told no tale. According to them, the situation at the front was satisfactory. At times they mentioned that the British forces made some strategic retreats, or made some withdrawals according to pre-arranged plans.

On the third day of the war, December 10, 1941; we heard that BBC announcement from London saying: "the Admiralty announced with regret that HMS the Prince of Wales and the Repulse had been sunk." The British fleet was ordered by Admiral Thomas Philip to intercept the Japanese fleet in the Gulf of Siam. As they were not protected by the air force, Japanese aircraft mercilessly bombed them. Admiral Philip went down with his flagship.

The sinking of these ships was a vital blow to the British Navy. They lost the supremacy of the sea….

We were living in a rented house on Freeman Road…We dug a hole in the front yard six feet deep and three feet wide. During the air raids, everybody in the house crowded into the grave-like hole – the five of us together with ayahs (maids) syce (driver) and kebun (gardener). We kept our ears glued to the radio for news and waiting for things to happen…We called a meeting of the Chinese leaders in Kuala Lumpur and told them to do three things: (1) the elder leaders to leave immediately to avoid being persecuted or made use of as puppets by the Japanese; (2) able-bodied Chinese to organize to protect the community and when necessary to participate in future guerrilla warfare; and (3) the rest to go into the mountains with their family bringing as much provisions as they could gather. [1]

Life was in chaos; refuge is the key to survival. My parents decided that mother and the two older girls were to leave immediately for San Francisco, to mother's homeland and her family. On Christmas Eve, 1941, my mother and two older sisters left by rail from Kuala Lumpur to Singapore. They, then, sailed on the British ship *SS Orion* routed through Australia then to Panama, transshipped on a banana boat to New Orleans, and on a train to San Francisco. Father said he needed to check on his own family in China.

1941- 9 Freeman Lane, Kuala Lumpur
May Lan Sun with Patricia, Gloria and Sylvia

But, what about me? At age seven months, I was entrusted to the care of Dr. Kim Lan Soo, the neighbor lady who delivered me. Almost immediately, Dr. Soo fled with me into the mountains some forty miles from Kuala Lumpur. However, she was not to remain as my guardian for the rest of the war.

There were no pre-arrangements, no financial agreement made with Dr. Soo for my care; was I a cast off? Dad would reason in his memoirs that he intended to come back and pick me up after visiting his mother in Chunking but the Japanese had cut the lines. It is difficult to imagine a diplomat deciding to risk life and limb to tote a baby out of a war zone when he was used to having ayahs change and feed his children. In later years when his own mother-in-law (my maternal grandma) berated him for leaving a female child behind, he claimed if I survived they would find me after the war and if I had died, I was too young to know the difference. In later years Grandma related father's responses and all I did was shake my head in disbelief. Obviously, I survived. Yet, it was because of father's response that I believed my survival had a purpose. I needed to seek out that purpose and to prove me worthy of living.

The evidence of my abandonment becomes more enshrouded when in the late 1960s mother gave me a cancelled but unused U.S. passport issued in my name. American Consul General K. S. Patton at the U.S. Singapore Office issued the document on December 26, 1941. Mother's signature appears on a chubby photo of me on my stomach at age seven months, one foot ten inches tall. She kept this passport in her possession for two decades and apparently took it with her when she departed for America.

Father joined mother in San Francisco shortly after his visit to China. The family first lived in Grandma Chew's apartment building and later moved to a flat on Clay Street near Powell Street. Decades later while glancing through some of my parents photo albums I found pictures of me taken with Mr. & Mrs. Tang. The pictures had the markings of a Penang studio. In one I looked about five years old, in a dress and sporting a big bow clipped to my short cropped Dutch Bob. No smile just posing besides a wicker stand. There was seriousness to my demeanor. I do remember that light blue, eyelet dress. The Tangs were a handsome couple in their early thirties. While I cannot remember their first names, I do recall they were childless and took me in for a short period.

These pictures are extremely important. For one, it confirmed that my parents did try to locate me by contacting friends and the Red Cross. Secondly, the imprint of the Penang Studio proved that I relocated to several cities during the war years.

Early Fears and Survivor Techniques

What are the earliest memories? Maybe at age 3 or 4? My recollections come in spurts. I know that I had been with masses of people running away when bombs drop. Along with many, I was a refugee and had moved up and down the Malay Peninsula. Guerillas helped those who fled into the highlands; in the cities, there were families who shared their home with other refugees. There is evidence that I had lived for a time in Singapore and Penang. I remember living with one family unit or another, for example with the Tangs.

Certain things continue to trigger fear in me even to this day. One of these is rapid movement below my feet; I still can envision making big leaps from car to car on a fast-moving train with the gravel and tracks speeding by below. I imaged my legs being cut off if I misstepped. The coupler connection wobbled so much it could not even serve as a temporary step. I get this same feeling on escalators, although now I blame it on my trifocals.

Mr & Mrs. Tang

Another fear is hearing the roar of airplanes and the whining sound when planes dived. I could only reason that there would be a blast and earth-shaking tremors at any moment. The barrel of a rifle, however frightening, was a common sight in my younger years. Somehow I learned to react quickly on command. When told to run, I would do so quickly – where? I didn't know and didn't care. I learned to duck and to hide. This rudimental thought of running away and hiding was implanted so deep in my mind that in later years I did it several more times. It was a personal mechanism to survive or at least to leave intolerable situations.

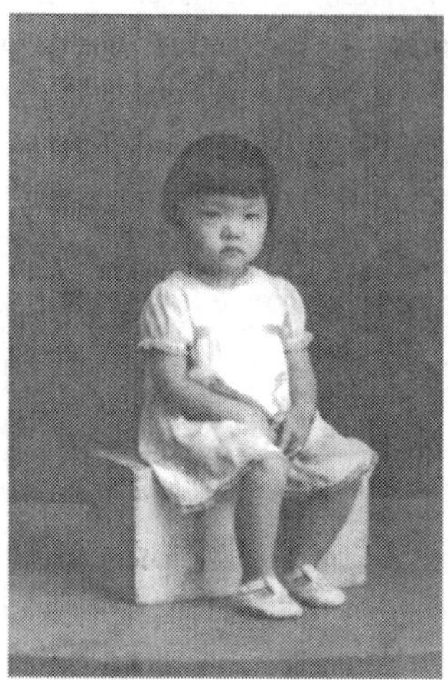

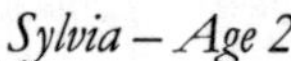

Sylvia – Age 2

Sylvia – Age 5

One time I vaguely recall walking somewhere holding on to a woman's hand and we saw some Japanese soldiers approaching. Next thing I knew she screamed, "Run" and then I heard her shrieking for help. I ran to a niche, shut my eyes, covered my ears, and screamed. I also learned to be suspicious of strangers, particularly when their eyes moved as if they are trailing some passer-by. I feared Japanese soldiers, those wearing khaki uniforms and carrying rifles. I could even identify who were Japanese and Chinese in civilian clothing. While about the same height and size, the Japanese appeared stockier and their facial features looked ruddier. Chinese men seemed leaner and their clothes loose fitting.

I don't know when I started to speak, but it seemed that I have always spoken English and Cantonese. English because Kuala Lumpur and the entire Malay country were under British rule; and therefore, by birthright, I was a British citizen. The majority of the Chinese living in Kuala Lumpur spoke Cantonese. I don't attribute any of my spoken languages to my parents even though my mother's ancestors are from the Toishan area of the Guangdong (Canton) province and my father was from Chekiang Province.

Was it a passion or was it to survive – but how I loved to eat. Squatting was a very comfortable position and eating with my hands, scooping up coconut rice, swishing it from the palm into the tips of my fingers in a cone-shape just before popping it into my mouth was glorious. Large banana leaves make great platters for holding food. Eating anything that requires the use of the hand is heaven, chopsticks may be a close second and the fork-knife combination puts great distance between the hand and the mouth. It is correct to say that I ate at the lower end of the food chain as in animal organs such as stomach lining, duck feet, and even snails. I was very appreciative of what I had. I still love that type of food. Spices, particularly those that pique the nose while startling the taste buds into submission such as curry and chili pepper, are now some of my cooking staples. The fruit of the tropics outclass that of the common apple and orange. Mangoes, custard apple, papaya, mangosteen, rombutan, and the heavenly-smelling Durian, fruit of the kings, have flavors beyond compare. Milk came from goats although it was not a steady diet. There were no cows and beef was an unknown commodity. However, early deprivation of proper nutrition, meat and, particularly the lack of vitamins and minerals caused me to have severe health problems by the time the war was over.

Considered quite sickly, I became accustomed to Chinese and folk medicine. One time a group of us were by the beach and I was told to go into the water for salt water had healing properties. It seemed I drank gallons of salt water during that visit hoping my insides would benefit. It was also during that occasion that jellyfish were in season; they looked so pretty swimming around that I wanted to capture one. But, even sea animals have their own way of defending themselves, I was stung so badly that the long red welt itched and burned for days. The sight of water is still pleasing to the eyes but getting into it is another thing. Insects love some people. They love me. As a folkway to relieve one- self from mosquito bites, I learned to used my fingernails and make a deep indentation into the bite forming an “x”. The idea was not to break the skin but segregated the bite into small sections and that seemed to stop the itch. Another remedy was to smear soap directly on the bite, somehow sealing it.

On this topic of health, I developed malaria as did many others during the war. American soldiers had the benefit of quinine pills, but for us natives, we resorted to eating bitter melon in Chinese cooking. Bitter melon grew all year round and I still crave this vegetable today. Unfortunately I cannot donate blood because of the particular strain of malaria in my system.

Families and Lifestyles

How much can a child remember? Dr. Soo was no longer my guardian, nor could I recall her face. However, from time to time other people's faces, insides of houses, locations, and colors flash across my mind, some more clear than others. Still vivid in my mind was a large, two-story, yellow house. Upstairs in the middle of what seemed like a drawing room, I sat waiting for someone who was taking piano lessons. The house belonged to a man who owned tin and rubber plantations. I was told to behave myself and was given a book with pictures of beautiful butterflies. That was the first time I held a book in my hand.

Perhaps my most vivid memory of early family life was that with the Tangs. They lived in a one-story, row house with a loft that served as their bedroom. There was no kitchen; Mrs. Tang cooked downstairs on an earthen single-pot stove with coal as fuel. We used chamber pots for number one and if one needed to do number two, one took a small pot of water for cleansing and went through the backyard to the open sewer drain. I had to squat with my feet straddling the drain. After finishing I used the pot of water to rinse off. One day a little girl, a bit older than I was also at the drain. She was only a few feet ahead of me. She finished and I had not, but something caught my eye about her deposit. Out of curiosity, as soon as I finished I went to inspect and saw worms squiggling in her mass.

I was in the Tangs' care when I was about four years old. I knew from the onset that my stay was temporary but it created a sense of family life. Mr. Tang smoked incessantly and one year a friend brought him a carton of cigarettes for his birthday. That was the first time I encountered the thought of people having birthdays and I looked forward to having one too even though I did not know when it would occur. Pleasant memories include hearing the soft *bok bok* sound in the late evening. Local food vendors, hawking their product, would strike two sticks together similar to that of a town crier to announce their presence in the neighborhood. A thought of a midnight snack, s*uey yeh*, a hot bowl of rice noodle soup woud be so inviting. The tantalizing aroma filled the senses and eating just before bedtime provided all the thoughts of comfort and safety. The peddler balanced his ware on a shoulder bamboo pole; on one end a basket filled with soup bowls, chopsticks and spoons and on the other a hot steamy pot of soupy rice noodles mixed with vegetables and a few morsels of meat. Never mind that the vendor had no place to wash, much less rinse off the bowls for the next person's use. Sidewalk food vendors' food always appealed to me, health standards be damned.

While living with the Tangs an incident left a permanent scar in the middle of my forehead. From the street level there were three fairly steep steps leading to the porch then the front door. The porch, stretching the width of the house, was not very long. As children would have it, jumping off the porch was an "I dare you" feat. I knew then I should not have done it, but I jumped. Dang, I landed head down, receiving more than a scratch in the middle of my forehead, and the blood poured profusely. I remember lying across both the Tangs' laps in the *sam law* (a three-wheel, peddled bicycle) as they rushed me to the nearest hospital. While Mrs. Tang implored the runner to speed up, I took note of various turns and landmarks as the blood trickled out warmly. Trying to stop the flow proved difficult. I thought about the mess I was making on the seat of the vehicle and her dress. The evening was fairly late and there was no wait when we finally arrived. After being stitched up we went home. I sported a huge bandage across my forehead like being a war wounded, much to the Tangs' embarrassment. The stitches were removed a week later and I was able to discern the state of the hospital. Even in the waiting area there was a decided disinfectant smell in the air. We sat on hardwood, pew-like benches positioned back-to-back. The wait was rather long. I saw others with bandages covering their eyes, head, and other body parts. The injured were all part and parcel of war – and I looked very much like them. The emergency unit treated Japanese soldiers and civilians alike. I bore the scar of my stupid bravado. Today as I look in the mirror at my center scar, in the shape of a star, it reminds me of a horse's markings on its forehead. I was to add another disfigurement on my face some five years later. One unexplained phenomena, this particular forehead scar was an ominous but predictable sign. In Chinese face reading, it indicates childhood problems (before the age of ten) with one's parents.

On another occasion I recalled the death of an elderly woman. As her body lay in state in the parlor, coins covered her visible orifices (eyes and mouth). We all wore white, the Chinese color of mourning in the Far East. The women wore white coarse hoods and their clothing was of the same material. I was more curious than frightened by this experience. Actually, visitors, mourners, commotion, food and continuous company created much excitement into the late evening. We waited for the return of this woman's daughter; who, when she arrived at the gate of the compound, appeared distraught and was stopped at the entrance. Attendants quickly tied a pair of chopsticks to one of her thighs before she moved forward on her hands and knees much like a four-legged animal, crossing the gravel-filled driveway. It must have been painful. Accordingly, this was a filial position and part of the custom of a returning daughter, particularly one who was pregnant. Pregnant women were not allowed to attend funerals and this disguise similar to animal movements was, perhaps, a way to protect the child in the womb from evil spirits lurking around. While the memory of this first funeral stuck with me, it served as a comparison to other Chinese rituals that I saw and participated in as an adult. Fifty years later I became a member of an internet group of international scholars whose focus was Chinese mortuary and funeral customs around the world.

A First Return

In 1984, when I was 43, I returned to Kuala Lumpur with my late husband, Richard. Upon arrival, a kind taxi driver took us for a quick ride around town. We passed the rubber plantation owner's yellow house. It was now dingy-looking, beige color, fenced in, and covered with graffiti. I said I'd been there before and described the inside. I was told it had now become a men's prison. As we rounded another corner, I stated that we were nearing a major train station with the hospital on the hill and a girls' school nearby. I had left 38 years ago, but my sense of direction was still intact. The driver said I was correct about the train station, but the hospital and school no longer existed. Thirty-eight years made a difference. A young Indian guide took Richard and me on another tour that included Tiger Balm Garden. As we walked the grounds I said that the steps and many of the carvings were made of marble. The 27-year old guide insisted they had always been made of plaster-of-Paris. His explanations did not ring true and only through queries with older people was my recall validated.

Jiang Qi Feng, my paternal Grandmother Sun in China, who lived to age 100. Her husband, Sun Hai-huan, a mining engineer lived to only 55 years old.

Leaving Kuala Lumpur

I was six when my whole life changed. I was told that I was going to meet my father in Manila, Philippines. American Consul General Paul R. Josselyn issued me a passport on April 21, 1947 and my transit permit showed a single journey, via Hong Kong, to Manila on June 13, 1947. I was then three feet and three inches tall and still sporting a Dutch boy haircut. Somehow or other I developed two infectious spots on both ankles and was given a salve to rub on them; the small can, about the size of a fifty-cent piece, was tucked into my pocket when I boarded the DC-3. There were no seats on the plane, just netting in the shape of hammocks slung along the sides of the fuselage. The hostess on board, Sally Chew, cared for me during the flight. She was a Filipina married to Tommy Chew, a Chinese American living in San Francisco. Little did I realize that she would witness the most excruciating moment of my life. When she returned to California she told her family about the occasion. Several decades later I met Jimmy Chew, one of her in-laws. He asked if I had any recollection of meeting my father. As I recounted with specifics Jimmy turned to his wife, Ruth, and said: "Yes, this is really Sylvia."

I knew my Malay life and that of World War II was over when we landed in Manila.

Chapter 2

Suns in Manila

It was 1947 and the war was over. I headed for the Philippines to meet my father who arrived there September 30, 1946. He became the First Secretary of the newly-established Chinese Legation on Valenzuela Street in Santa Mesa. A father was a new concept considering I never thought I had one. The plane ride from Singapore to Manila did not seem long. As we touched down at Neilsen Towers, the Manila airport, a tall set of stairs was wheeled to the door and we passengers disembarked. I was the last to leave and Sally Chew walked me down. At the bottom she said gently: "This is your father."

There he was, a slightly built man in a white gabardine suit, jet-black hair, round face, sporting a trimmed, thin moustache. He stood about five foot five. To others he might be described as dapper. I looked at him long and hard and was horrified. The most unforgivable thought came to mind and popped out of my mouth. I said rather loudly, "He looks like a dirty Japanese." Just as quickly, my father slapped me across the face. I turned and ran back up the stairs into the plane and just wanted to fly away. I cried because for years I was taught to flee the Japanese and now my father was or looked very Japanese. For every action there definitely is a reaction. This terrible split-second action set into motion a lifetime of brutal pain. The war might be over, but, I was entering my own living hell.

On my father's part, he had already weathered some subliminal guilt about my abandonment and surprising existence. Much to his embarrassment, he was facing a barely three feet tall, skinny girl with malaria and lice in her hair. While I must have been a disappointment in appearance, I had the audacity to be so outspoken. His background, personal achievements and that of his family lineage were beyond reproach and now to be so insulted.

The Sun Legacy

Father came from a distinguished line. Patrick Pichi Sun was born on May 23, 1908 in the small village of Hsiao Wang Miao, Fenghua Magistrate of Chekiang Province. Father was the oldest of three boys and one girl. Of note President Chiang Kai Shek also came from the Fenghua area, actually only seven miles away in the village of Chi Kuo. Father had a shirt-tail relationship with the Generalissimo in that Chiang's first wife was father's aunt. She was killed when a brick wall fell on top of her. Father's ancestors were originally farmers but they knew that education was the only way to future success.

Sun Chiang (my father's grandfather and my great grandfather) was the first in his family to pass the highest public exam and be declared an Advanced Scholar in 1895; this achievement brought great prestige to the family name and a plaque placed on the front door called attention to this special honor. Great grandfather was given the rank Secretary of Cabinet of Central Government and appointed Prefect of the District of Yuehhsiting in Szechuan Province in 1901. This small county's land was barren and its people illiterate but it did not deter Sun Chiang who set out to establish schools, hire teachers to teach irrigation and agriculture, and even sponsor scholarships for studies about foreign countries. While the populace appreciated his efforts, he made too many enemies higher up and was demoted. In 1911 when the Ching dynasty was overthrown and the Republic of Nationalist China born, great grandfather and his family moved back to Hangzhou where he devoted the rest of his life editing favorite writings of well known authors. He passed away after suffering a stroke in 1933.

It was through Uncle Samuel Sun's writings that I learned of Sun Hai-huan, my grandfather, born in 1876. As part of the young intellectuals, Sun Hai-huan and his colleagues realized that China was basically weak in many ways and the path to salvation was to learn foreign languages, education, and modern techniques. Grandfather Sun studied English, mathematics and sciences in a Japanese school in Beijing. By 1902 he was learning mining and assaying at Osaka Institute of Technology in Japan. After passing the Imperial Exam, he received the degree of Elevated Person in Engineering and was appointed chief of the Penghsien Copper Mine Administration in Szechuan. The plant he built at White Water River in the northern part of Pengshien produced fine quality copper ingots used for minting coinage, pots and pans and bullets. He was later appointed Deputy Director of the Bureau of Mines in Fengtien Province. The mining talent led to inventing a refractory furnace to refine the copper. He named his invention "Sun's Furnace" and published a book with full diagrams and notes that he distributed freely to the science and technological community. The breadth of his knowledge included writing a text book on physiology used in Shanghai and Ningpo schools. During the revolutionary period of competing armies and warlords, grandfather was captured by bandits. His employer, a Mr. Song, paid an enormous amount of ransom money to free grandfather. Grandfather suffered serious setbacks mentally and physically because of this incident. In 1925 Grandfather Sun Hai-huan contracted tuberculosis and passed away at the age of 54.

Grandfather Sun Hai-huan oversaw his children's education insisting they begin their schooling by studying Confucius' Canon of Filial Piety and moving on to Confucian Analects and the Works of Mencius.

Father's other brothers also received an education in Japan and followed in grandfather's footstep in the field of engineering. Father's younger brother, Samuel, continued the family tradition and became an engineer having graduated from Shanghai's St. John's University in Civil Engineering. He became involved in many transportation and construction projects. He edited the Chinese Encyclopedia of Civil Engineering and co-authored Hangzhou stories including one entitled: *Pieces of West Lake.* Unfortunately, Uncle Sam became a victim of the Cultural Revolution and was sent to hard labor in 1967 and released a few years later. It was not until 1984 that he was absolved of having capitalist thinking. In 2010 Uncle Sam passed away peacefully at the age of 92 in Beijing.

Without a doubt, father was well rounded as a Confucian scholar by the time he received his formal education. Initially, he entered Chiao Tung University in Shanghai to study Mechanical Engineering but found his real academic interest in Economics. He transferred to the prestigious Tsing Hua University in Beijing where he graduated in 1929. He took a job with the Nanking Legislative Department and quickly entered the Treasury Department in Shanghai then the Nanking Diplomatic Corps. In 1931 father was appointed to the San Francisco Chinese Consulate on Montgomery Street as a consul secretary. While working he furthered his education enrolling at University of California, Berkeley, then earning his Masters in International Marketing at Stanford University, Palo Alto.

Dealing With Me

A diplomat and Confucian scholar, father naturally found my behavior despicable. He did not know how to handle me; I was not like any person he had ever encountered. The very next day father enrolled me into St. Paul's Convent and College, actually a girls' boarding school located in Quezon City. Part of the complex was destroyed during the war; however, the dormitory was large enough to hold at least 50 beds, lined up in uniform rows with the younger girls being in the first row. A small cabinet for personal belongings separated the beds. My bed, in the first row, was generally the first or second bed. Because of my malaria, I was pretty much in isolation with a white curtain pulled around the bed. To see what the other girls were doing I knelt on the mattress and parted the curtains ever so slightly so that I wouldn't be caught by the nuns. Actually the nuns were very kind. Sister Patrice, the second in command at St. Paul's, was my favorite.

At St. Paul's College & Convent - 1947

The class size was small and I enjoyed learning. I even learned to hem handkerchiefs. I would drool over the sweets on the snack rack.

One needed spending money to purchase a candy bar or a small bag of sweets. There was no extra allowance in the money father paid for my board. Although I never became a Catholic, St. Paul's gave me an appreciation of the dedication one commits to faith and a sense of purpose. Even when I was 14, I thought that life in a nunnery would not be so bad. It seemed safe to live one's life in a cloistered environment and pray for the souls in the outside world. Sister Patrice had an administrative presence and also personal warmth. She was one of two women who made the greatest impression in my young life, the other being my maternal grandmother. In later years Sister Patrice became the head of the order in Rome.

People Who Cared

On very rare occasions Father brought me to his residence. However, when he did he asked Amparo Wong to look after me. Amparo Wong was a 16 year old Filipina who recently married Peter Wong, a junior counsel at the office. She was from the province and was hired to pour tea for the workers. Peter was smittened by her and did all the paperwork necessary to marry her. In those days marriage between different nationalities, even among Asians, was greatly discouraged. Peter studied very hard and received his college degree while working in the legation. Amparo recalled how they lived above a garage and had one child after another. Eventually with his effort and education, Peter Wong also moved up the diplomatic ladder. Today I am still in touch with Amparo who now lives near Houston. The Wongs had a very exciting and challenging career. Peter served the Nationalist Chinese government in Argentina and then became the Chinese ambassador to Mexico before they retired to Houston. I came to admire Amparo, as her husband's career ascended she developed her own style and grace. One truly did not need to attend finishing school or even get a formal education to stand shoulder to shoulder with world leaders' wives. Quality and dignity come from within. The Wongs had seven children and Amparo tells her brood that they had an older sister long ago – meaning me. She felt I was her family in her early married life. I asked what she remembered about me and without hesitation she said I was nosy and asked lots of questions. I believe she meant that I was always curious.

I seldom saw my father while living at the convent but I became a pseudo-adopted member of the large Tankiang family. Friends of father, the Tankiangs, were quite affluent and lived in a big mansion on Dewey Boulevard (the name was later changed to Roxas Boulevard). Part Chinese and part Filipino; they were members of pre-War high society. As in the Asian tradition, I addressed them all as my "aunties" and "uncles." Betty Tankiang, the oldest of the sisters, was very warm and motherly. She came to the convent every other weekend and packed me off to spend time with her family. Her boudoir had fascinating jars of creams, powders, perfume, and some wonderful cosmetics to try when I was not roaming around the large house. There were always visitors and activities. We would go to the amusement park after dinner and the crowds were thick and bright color lights glowed everywhere.

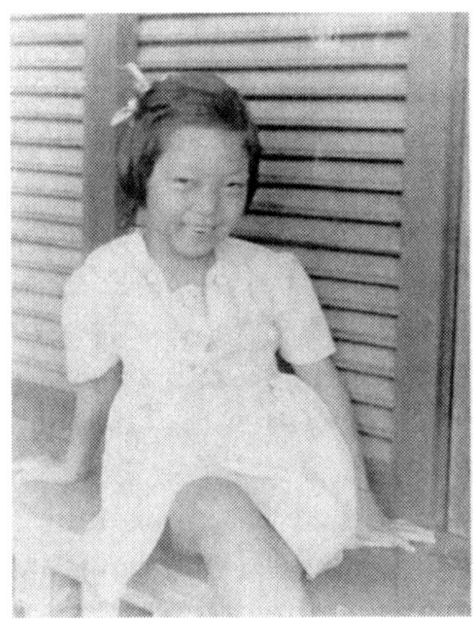

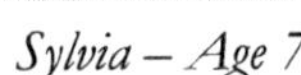

Sylvia – Age 7

Betty Tankiang (white dress)

Auntie Betty enjoyed going to fortunetellers. Her favorite was a Mrs. Ledesma. In a span of forty years, I returned twice to the Philippines and each time Auntie Betty and I traipsed off to Mrs. Ledesma. Betty enjoyed keeping track of my life and thought Mrs. Ledesma very reliable. This clairvoyant proved quite accurate as my life played out. I later sought psychics in other countries while traveling, often comparing their techniques and watching for the similarities or accuracies from one individual to the other. Psychics have their own sense of what is important in life, mostly based on their own priorities, backgrounds, nationalities and perspectives.

Chinese fortune tellers use a published date book which they consult researching the elements associated with the date, year and time of one's birth. They pair this information with the five elements of wind, water, earth, fire and metal, the twelve animal signs and seasonal charts. Some also look at the hands and do some face reading. On the Chinese calendar I was born in the metal year of the Snake (often described as a golden or silver snake) and my Chinese birthdate is April 1st. I am told it was not an auspicious day. Maybe this might have something to do with my parents' abandonment of me? Or that they considered me an unlucky child, a third girl at that.

Filipino fortune tellers are big in the field of romance. Japanese psychics often size up one's health and physical being. A general reading covers only a small smattering of wealth and health. The elderly and many business people frequently study faces as a guide to measure one's persona. In later years I developed my own interest in face reading. Although a novice I found it interesting to study people's ears, nostrils, forehead and lines around the mouth. Long ears suggest wisdom much like those found in statues of Buddha and, I have found, many judges have long large ears. I can't say the same for all lawyers. Rounded nostrils indicate the person is generous as oppose to slit-shaped nostrils. Deep, uninterrupted lines going across the forehead suggest one's ability to think clearly on complex issues. Faint lines emitting from the creases above the mouth suggest pains in the extremities such as hip problems. I don't tell fortunes but find that vocation interesting.

Time spent with the Tankiangs afforded an opportunity to be absorbed into a semi-Filipino, yet Chinese, environment. I developed an ability to eat *balut* the native embryo-egg on which the feathers of the baby chick were clearly visible. And, of course, my love of *bagoong* (shrimp paste) and *patase* (fish sauce) were favorite seasonings. Hence, the craving of both salty and sweet flavors were well set in my palate. Sprinkling salt or dipping with soy sauce became a ritual while eating mangoes, pineapple and other fruit. The Tankiangs enjoyed music and dancing to Latin rhythms in particular. Father was also a good Latin dancer and even a singer. His favorite song that he sang or played often was *Besame Mucho* (Kiss Me A Lot). Father even sang Chinese opera but I never understood or appreciated this talent in him.

One of my fondest memories of the Tankiangs was Uncle Paquito's wedding. I was a flower girl. It was a magnificent wedding with many beautiful bridesmaids (all the sisters and cousins). My dress was a floor length Chartreuse taffeta. The cathedral was filled to capacity and the ceremony, including High Mass, was long. So very long that I catnapped. The wedding dinner, held at the mansion, had so many round tables it filled up the living room as well as the dining room and foyer.

About twenty years later Auntie Betty came to visit me in Stockton. We went to Disneyland together. Periodically I would hear from her and after Auntie Betty's passing I also lost touch with the entire Tankiang family. But my memories of this warm and wonderful family live on.

Family Dynamics

On February 22, 1948, father and I arrived at the Manila pier bright and early as the *S.S. Contest* docked. He had been anxiously waiting the arrival of his wife and two other daughters. They had been at sea for two months. Their arrival united the family. I was almost seven years old when I first met my mother and two older sisters.

Mother was diminutive, with oval shaped face and a sharp pointed chin (a family characteristic inherited from her mother's side). In essence mother was dainty, very attractive and there was a lilt to her voice. However, I did not sense her to be very demonstrative; she lacked the motherly warmth Auntie Betty possessed. She never embraced me, nor did I ever see her do the same to her other children. Mother, or rather Rose May Lan Chew, was born in Alviso, California in 1912. She was the oldest girl in a family of nine children. Her father was Thomas Foon Chew and her mother, Lee Gum Ching. She went to school in Los Gatos and San Jose and received awards for her excellence in typing. She bragged that among her classmates were two sisters- Olivia De Havilland and Joan Fontaine, both became world renowned in the movie industry.

The courtship of my mother and father is rather legendary. Father, a young Masters' candidate at Stanford and a junior counsel at the time, was standing on the sidewalk in the heart of Dupont Gai (Grant Avenue) as a funeral procession slowly marched by. The band played a mournful dirge and preceded the immediate family who followed the hearse. Mother, in the procession, was driving a Franklin car. He spotted her. She was extremely attractive and, obviously, her ability to drive was rare for a woman in those days. He equated that she must have an independent nature. Quickly he queried who was the deceased and, audaciously crashed the reception dinner following the burial. Father courted her. She saw that he was a promising suitor. They married in 1934 the same year he received his graduate degree in International Marketing.

My oldest sister, Patricia, turned 12 the day they arrived in Manila. She is five years older than I. She was called Dida, a shortened version of Patricia. Di or Dida enjoyed two talents, playing the piano and being a young diarist. Dida brought with her a rag doll named Mary that I thought looked rather dirty. But then it was Dida's and I was not allowed to play with it. For that matter, I don't remember ever having a doll myself.

For the model first child that Patricia was, my second sister, Gloria, was entirely different. Her nickname was Gloco, later shortened to Glo She wore her hair in double braids which the maid plaited daily. She has very fair skin whereas I am as dark as Malays. In comparison she looks very Chinese American and people often wondered if I was Hawaiian, Filipino, Japanese or even Chinese. Gloria was only 13 months older than I and was quite tomboyish. Moreover, she thrived on maintaining that visage for the better part of her life, partly or mostly to gain father's attention. She became the boy that he wanted so badly. My parents even made her a white military uniform, cap and all which she wore mimicking children of servicemen. Glo looked at me most curiously and, I think, was expecting someone who just walked out of the jungles. It might have been that the Tarzan movies were extremely popular at the time. Very quickly I was to understand Glo's rambunctious nature, much to my misfortune.

Life At Fernando Rein

I left St. Paul's Convent when our family moved into No. 7, Fernando Rein Street in Pasay City, a short quiet street. The house seemed large, built fairly high off the ground with a full open-lattice work basement which made into a very nice play area. I quickly found a hiding place in a large tree off the front left corner of the house. On one side of the tree was a hollowed-out area perfect for hiding. One could see the termites having a field day feasting farther into the wood. I stood inside the tree to test out its serviceability and came out covered with termites.

In the house the parents had the front bedroom and we, girls, all slept in the adjoining bedroom. A maid, houseboy, cook and gardener took care of the household chores. Father had already established a reputation of a *bon vivant* and mother's looks and charm captured not only the heart of high society but also the diplomatic corp. She was very photogenic and newspapers found her delightful for they featured her in many articles. She was selected as one of the ten most glamorous women in Manila a year later. My parents, a dashing couple, were socially active; they were literally the toast of the town. My two sisters also gained fame as they participated in a weekly radio program called the *Ave Maria* hour. One could hear over the radio the clarity and innocence in Gloria's voice as she read her script.

I tried very hard to fit into the family but failed miserably. One of the very first punishments I received was when Glo talked me into playing cowboys and Indians. I did not know what she meant until she began to tie me up. At that point I spat and scratched at her. No one was going to tie me up; my survival instinct kicked in. Glo screamed to mother that, "Sylvia spit at me." Mother thought no civilized person spits and I received a spanking. Glo thought up other antics whereby, because of my gullibility and the want to get along, I found myself being victimized. She thought it clever when she talked me into stepping into a trunk, put the lid down and closed the hasp. I couldn't get out; Glo told mother she threw away the key. I didn't think it was funny. When we played Crack the Whip, I was always put at the end of the whip and trying hard to keep up at the unexpected signal to break. I would be hurled into the wall or furniture. I didn't think that was funny, but the others did and they laughed. Many years later my cousin Cherk remembered when he was a child and visiting the family in San Francisco, Glo chased him with a screwdriver and threatened to gouge his eyes out. His recollection only validated my childhood fear of Gloria's intentions.

My relationship with father did not improve when the rest of the family arrived. He was extremely short tempered, perhaps due to the stress of work. Our earlier bad start was still part of the underlying poor relationship between us. Once, I looked at him, not actually glaring; but, clear out of the blue he said, "I don't owe you anything." Catching me short, I immediately retorted, "I didn't ask to be born." Whack! I got it again.

Family portrait in Manila - 1948

Every time father got ready to do something physical or violent, I noticed that he bit his lower lip. One time father locked me in the closet as punishment and he and mother went out for the evening. I didn't mind that because there was no physical pain associated with being locked up, except I really had to pee. The servants were not permitted to let me out, so I conveniently used father's shoe as a commode. When they came home, I really got the physical part of the punishment. Another time I forgot the reason why but we were just getting out of the car and walking on the graveled driveway and he kicked me. I fell, skinned my knees where now I still sport a scar.

One day mother opened a desk drawer in the living room where the telephone rested. She spied a small piece of unwrapped hard candy, half eaten. She asked Glo and me who put it there. We both denied doing so. I swore, even to this day, that I had nothing to do with that candy. At dinner that night, mother made mention of the incident. Dad may have had something else on his mind and did not want to hear mother's ranting. Acting out his frustration, he took his rice bowl and threw it straight at me, with food and all. The round dining table was only five feet in diameter. The bowl shattered in my face and cut my forehead about an inch left of my center scar. I cried, mom couldn't stop the blood, she wanted to take me to the hospital but father wouldn't consider it. She wanted to call the doctor, he yelled, "No!" With cold wet towels and a couple of band-aids pulled tightly across the wound it eventually healed. That was the second of three permanent scars left by my father. The beatings were so frequent I lived in fear of the man. Strangely, mother never lifted a finger to stop him or help me. Even today I remain troubled by mother's passivity.

I attempted my first running away to escape one of the beatings. I thought running away was literally just that. So I ran out of the house down the middle of the street and kept on running until I tired. I even asked for a ride from a *carata* (a horse-pulled wagon) loaded with garbage but was refused. I forget who picked me up and brought me home.

My parents were proud of my sisters and took them to many places but often chose to leave me at home. One reason may have been that I was frequently car sick. Father smoked cigars and the smell coupled with the leather seats and the inability to look out because of my height made traveling miserable. After a while I developed such a low self-esteem that my life seemed to be that of the poor step-sister like Cinderella. How I missed the Tankiang family and even life at the convent.

In 1949, mother became pregnant. On November 30, 1949, at last, there was now someone to carry on the family name, my brother Philip. Father finally got his son. And one could see a change in his personality, he seemed to soften a bit. Regardless, my relationship with him did not improve.

My final memories of Manila and our family life include, of all things, livestock. We had a police dog named Alec, but I didn't like him for he would attack or chase me when given the opportunity. Someone gave mother two turkeys as a gift. She told me to watch over them, as if I was a shepherdess so they would not fly away. It was my first babysitting job and I diligently followed these turkeys around for weeks. I think they later graced our table. When the folks decided to raise chickens they bought some Rhode Island Reds. This type of chicken laid very large brown eggs and the prize was when one was served eggs that had double yolks. The cook fed them, and they kept us fed. I remembered how the cook would grab a chicken, tighten his grip, hold it between his legs, take his knife and, with lightening speed, slit its throat while twisting the head at the same time. I learned the term, *running like a chicken with its head off.* It was not a pleasant sight.

In early Spring of 1950, father was re-assigned. This time it was Counselor to the Embassy of the Republic of China to Thailand and the duties of the Charge d'Affairs in Bangkok. He was definitely moving up the diplomatic ladder. As the rounds of farewell parties for the folks were in full swing, I tried to ask each of the servants if they would take me home with them to the outer province. I did not want to live with my family anymore and thought this was a good opportunity to leave. Of course, they could not and would not. Being simple-minded the thought of being a permanent member of a unit, much less a family unit, never entered my mind. It seemed from past experience in Malaya I went easily from one family or one group to another. Why couldn't it happen here?

Almost everyone looked forward to the new post and the excitement of travelling to a new country. Unfortunately I did not share this feeling. I did not feel anything would change, new country or not.

I was wrong!

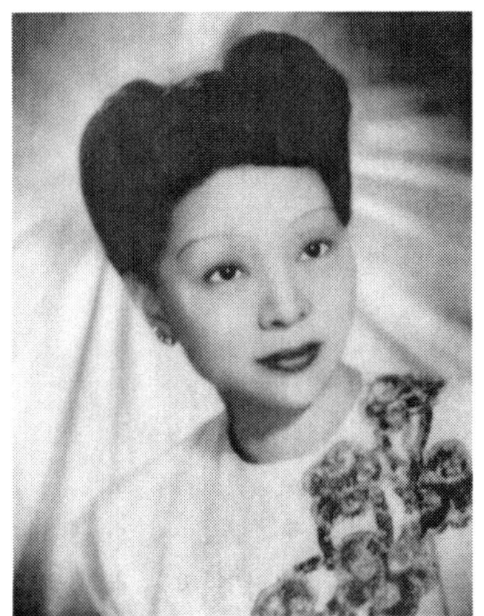

My parents were extremely photogenic and fitted well in the diplomat corps.

These pictures were taken in Manila in 1948

Chapter 3

A Bangkok Palace

The Sun family set sail for Thailand on board the S.*S. La Marseilles.* It took ten days. Actually it would have been shorter but the ship turned around and made a rescue at sea. Traveling was rough and the water choppy. I was so seasick I laid in the bunk throughout the journey and drank only consommé as nourishment. We stayed in Saigon (Ho Chi Ming City) for a few days at the famous Intercontinental Hotel. Once we took a *sam law* (three-wheel tricycle with the man pedaling in front) for some sightseeing. There was nothing too memorable except that there were a few bombed out buildings which had not been repaired or demolished. The driver had the biggest leg muscles I had ever seen. Then it was onward on an Air France airplane to Thailand. We landed in Bangkok on March 3, 1950. Philip was only three months old.

Our first hotel in Bangkok was the Suriwong, not a very nice one but it was owned by a Chinese. Apparently its reputation was a bit questionable. We moved out very shortly to a much nicer one on Raj Damnoen Road. I can't remember the name of the hotel but there was a nearby roundabout with a large victory monument in the center with uplifted wings commemorating one of the Ramas (Thailand's many monarchs). Our arrival coincided with the end of the four-year mourning period for Rama VIII, King Ananda Mahidol. The king had committed suicide with a bullet to his head. No one knew the reason and the prolonged mourning might have been compounded by a lengthy investigation.

My parents, as officials in the diplomatic corps, participated in the foreign delegation aspects of the state funeral and cremation. Father said he perspired profusely in his "tux and tails." A newspaper photograph captured a picture of mother in her chic long, black Chinese *cheongsam* showing her several paces behind father. Observers thought it quaint that she walked behind her husband; but, mother complained that that was not her intent; it was because the slit on her dress was so short that she couldn't take long enough strides to keep up.

Following the funeral ceremonies, the nation prepared for the coronation of Rama IX, King Bhumibol Adulyadej and Queen Mom Rajawongse Sirikit. His majesty King Bhumibol Adulyadej was the late king's brother. Father had a white military uniform made for the occasion, equipped with all the regalia even down to a dress sword. We followed accounts of these spectacular events with great interest when they returned to the hotel. The newspapers' extensive coverage included many photographs. This was history and my parents were participants.

The new monarchs were quite popular with the American press. The king was born in Cambridge, Massachusetts and received his education in Switzerland. Most endearing was that he played the clarinet and loved jazz. Their majesties have continued to warm the hearts of the Thais for decades because of their humanitarian efforts although their countrymen see their role only as a constitutional monarchy. Little did anyone realize that in 1951 Thailand would undergo a coup d'état.

Patrick Sun and Generalissimo Chiang Kai Shek

From the hotel we moved a couple of times to different houses. One was on Chai Yat off of Bankapi, the main road. Chai Yat translates to Seven Soy, a "soy" was a lane or road spinning off the main street. The even numbered soys were on the right side and the odd on the left and as the city grew the numbers of soys extended. Now they number in the hundreds whereas in 1950 there were less than twenty. Bankapi's name later changed to Sukhumvit. The house, with two stories and three bedrooms, was charming. A square pool or pond separated the main house from a smaller single-story guesthouse. It must have been a pool but the water was green and filled with algae. I was fascinated by the aesthetics and layout of that house. Built in the late thirties its windows, trim and stairs were of a rich brown wood with light green walls as the basic interior colors. Just off the living room to the left were two ascending steps and a moon-shaped doorway leading into a small study with a balcony that overlooked the pool.

The neighbors next door hung a large sheet off their downstairs lanai and showed Hollywood movies. All our bedrooms were on the second floor and it was comfortable to sit on the window ledge on warm summer nights and watch the movies on the backside of the sheet. Of course, we saw everything backwards and the sound was muffled. That's how I will always remember Cole Porter's *Day and Night* and Gene Kelley in *American in Paris.*

We stayed in the Chai Yat house for only three or four months, one reason may have been an act of man against nature. The gardener had found some python eggs and removed them. The mother python was quite angry when she went searching for her eggs. My parents' fear of that snake thrashing around was enough reason to vacate the premise.

Living in a Palace

Luckily, a minor prince's palace on Ploenchitr Road became vacant thus allowing the family as well as father's office to be under one roof. It became the official National Chinese Embassy and father was its Charge d'Affaires. A turbaned Indian guard in his kiosk manned the entrance to a long driveway. While he looked very official in his role, I thought it rather ironic for he did not speak Chinese, his English was hard to understand and he did not look like he could protect against intruders.

The palace, rather the residence itself, was two stories tall. Offices for all the business and formal activities were on the ground floor and a grand staircase led upstairs to the living quarters. At the base of the staircase stood a wonderful grandfather clock and its chimes were deep and resonating. There were several sitting areas, large open verandas and a formal dining room. One sitting room opened down to a set of steps leading to a large, natural lake on which there was a wooden rowboat. The setting of the room and steps was very reminiscent of a scene from *The Sound of Music.* The lake fed into the *klong* (a minor tributary of the delta) that flowed along the entire back side of the lot. A row of trees hid the klong from view. Access to the rivulet was possible through a small wooden gate that led to an old, small rickety pier. The river served as the transportation route for vendors paddling their way to market carrying fruit, vegetables, fish and other merchandise. As the water merchants sailed down the waterway to the famous Floating Market, they hawked their wares to interested landowners along the way. I had always wondered why we never bought most of our produce from these people; but, perhaps it was for hygienic reasons.

Upstairs in the embassy there were four bedrooms, several large sitting areas, and a front balcony that was on top of the porte cochere. Father's office was on the right front corner of the building and adjoining that a second and smaller dining room for family use. Off the dining room was an even larger balcony. The size and length of the balcony covered the entire breezeway below which connected all the downstairs' offices. This large balcony easily held one hundred round tables for formal banquets. I loved this particular balcony; it was seldom used, very open and I would play house by climbing under one of the wooden tables or I would run from end to end and not bother anyone. I had to make sure that father was not in his office before I would venture out there. From the dining room there was a small bathroom that adjoined my two sisters' bedroom. Our parents' bedroom was just beyond.

Philip slept in a separate room with his amah and I had a small room way in the far corner of the building. To reach Philip's and my room one entered through a separate sitting area. Frankly, I thought it was wonderful to not only have my own room but to be away from everyone. My humble area also served as a storeroom for it housed two large steamer trunks, several wooden crates and large boxes and an old refrigerator. The motor to the refrigerator was quite loud; but I did not mind. There was a small window but it did not open out. To pass away time I retreated to my room and read. It was about this time that I started copying contents of books thinking that was the skill needed to write books. I did a lot of copying.

When the weather became too hot in my small area because of the lack of ventilation, I slipped into Philip's room. Aside from his crib, the amah slept on a mattress on top of two trunks laid in tandem and there was another set of trunks in similar fashion where I frequently napped.

It was in Philip's room that I witnessed a horrifying sight. There was a small balcony and a tree just beyond. Someone had given the family a baby gibbon; it was almost like a child and loved to stay in that tree. One day I noticed something was wrong with the monkey for it was lying on its back on a big limb but it wasn't moving. Apparently, a snake had killed it and had eaten half of its stomach, my stomach turned. Since then I have never been fond of the documentaries on *Wild Kingdom*.

Low self-esteem continued to plague me and I learned very quickly to stay out of my parents' way as much as possible, especially when they entertained. Dida and Glo, of course, were included in all the functions and even when the family went on excursions. I was continually excluded and recognized as the black sheep of the family. Father's temper was still fierce and he continued to strike me whenever occasions arose.

The family vacationed at Chiang Mai (to the north) or Hwa Heen (the shores to the south). I never accompanied them. Once they left for three days. For whatever wrong I did (which I can't remember), I was locked in the bathroom between the dining room and my sisters' bedroom. Perhaps it may have been my being locked in father's closet in the Philippines and my soiling his shoes that the bathroom was a sure way for punishment and a guarantee that I would not run away. The servants brought food but were not allowed to let me out. The water tank was high above the toilet and one pulled a chain to flush; I had difficulty reaching for the chain while in a sitting position. There was a small window that looked onto the garden. I fantasized that I was a princess imprisoned in a high tower. I did not have any books or toys and I did not want to take a bath for the tub served as my bed. Actually, staying in the bathroom was a tolerable punishment, one without pain.

Living in the embassy was quite different with so many people and activities occurring daily. On June 29, 1951 there was a three-day coup d'état whereby the navy captured Prime Minister Pilbul Songgram. The air force joined the army-police line up; thus, the navy with its erstwhile coup was completely squashed and the prime minister rescued.

During times of civil unrest in a foreign land, ex-patriots sought asylum within their own country's domain. The Chinese were no exception. Countless Chinese took refuge in the embassy and for about three days people slept in the sitting rooms and even in the hallways.

To pass the time away, mahjong tables were set up and I could hear the clicking of the mahjong tiles in the wee hours of the morning. The cook provided food for all, the number escalating as conditions warranted. Mother was afraid that we would run out of food. Father claimed that in the early days of the coup while he was in his office a bullet whizzed by; but that was the only close call the embassy received. However, the Australian Embassy got hit by a naval shell and one of its personnel took some shrapnel in his leg.

Becoming Anglican

Several events affected my life in Bangkok. Father decided that the family should be Christians and he decided the Anglican faith the best. In August of 1951 the entire family was baptized at Christchurch on Sathorn Road. The Reverend Cecil Eagling performed the ceremony with his wife, Ruby as the sponsor and daughter Rosemary as witness. Rosemary gave me a King James bible that day which I still have. In addition, the Eaglings operated a school on the church grounds which Gloria and I attended. Dida took correspondence classes for her high schooling. My teacher, Miss Pamela Pring, was half Thai and half British. At the end of the semester the Eaglings awarded prizes for the best students. I was so proud to receive the book, *WHAT KATY DID* by Susan Coolidge. It still sits on my bookshelf with the faceplate boldly showing my achievement. The last time I saw Miss Pring was in 1978 when she circled the square in Henley-On Thames in England to pick me up and we had a grand reunion. At that time she was raising a family of three children.

Gloria and I went into scouting as an after school activity. The four categories of scouts, according to age and grade, were: Gnome, Sprite, Pixie and Elf. I belonged to the Pixie group. These gradations were similar to that of the American scouting program. I thoroughly enjoyed scouting under the British system.

The Eaglings and I kept in touch through the years. Reverend Eagling died and Mrs. Eagling became a conduit for former students of Christchurch. Richard and I visited with her in Bingley, West Yorkshire. Among her proud possessions was a silverware box displayed in her dining room. The Eaglings received this gift when they left Bangkok in 1951. A silver plaque affixed in the inside lid showed the signatures of the students from the second grade and my name was clearly visible. Daughter Rosemary married the Reverend Bruce Grainger and they have three children and several grandchildren. They are active in the church and also with educational events following in the footsteps of Rosemary's parents.

About the time the Eaglings left Bangkok we transferred to the new International School, serving mostly diplomats' and military children. It was a new school housed in an old wooden building with a large assembly space and classrooms on all three sides, more in a shape of a "U". While the school was quite international it had some uncomfortable incidents when German children would not sit alongside the Jewish children. But for the most part, everyone seemed to get along. Mrs. Mitchell was my teacher and we were under the Calvert System of education. I remember once a girl asked if my blood was truly yellow and would I cut myself to show her. I didn't accommodate her. We did take part in other nations' holidays. More specifically, on July 4, 1951, the whole family went to the American Embassy for the Independence Day Celebration hosted by Ambassador and Mrs. Stanton. It was my first glimpse of an old-fashioned Red, White & Blue July 4th with hot dogs, hamburgers and all the trimmings. They, too, had a lake and gave boat rides to the children. Many of our school friends also attended this festive occasion.

A favorite hangout for the international children was the famous Royal Sports Club. It had a swimming pool, tennis courts, a race track and even offered equestrian lessons. Both sisters were swimmers; I don't know if they ever had lessons. In fact, Gloria was so good that she entered and won the women's division and she was only 14. She excelled in athletics. The only time I remember trying to swim was when Dida said she would teach me and got me down to the deep end of the pool. She was kneeling along side of the pool. She said: "Hold on to the side, stretch out and kick." After a while she thought I was doing well enough that she said, "Let go." I sure did and down I went. Funny, but as I was going down I had the feeling that I was drowning and in those quick moments I realized that I didn't have a will and I had specific thoughts about where my sparse belongings should go. Next thing I knew I blacked out. I woke up poolside stretched out on my stomach and a man was pumping the water out of me. Apparently, when I went down Dida screamed for help. Although she was a good swimmer she decided not to jump in because she was wearing a dress.

While Gloria and Dida had opportunities to make friends and visit with other international children, I played with the gardener's children. There were about five of them, all boys. Mother frowned seeing me frolicking with what she considered urchins. If there were guests about I was prohibited from running around in the garden. Once Gloria convinced me to sneak into the cookhouse, a separate shed behind the main house. We thought of cooking but decided to make candy. We fired up the burner and got hold of a wok. Into the hot pan we dumped lots of sugar and flour. The sugar melted and the flour gave it consistency. It didn't taste bad, but the cook was not pleased when he entered the kitchen. Mother prohibited us from ever returning to the kitchen again.

Freedom

In September 1951 my mother's mother, Grandma Chew and her daughter, Aunt Frances, and son, Uncle Tim came to Bangkok to visit. This vacation coincided with the recent death of her second daughter, Taidy. Her children thought she would get passed her sadness with a change of scenery.

My mother was a spitting image of grandmother. But she did not exude the latter's instant warmth. Grandma said I looked like my mother when she was my age. I steadfastly remembered Grandma was my sole booster during World War II when she berated my father for having abandoned me.

Mother quietly asked if grandma would take me to the United States. Mother told grandma that she feared father would really think about killing me one day. I now suspect that Mom felt she was expressing filial piety to her mother as well as removing me from an untenable situation.

The Sun children with Grandma Chew in Bangkok

The thought of leaving this household was far more exciting than going to America. Glo said the weather in the States was so cold that butter left out would still keep its shape and not melt as it does in Asia. I dreaded the thought of living in cold weather, however the excitement of a new beginning overcame all fears.

I remember distinctly the day I left Bangkok. Just as everyone was getting ready to leave, father called me into his bedroom. He said in a rather matter-of-fact manner, "Where do you think you are going?" And I replied, "To California to live with my grandmother." He then said, "I want to give you something to remember me by." And with those words he hit me so hard I fell against the corner of the large wooden desk in his room. As I picked myself up, he hit me again. By the time I went down to the car I was bleeding from a busted, swollen lip and sported a shiner on my left eye and I chipped my front left tooth when I hit the desk. Both Aunt Frances and Grandma were furious, mother didn't say a word nor did she hug me good bye. Some forty years later I had to have a root canal on that tooth, the dentist surmised it was caused by a severe impact when I was young. I did not mention the incident, I was embarrassed. Yes, father gave me something to remember him by all right. How I hated him for so many years.

As an adult I searched for an explanation for his cruel treatment. I could only conclude that they might have felt a societal "loss of face". Telling family and friends in San Francisco about their escape from Kuala Lumpur included losing a daughter to the ravages of war suggests pain associated with sacrifice. I don't really know what my parents expected when they found me; but, it certainly was the opposite of elations. At that point in 1951 I did not care and looked to begin a new life.

To Hong Kong and Beyond

We flew from Bangkok to Hong Kong and stayed at the Peninsula Hotel in Kowloon for about two weeks. It was a swanky hotel; the lobby was beautiful, thickly carpeted and soft classical music in the background. Rather than using a loud speaker to locate people a bellhop marched through the lobby carrying a placard as a discrete way of finding the individuals. Hong Kong had water rationing but the hotel was not under that restriction. One visiting relative came often and invariably ended taking a bath before she left. Grandma and Aunt Frances took the opportunity to check on some of grandfather's holdings, one of which was a theater. Other days they went shopping looking for boxes of dried shark fin, scallops, Chinese beef jerky, herbs, Chinese folk medicine, oils, balms and even dried pressed duck. Grandma visited with many of her relatives and also went shopping for food products that were difficult to get or were too expensive in San Francisco. She spent a small fortune on herbs. Much to her distress the majority of these items were confiscated as she passed Customs at the port of entry in Honolulu. She never liked Hawaii after that.

Grandma also had an eye for good jade jewelry. Among her purchases were two special items: an apple green jade ring encircled with diamonds looking like a daisy, the other was a bracelet made up of a series of apple green jades separated by diamonds. I believe these two pieces were handed down through Aunt Frances' children.

One day when Grandma was out shopping, I remained in the hotel. There were pigeons roosting on the clay tile roof. I wanted to chase them away because they were making such a mess so I lit some matches, threw them out the window to scare away the bird. It didn't do any good and I almost caused a fire on the roof.

Another day while walking up a hilly part of a native shopping area in Hong Kong, we passed a young mother and child about three years old squatting besides the set of stairs that we were climbing. As Grandma walked ahead, I was visibly struck and thought I saw a bad omen, no matter how innocent. The child, entertaining himself, was

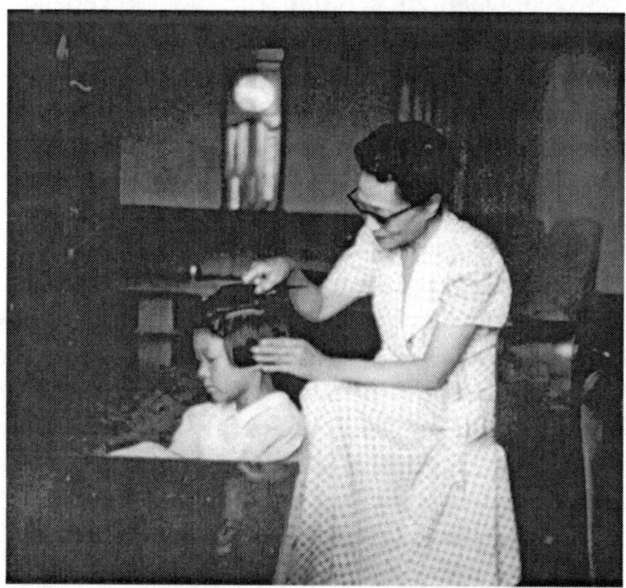

1951 Bangkok – Grandma Chew and Me

playing with the Nationalist Chinese flag and using it to flip muddy water out of a pothole. I had been taught that a Communist Chinese was something horrendously bad and Nationalist Chinese as good. To see the Nationalist flag first being dipped to the ground and secondly having it be used as a toy was appalling. Perhaps this scene was a precursor to the thought of that government's failure followed by the possibility that father might lose his job. I stopped and stared at the woman and told Aunt Frances about the incident, but she thought better of making a scene. She just shrugged it off saying that the people were just ignorant. If she didn't know it by then, Aunt Frances soon learned that I never hesitated to speak my mind.

The flight from Hong Kong to Hawaii was long. The plane was a Pan American double-decker with a huge underbelly. The plane ride was so luxurious compared to my first airplane ride sitting in netting strung along the inside of the plane. This plane had overhead compartments that pulled down and converted into sleeping berths. Poor Aunt Frances gave up hers for me and she slept in the reclining chair. We refueled in Guam and Okinawa before reaching Honolulu. All the while we were in transit in Honolulu Grandma grumbled and cursed the custom inspector under her breath. Today even with larger fuel tanks the flights still feel long without making all those stops

We reached San Francisco on October 12, 1951. Christopher Columbus landed on American soil that very day in 1492; I take great joy in recognizing that he and I celebrated the same anniversary date. The airport terminal was a long, one-story building. After disembarking we saw Aunt Ethel, Grandma's youngest daughter. What a warm and fun-loving person, one can tell from the gleam and a hint of mischief in her eyes. Walking through the terminal was a moment to remember. We passed a cocktail lounge and I was asked if I wanted to see a television; without any encouragement, my aunt pulled me into the doorway as libating customers turned their heads to see who was coming in and there I stood on the threshold watching Del Courtney in his afternoon talk show. The television reception had a lot of static; the unit itself would be comparable to a nineteen incher with curved corners. Nevertheless, it was the first time I saw television and was fascinated. Today I continue to marvel at the wonderful colors that present-day television brings into our living room.

Our arrival to San Francisco included some minor glitches. A Mr. Herzog was in charge of inspecting those entering the country. It was a good thing that Aunt Ethel was with us as the immigration agent queried Grandma about her passport and also mine. We immediately went into detention at the Sansome Street immigration station. Grandma was released rather quickly but I remained. The agents wondered how I was able to obtain a United States passport when I had never been in the United States and was not born here. I was quartered in a small windowless room. It took a while before Aunt Ethel came to get me out. She was working at the Chinese Consulate and knew immigration formalities. Once through immigration I began my Chinese American life.

Chapter 4

A California Legacy

Just as I laid out the early beginnings of my paternal lineage, my maternal side had an equally stellar beginning, however, in California. When people hear of the mid-nineteenth century Chinese Argonauts, they immediately think my ancestors participated in the California Gold Rush or maybe laid rail tracks over the High Sierra. No, my ancestors had more brains than muscles. It is fitting that I lay the blueprint to claim my California heritage. Grandmother's father, Mr. Lee, was the earliest of our pioneers. A native of the Toishan area of Guangdong province, he arrived in 1869 and settled in San Francisco. Great grandfather noticed the Chinese in California exchanged the soft, cotton-paddled slippers for the more practical western leather shoes. The Chinese, however, had to stuff them with newspapers to make them fit. As an entrepreneur, he saw this need and quickly built a shoe factory in the heart of Chinatown, on Washington Street just above Stockton Street. Business was good and great- grandfather Lee's capability provided well for his large family.

Thomas Foon Chew

The most notable in my mother's side of the family was her father, Thomas Foon Chew. He was described as "larger than life." According to many old timers, he was "a man's man." He had a commanding appearance. Pictures of him indicate a rather handsome man standing about five foot eight, square-shaped face, with a high forehead (indicating intelligence), fairly large ears (suggesting wisdom) and a stock of black hair with a hint of white at both temples. It seemed he was more western than traditional Chinese. He never wore the customary Chinese robe one often sees in other people's period family portraits. He dressed mostly in either a western suit or at least wore a vest over his shirt and tie. Rather than a queue he preferred a fedora.

Grandfather, better known as Tom Foon, was born in Loong Kai District of the Guangdong Province in 1887. His father, Yen Chew, migrated to San Francisco and brought along his only child, Tom, age ten, so the youngster could have an opportunity for western schooling. Yen Chew started the Precita Cannery on the corner of Sansome and Broadway Streets just prior to the turn of the twentieth century. The Loong Kai men had a reputation for their astute business acumen and Yen Chew was no exception. The 1906 San Francisco Earthquake destroyed the cannery. Quickly, Tom Foon sought help from one of his best friends, A.P. Giannini from Los Gatos. They had been classmates in their teens.This is the same Amadeo Pietro (Peter) Giannini who founded the Bank of Italy in 1904, later renamed the Bank of America. A.P. had a propensity for helping many fellow immigrants, particularly after the San Francisco disaster. History tells that Giannini set up his bank on the street using two barrels and a plank as a desk from which he generously handed out loans - regardless of ethnicity. Many years later Giannini boasted that every single loan was repaid. This tells also of Tom Foon's integrity.

Birth of Bayside Canneries

Helping his own father recover his business, Tom Foon, at age 20, moved the plant down to the mud-flat borough of Alviso, not far from San Jose, and renamed it Bayside Cannery. He later built another at Mayfield near Palo Alto and, in 1919, a third cannery in the little town of Isleton, on the Sacramento River. The company's tugboat, *Progress*, pulling a train of barges, bridged the waterway from the Sacramento delta to the South Bay and north to the market in San Francisco.

Grandfather's enterprises depended heavily on agriculture. The Tom Foon Ranch consisted of both purchased and leased land in several Northern California counties. The California Alien Land Law of 1913 prohibited non-native born Asians from owning property; but, this did not stop my immigrant grandfather nor other Asians who took to putting title in their children's names. Records show he leased 180 acres in Yuba City to grow peaches, several hundred acres in Dos Palos to plant rice and he planted fruit trees in the Grass

Valley area of Northern California. The Tom Foon fame included the cultivation of asparagus, more specifically that grown on the San Joaquin Delta islands of Andrus and Bouldin Islands. Green asparagus was a known commodity, but Bayside Cannery's tasty white asparagus took more effort to cultivate. This specialized crop catapulted the cannery's name and fame. Daily, stoop laborers packed dirt around the growing stalk to prevent light from turning the plant green. One estimate showed Bayside canned approximately six hundred thousand cases per year, or an estimated three million dollars worth. As in all cannery businesses safety was foremost such as keeping a close watch on pressurized cooking of fruit, especially tomatoes. Furthermore, family legend has it that Bayside Cannery was the first to can fruit cocktail.

After the 1906 earthquake the agricultural area of San Jose burst with entrepreneurism. Tom Foon made agreements with neighboring farms and orchards to buy their harvest. One old-time fruit company, Mariani Fruit Company in the Santa Clara Valley, provided much of the fruit Bayside Cannery needed. Similar to Tom Foon's efforts, Yugoslavian Paul A. Mariani arrived in 1904 and started his company in Cupertino. His farming involved growing various fruit trees and, today, a hundred years later, the four generation company now continues to thrive in the dry fruit business. I am struck by the various immigrant nationalities' ability to form working agreements across ethnic barriers and as each declared "It was done with just a handshake."

Cannery Operations

Bayside Canneries' early workers were relatives, fellow clansmen, and friends. Eventually the crew became multi-ethnic but the supervisors were generally Chinese. One group, the "Chew" boys, although not blood relatives but clansmen, took greater supervisorial responsibilities. Frank, Johnny, and Tommy stayed with the Bay Area canneries while Grandfather sent Jimmy to oversee the building and operation of the cannery in Isleton. Prior to his assignment in Isleton, Jimmy served as a driver and companion for Tom Foon's children. Tommy Chew's wife, Sally, accompanied me on the airplane when I flew from Singapore to the Philippines to meet my father. This is truly a small world.

Tom Foon treated his workers in typical Chinese fashion – he expected them to be diligent and productive, in other words, they worked long and hard. Meals were always provided and, in some cases, as in Isleton, so was lodging. Grandfather went further by lending the workers funds when they ran short or had to send money home. The workers, themselves, contributed to the construction of each individual cannery. Each cannery complex consisted of a series of buildings including warehouses, processing facilities and cottages for the workers. After a day's work and after the evening meal, men employees mixed cement and poured a section of the warehouse wall until the building's completion. One could tell how much was accomplished the night before by the different layer and color of concrete laid. Even the canneries' trucks were expedient. Portable wooden benches bolted onto the truck floor provided transport for workers living in the cities. Upon arrival at the plant the benches were removed and the trucks used for hauling produce and products.

A current picture of the once functioning Bayside Cannery in Alviso, Ca.

Tom Foon also knew when to leave well enough alone. The late Jimmy Chew told of one incident. Mr. Ito, a Japanese farmer in grandfather's employ, was in charge of growing asparagus on nine hundred acres. One day Tom Foon, interested in greater productivity and having read a smattering of agricultural books, thought of a way to increase production and wanted Ito to try his idea. Ito, with patience and wisdom, countered by suggesting that of the large acreage he would set aside 25 acres so that Tom Foon could plant the way he wanted to his heart content. But the rest of the land was to be done under Ito's instructions. Both men agreed. When harvest came, Tom Foon's section was a dismal failure but the company's overall crop was bountiful due to Ito's expertise. Tom Foon never again meddled in Ito's decisions. [2]

Tom Foon's relationship with Ito was close, so much so that Ito forewarned Tom Foon that if he did not change his lifestyle what with continuous work, hard drinking, and smoking he would die in his forties. Ito read "faces" like many other Asians and could foretell one's fortune or in this case his fate. Ito was correct. Grandfather Tom Foon died in 1931 at the age of 42.

A Member of Many Communities

In his short lifetime Grandfather Tom Foon Chew built a financial empire with impressive land holdings. Grandfather believed in giving to his community both in leadership and generosity. He took an active role in providing for the needs of his clansmen through major donations to the Lung Kong Association as well as to the building of the Ning Yeung Chinese Cemetery in Colma, just south of San Francisco. He also invested in a number of Chinese enterprises and stores in Guangdong, Hong Kong and San Francisco's Chinatown including *The Chinese Times*, a local Chinese newspaper, and *Tin Fook*, a jewelry store on Jackson Street. This jewelry store was known to help early Chinese melt their gold and convert it to utensils disguised with soot so the returnee could bring his riches back to China safely and then re-melt it back into the original ore once they reached home. Grandma once told that she made a trip to China in the 1920s on a freighter and she had gold bullion hidden in a false bottom of one of her trunks. Apparently word got out and someone on board made off with the gold during the voyage which Grandma did not discover until she reached her destination.

Grandfather Chew also participated in the greater community; he became a Mason in the San Jose Lodge No. 10 as well as a member of the Scottish Rite and Shrine. Among his wide circle of Caucasian friends was Governor James Rolph, Jr., a former mayor of San Francisco. Grandfather was also quite the family man for he sired nine children although two died in infancy. There were two family abodes, one in San Francisco where the family stayed for prolonged social engagements and the other in Los Gatos, an adobe style house with a large yard for the children. The address was 132 Loma Alto Avenue. However, one of the family's favorite places was a cabin that he owned in South Lake Tahoe near Camp Richardson. Unfortunately, Tom Foon asked his trusted lawyer to purchase the cabin but he did not check the title and the lawyer had put the holding in his own name. At his death when the family went to claim the cabin the lawyer denied any transaction.

Tom Foon's fame was as memorable in death as his life. The story goes that when his first-born, Charlie, got married Tom Foon threw the biggest celebration ever. The festivities included several wedding banquets, each with well over 500 guests including dignitaries and leading businessmen in the State. All these were held over a period of several days. What with excitement, stress, and hangovers, exhaustion followed. It was no wonder after a three-day hiatus Grandfather, always troubled by severe asthma, developed pneumonia and shortly passed away in the O'Conner Sanitarium in San Jose.

The *San Francisco Examiner* announced on February 23, 1931, "The Asparagus King is Dead." And *the San Jose Mercury* 's article noted that his funeral would be delayed until March 8$^{th.}$ However, the same paper reported that the actual funeral took place on May 9th. The lengthy delay was common, for grandfather's death occurred around the Chinese New Year period and funerals generally took place either before or after Chinese New Year but not during. The *Mercury* recorded grandfather's funeral as "the largest funeral ever held in San Francisco's famed Chinatown... and it drew an estimated 25,000 spectators." Grandmother later told me that there were two separate services held in nearby locations because of the numbers of people wanting to pay their respect. One service performed in traditional Chinese style and the other a Masonic funeral. More than 200 San Francisco Masons participated, as well as five ranking Rose Croix officers from the local Scottish Rite, and the San Jose Lodge. Many prominent people including the San

Jose City Manager, the Mayor of San Francisco, the President of the State Chamber of Commerce and many Chinese dignitaries walked in the procession through Chinatown. Testimonials even by those in the twilight of their years held Grandfather Tom Foon in the highest esteem. He touched many in all walks of life.

This giant of a man instilled in his children the belief that they too, without a doubt, could function in both the white world as well as in the Chinese. However, his fame and good deeds became a tremendous pressure and challenge for his children to follow in those same footsteps. It is a pity that none would come close to matching the legacy that this man built.

When Grandfather died his wealth was estimated at $150,000 but after paying the bills and assessing the net worth grandmother was left with $10,000 and an apartment building on Powell Street. The canneries failed to operate as efficiently and profitably. [3]

Plaque honoring Thomas Foon Chew in Alviso, Ca.

Quickly, the business went into receivership. In addition, eldest son Charlie took to gambling and lost some of the family's meager funds, leaving the apartment building as grandma's only asset. Grandma still had to support her six children: Charlie, May Lan (my mother), Lillian (Aunt Taidy), Henry, Frances, Ethel, and Timothy as well as her mother-in-law, Tom Foon's mother who lived with the family well into the late 1940s.

Mrs. Tom Foon Chew, nee Lee Gum Ching

Grandmother's California heritage is much older than grandfather's. Her family was in California at least three decades before Tom Foon's father, Yen Chew, set foot in California. Mrs. Tom Foon Chew, my *Ah Pau* (Chinese for grandmother), was as strong in character as her husband. It was a good match for both derived from the Toishan area, were raised in wealth, and both intelligent and physically attractive. Ah Pau, Lee Gum Ching, was born in 1889 in Oakland. She was one of 16 children of which 10 were natural siblings and the rest adopted into the family. She was the third daughter. Perhaps that may be why she had an instant fondness for me. She said her English name was Jennie Lee. She went to Chinese school for a few short years but was basically self-taught. She believed in reading the Chinese newspaper daily as did her siblings who had a fair knowledge of world and community affairs. Grandma recalled the 1906 earthquake and fled by ferry with her family to Oakland. Grandma married Tom Foon the following year. By 1908 she was seventeen years old, married, and had her first child.

Grandma Chew – Lee Gum Ching

Grandma Chew, often referred to as "Mama Chew" was a beauty. She was diminutive, less than five feet tall. She had a very pleasant oval face that ended with a rather pointed chin which all her children and grandchildren inherited. Her skin was wonderfully smooth – not a wrinkle, even though she was 63 years old when we met. I thought that was old. Not one to spend lavishly on creams and powder she used only Pond's Dry Skin Cream at night and Pond's Vanishing Cream during the day. She shuffled rather than walked because of her bound feet. All her shoes, size two, were specially made in China. They were mostly made of cloth with leather soles and had a very high instep. Even with such infirmity she managed to get around quite well. One hardly noticed another handicap of hers' – she was blind in one eye. She lost that sight due to glaucoma. She always wore Chinese dresses and never trousers. When she went out she was bedecked with jewelry and her full-length mink coat. Ah Pau was not the normal, old-fashion grandmother; she possessed other enduring qualities - smoked Viceroys, drank Scotch, and loved to gamble. This, too, she passed on to her children and even to some of her grandchildren.

The Aunties and Uncles

The story of my arrival in San Francisco and my youth at 1122 Powell Street, the apartment building Tom Foon Chew left for his widow and children, would not be complete without an introduction to the Tom Foon and Lee Gum Ching's children. These aunties and uncles, a collective set of surrogate parents, influenced my upbringing greatly.

Charlie

Ah Pau's first born, Charlie, had all the privileges and opportunity afforded him. He went to Bellarmine College in San Jose and followed in his father's footstep to become a Mason and a Shriner. His life was not exactly stellar in that he got involved with gambling and was a member of the Suey Sing Tong, a less-than-violent organization with cooks as major members. His well celebrated marriage did not last long. When I met him he had moved to Seattle, Washington. In the late 1950s, for some unknown reason, he had to quickly leave Seattle. Rumor had it that there was a price on his head, perhaps over a gambling issue. Charlie married his second wife, Auntie King, in 1955, settled in Reno, Nevada and opened the Cosmo Club, a gambling house near the railroad tracks in the downtown area. I adored his stepchildren, Hwa-Di and Cherky. Their names seemed a bit strange, but they were a lot of fun and my age. I remember spending some time with them one summer at Lake Tahoe. To this day we remain close. Uncle Charlie's own daughter by his first marriage, Joan, was ten years older than I, and was a wonderful person. She always had it together. Upbeat, slim, talented, she married Martin Taam, eldest son of the Chinese Methodist minister Reverend T.T. Taam. Initially Grandma was disappointed that Joan married so young. But once Joan began to bring her toddlers by everyone was so pleased. One particular Easter Joan visited with her three-year-old daughter, Janice (we called her J.J.) who looked absolutely charming in her Easter dress, parasol and all. One look at her and I knew I wanted children and I wanted girls so that I could dress them up.

Lillian

Auntie Taidy (Lillian), a spinster, died at thirty-eight years old. She worked for the Chinese Consulate on Montgomery Street. She passed away a year before I arrived in the States. It would be decades later when I fully understood Grandma's pain at the loss of this daughter. Half a century later I, too, faced the same situation.

Henry

Uncle Hank, Grandma's second son, worked for the Division of Highways in Redding, a six-hour drive north of San Francisco. Because of that distance he and his wife, June, and their three children were not often at family gatherings. Visiting them proved difficult for Redding was extraordinarily hot in the summer and we were not accustomed to the heat. Uncle Hank was never in good health and was plagued with lung problems. He passed away in 1977 shortly after having half of his lungs removed. I remember the aunts did not want to tell grandma of his passing. They did not want her to feel any more sorrow as she too was near death. Aunt June, his widow, moved the family to Oakland. In later years the family lost track of that branch of the family. I've always felt a bond with Uncle Hank and Redding. They played a pivotal role in another of my escapades dealing with my father.

Frances

Third daughter, Frances (or Auntie Fran), along with Ah Pau, brought me to this country. For that I am eternally grateful. She and Uncle Hank looked so much alike they could have passed as twins. They were only a year apart. She received an Associate of Arts degree from San Francisco City College and immediately went into the financial workforce. She served as assistant manager at the Chinatown branch of Bank of America under Dolly Gee, a flamboyant, outgoing bank manager. I used to sit there and try to digest the meaning of Dolly Gee's risqué statements. They must have been bawdy because everyone around would burst out laughing – but

I was stumped. Dolly followed her father into the banking business and rose in the banking field. She eventually succeeded her father as bank manager. Several years passed before she realized that her father made some bad loans but being a filial daughter she didn't want to report on him. Soon the banking authorities caught up with what we call today "cooking the books." Aunt Dolly Gee served prison time for the sins of her father.

Auntie Fran owned a 1952, light-green Studebaker coupe that she kept in the garage next door and took it out only on weekends. She also had a sweetie, George Lim, a graduate of Cornell and an engineer for the Bechtel Company. He looked like Jack Benny, a Chinese one at that, although he played no instrument nor was he a comedian. Previously married, Uncle George had a daughter, Valerie, just a few years younger than I. Valerie's mother's side of the family raised her. George used to stand across the street for hours waiting to catch a glimpse of Auntie Fran hoping she would spend a few minutes with him. I used to check to see how long he would wait. On many a cold San Francisco night he stood in his heavy overcoat right by his two-tone, pink-and-white 1954 Buick, well in sight of Grandma's building – just in case Auntie Fran peeked out through the blinds. He tried so hard to please Grandma during the courting days and Grandma was persistently aloof. It may have been that with Aunt Frances' marriage the last of her children would leave her abode. All mothers prefer their children to never leave the nest. When George and Fran married in 1957, I was able to see Valerie a bit more. Later as an adult, Valerie made a career in library services and raised her own family in the South Bay. In 1960 Auntie Frances gave birth to Janet and it surprised me. By then, Auntie Fran was forty years old and I thought "wasn't she past the childbearing age?"

Ethel

Ethel, the youngest daughter, has the most interesting life and, truly, was the liveliest. Known as "E" she is quick, witty and has a gleam of mischief in her eyes. I called her Auntie E. She graduated from the University of California, Los Angeles and joined the Sprites (Merchant Marines) during World War II. Ethel was fluent in English and Chinese so the Navy Department in Maryland asked to have her temporarily assigned to their decoding section. She said it was one of the shortest but most interesting jobs she ever held. Another adventurous and short-lived occupation was serving as hostess to the second and third class passengers on the Matson Line. It was an experiment to assess passenger needs. Unfortunately, during the ship's stop in Manila, Ethel came to visit our house on Fernando Road. Father was less than pleased and ordered Ethel out of the house. He felt her job was too lowly and suggestive of risqué activities. After Aunt Taidy's death, Auntie E took over her sister's position at the Chinese Consulate on Montgomery Street. She even worked for the San Mateo police department for a number of years. When she retired from that law enforcement agency her friendship with various detectives and officers continued with poker and Auntie E's home cooking.

Auntie E had many suitors but chose Paul Richards, half-Hawaiian half-Chinese from Hawaii. Now, he really had a swagger and something very appealing that reminded one of John Wayne. To please Grandma, Uncle Paul changed his last name to Chang, his mother's maiden name so Aunt Ethel and their children would have a Chinese last name. Uncle Paul started out as a longshoreman and moved on to become a restaurateur and eventually an entrepreneur. Their first company was Cathay Kitchen, a take-out restaurant on El Camino Real in San Mateo near St. Matthew Episcopal Church and Mills Hospital. Uncle Paul designed a trailer that served as a full kitchen with two woks, quite similar to today's version of a taco truck. He towed this wok-on-wheels to fairs and other events throughout California and even as far away as Washington, Utah, Colorado, Michigan and Minnesota. As a consistent and dependable vendor, the Alameda County Fair officials allowed him to build a permanent building on the fairground which he operated for several decades. The Changs' Chinese Food company expanded into kitchenware. Their red colored woks and ancillary pots and pans were much in demand as they were attractive and practical. I remember even in small communities such as Pullalup, Washington customers flocked to the demonstration stand when Auntie E stir-fried simple vegetables such as bok choy or even bean sprouts. Auntie E had real talent, she was quite a showman demonstrating cookware and advocating healthy eating. In their travels, the Changs saw a cross section of the true Americana spirit.

Ethel and Paul had two daughters, Paula and Clarissa. Paula followed in her mother's footstep and graduated from UCLA. Paula is actually a gifted artist. She created a unique cottage industry in jewelry-making. Most artists work with beads, Paula's were made of heavily-starched cloth and her designs have an Asian flair. The earrings and pins are much in demand and, like her parents, one can find her at various art shows and special events throughout the western states. Clarissa, the youngest daughter, married and had three children. Unfortunately she died at the age of 38 from a reaction to diabetes medication.

Timothy

Timothy, Tom Foon's youngest son, had polio when young but that did not deter him from being active in school. Very handsome, he was quite popular and served as president of his fraternity at the University of California – Berkeley. He often brought his frat brothers home to Grandma who thoroughly enjoyed the company of many lively young men. They considered her as their godmother and continued to visit her well into their marriages and careers. Tim majored in mechanical engineering and took on a variety of occupations. Out of college, he worked for the State of California for a short period.

Upon Uncle Tim's return from Bangkok in 1955 he brought his lovely Caucasian wife, Carol. We called her C.C. She was born in Burma to missionary grandparents and her father, Bill Cummings, at one time served as General J. D. "Vinegar Joe" Stillwell's interpreter. In his retirement Bill Cummings belonged to the prestigious, government-backed, Rare Fruit Society raising many fruits from the Orient in Florida. Tim and Carol had two children, Robyn and Tom. C.C. tried very hard to please Grandma learning ways to being a Chinese wife. But it was Tom's birth that made Grandma very happy for he was not only a Chew but had his grandfather's name.

Uncle Tim with several of his fraternity brothers formed a pharmaceutical plant, Allied Biochemical Company, on Clay Street between Powell and Stockton. It manufactured and packaged pills for sales overseas. Aside from slinging Chinese food for the Changs at local fairs, for two summers I worked at this plant as a receptionist, telephone operator, and even once on the assembly line. It was also during this period another item remained indelible in my mind Uncle Tim had a hot pink and black 1956 Cadillac De Ville. What a beauty!

In later years Tim and C.C. divorced and she married Howard Grieves of Florida. Upon Grieves' death C.C. moved back to the Sacramento area. Tim met and married Aunt Sally in Hong Kong in the 1990s. Sally Grimsley is an Australian and well versed in the world of South East Asia. Although many years her senior, Tim has been extremely fortunate for she has been quite insistent in taking care of his health.

The children of Tom Foon and Lee Gum Ching were typical of third generation Chinese American families. They straddled both the Caucasian and Chinese worlds, speaking English for the better part of their lives with only a smattering of Chinese thrown in. But when addressing their mother they reverted back to their native Toishan dialect. Educated, professionals they partook in social activities such as smoking, drinking and gambling.

The greatest asset left by their father was the apartment building on Powell Street. It was their family home, one that had no mortgage and a modest income. Without Tom Foon and with many mouths to feed, the apartment building provided the security needed during the difficult years of the Great Depression. Even my parents sought the shelter of this building when they escaped World War II. I, too, found refuge there when I came to America in 1951.

The Thomas Foon Chew Family
Back: Taidy, May Lan and Charlie. Front: Frances, Grandma, Ethel Great-grandma Chew, Timothy, Grandfathr and Henry.

Chapter 5

Powell Street Living

I fulfilled a role when Grandmother brought me to this country. The closest job description would be that of a *muy jei*. A *muy jei* is a young person taken into a household, not as a servant but rather as an adopted or distantly related member of a family. The person is expected to perform certain household chores and provide companionship in return for food and lodging. At age ten this responsibility never occurred to me. All I knew was that this transition in life ended my previous miserable existence. I had the opportunity to start anew. It was the best of all worlds; no father to fear, my mother no longer worried and, by giving me to her mother, she made a filial sacrifice. Aunt Frances was able to get a life of her own instead of being the caregiver to her mother. Grandma, whom I now called Ah Pau, had someone to assist her as she entered her senior years, someone on whom she could focus her maternal instinct and help her lessen her grief over Aunt Taidy's passing.

Quite early in my stay with Ah Pau I gained an appreciation for the strong legacy my maternal grandparents built teaching their children to strive for success in both the Chinese and the Caucasian community. Through Ah Pau I had the opportunity to absorb folkways and traditions. This was a lifetime of learned survival skills and instilled cultural folkways that enriched my knowledge of Chinese American history.

Ah Pau's apartment building, 1122 Powell Street, was in the middle of the block between Washington and Jackson Streets. Just half a block up Powell, on the corner of Washington and Powell, stood Margaret's, a large candy store. Mrs. Winnie Lum ran the laundromat on the opposite corner. Next door to our building to the north was the Powell Street Garage serving as a service station, mechanic shop and garage. The apartment was directly across from the Korean Methodist Church and the Chinatown Public Library. My father believed that our building's *feng shui* was not good for it faced a church. And that Ah Pau would not be lucky. Whether he was right is a matter of interpretation for the building provided for the family at our most crucial period.

The cable car route connecting Market Street to Fisherman's Wharf passed the apartment every twenty minutes; this was followed by another cable car serving the Hyde Street system. The roar of the cables was accompanied by the conductor clanging the warning bell in sharp rhythmic tones as the car swung widely uphill onto Jackson Street. On return routes the conductor's music could be heard again when it sped down towards the curve on Washington to Powell Street. The car passed the Nob Hill area then down hill to Union Square on route to the end of the line at Powell and Market Streets. The cable car company held an annual bell ringing contest; it was a rather big deal for the streetcar aficionados. Competing conductors would practice their cadence with the music surging to an energetic crescendo just when they passed the front of our apartment building. To awaken in the morning to the melodic sounds was better than depending on an alarm clock.

The Powell Street building seemed small by some standards: three-stories, six units with a basement studio unit and a small, one-operator beauty shop near the front entrance. Ah Pau reserved the basement unit for Uncle Charlie when he came to visit. There were two one-bedroom apartments on the second and third floor. The apartments' numbering system was very odd. It was neither systematic nor logical. Apartment #1 at the top of the first landing connected to apartment #2 with #1 serving as the living room and dining room and #2 the bedroom. When I arrived our living arrangements were such that Aunt Frances lived in #2 and Ah Pau and I lived in #4. The other three units had a Mrs. Emily Wong in #6, Sarah Leung who worked with Aunt Frances in #5, and Ho You in #3. Mr. Ho was a quiet man and kept to himself. His name was written differently in Chinese but when spoken it was the Chinese word for "oyster sauce." He managed a small parking lot on Jackson Street next to the Chinese Hospital. Grandma collected about thirty dollars from each of the apartments and forty dollars from the beauty shop. Ah Pau's cousin, Aunt Jessie, used to rent the beauty shop but when she moved to a bigger place on Mason Street, Vi became the renter. I called her Auntie Vi (out of respect). She was the epitome of a hair dresser for her hair was always disheveled and she always wore a towel pinned across the breast of her black dress. I got my first permanent from Auntie Vi, a frightening experience in that the metal bonnet holds massive electrical cables with clamps at the ends. These were clamped to the curlers on my head. Then she threw a switch and the wires sent heat into the clamps. If the treatment lasted too long or the operator did not pay attention one's hair got fried. The next time I needed another permanent Auntie Fran used a cold water chemical solution known as a Toni kit.

Duties and Expectations

Ah Pau frequently reminded me that she paid for my air passage. Therefore, to earn my keep I was assigned duties and responsibilities.

Foremost was to keep the building clean. For seven years (from age 10 to 17) I vacuumed all the hallways and stairwells. Only 4'6" and weighing about sixty pounds, I lugged that vacuum cleaner and all its attachments up and down all three flights and even cleaned the deep crevices of the steps. The landings and steps had a muddled green carpet, it must have been fairly deep and sculptured when new but by the 1950s there were worn areas and other places were matted down. The railing rungs spaced only an inch apart were tedious; thus, weaving the dust cloth through several rungs and a quick jerk pulled the cloth through and the dust was gone. I alternated cleaning the stairs with washing the tiled interior foyer and the outside alcove; it was bucket, mop and Spic N Span followed by two rinses. Of the two major chores I preferred the stairs for I was embarrassed to be seen doing menial chores such as washing the outside walkway -- particularly since I knew many of my friends did not have to work as hard. The dust and dirt from the dang parking garage next door added greatly to the weekly grime. My other duties were the typical dish washing and helping with the general cleaning. Laundromat owner, Auntie Winnie played poker with Auntie Fran on Friday nights. Sometimes I was late picking up our clothes but Auntie Winnie did not mind and always had them folded, packaged and ready to go.

Dumping garbage required special skills. There was an exterior garbage chute affixed to the building. I climbed on to a chair, opened the kitchen window, lifted a lid and threw out the garbage. However it was not always a straight shot as garbage from the upper floors sometimes jammed the chute. To unclog the passage I needed the handle end of the broom to push it slowly down making sure not to break the garbage bag. I could not keep the kitchen window open for fresh air; rats frequented the garbage area and even had the capability of scaling the garbage chute. Once when I decided to soak in the bathtub down in the basement unit (Uncle Charlie was not in town) I heard some scurrying and suddenly between the crack in the wall I saw three rat tails. It scared me so much I quickly jumped out, put on my clothes and ran up stairs to Ah Pau's. After telling her what I saw, she looked at me very calmly and said in Chinese, "why didn't you chop off their tails?" Was she kidding me by reciting a lyric from *Three Blind Mice*?

On the first and fifteenth of each month in the Chinese calendar (dates that coincided with the new and full moon) I tended to the ancestral altar (*sun toy*). Ah Pau believed in ancestral worship and Daoism. The altar was actually a closet in Apartment #1 with the door removed and a shelf inserted midway up. In large calligraphy the words written on a red paper served as the focal tablet in a 24"x18" frame encircled by a red cloth sash. It honored the Chew lineage. A pair of decorative vases sat on either side of the tablet. In front there was a brass urn containing copious amounts of ashes and stubs from incense sticks showing years of accumulated offerings. In my time with Grandma I never saw anyone remove any ash or burned out punk sticks. In front of the urn were neatly placed three tiny ceremonial teacups, just a little bigger than a thimble with a pair of chopsticks laid to the side of each cup. My job was to clean the ceremonial cups containing dried tea leaves and tea stains from previous offerings. Tannic acid stain is difficult to remove with just soap and water but a quick rub with Old Dutch Cleanser worked wonders. Once the cups of tea were in place, I lit three sticks of punk and kowtowed three times before the tablet and then stood the punks on end in the urn. Dutifully, I bowed even with no living person present for the Gods may have been watching. Admittedly, I was a bit superstitious and fearful of retribution if the ritual was not performed correctly. On special holidays such as winter solstice or Chinese New Year, there was a more elaborate presentation at the altar - a whole cooked chicken, whiskey, and paper money folded origami style into the shape of gold bullion. A cloth draped from the altar hid household supplies and other items such as mahjong sets, playing cards and poker chips. This was truly an example of counterculture at its best.

Chinatown

My favorite chore was running errands. If Au Pau needed a piece of pork it meant going to Quon Yick, the corner store on Powell and Washington Streets, kitty corner from Margaret's Candy Store. For ten cents' worth of pork the old clerk threw in a pork soup bone or two. Bread cost only a nickel. If we needed something more substantial such as produce, I ran farther up the hill to Tom's Market on Powell and Clay Streets. I probably was the only youngster ever to walk out of that store with bottles of White Horse Scotch Whiskey. That was Grandma's favorite drink and storekeeper Tom Hom knew that the $5.25 I laid down was not for me. More extensive shopping took planning. Chinatown was only two blocks downhill from Powell Street. To get there hurriedly I literally had to weave in-and-out looking for openings or spaces between groups of people and squeezing through even if I had to side step. It was the matter of being passively assertive.

I preferred to walk down Washington Street. There was more to see: children playing at the Commodore Stockton Elementary School playground, the school's annex across the street and next door housed *Gum Moon* (a residence for young ladies). Finishing the left side of the block was the Chinese Methodist Church at the corner. Right across the intersection (Washington and Stockton Streets) was the drugstore stuffed with lots of pharmaceutical merchandise. Just a few doors down on the same side of the street was Uncle Lee Gin's shop where he made bean sprouts and various types of noodles. As I headed towards Grant Avenue there were several street level small shops and restaurants. My favorite was a Chinese confectionary store which sold a variety of dried plums, cracked seeds, dried squid, abalone and octopus. To attract customers the owner extended his storefront display out to the middle of the sidewalk, thus narrowing the walk path. I would chew a piece of abalone or suck on the seed of the dried plum at length just to slowly savor its sweet and saltiness. This was much tastier than sugary candy that only melts in the mouth.

From the heart of Chinatown I would return home on Jackson Street. It paralleled Washington and had about the same amount of shops as well as the Chinese Hospital and *Tin Fook Jewelry Store*, where Grandfather Chew was, at one time, an original part owner.

If Grandma had a craving for filet mignon (at that time a fairly decent piece cost only fifty cents and was sufficient to feed both of us) she sent me to El Dorado Meat Market on Stockton and Pacific Avenue, less than three blocks away. The meat counters were rather high and I couldn't be seen. So I squeezed in between the two meat cases and yelled for Mai Day, the kind-looking woman butcher. Then with one of my "please, please" pathetic looks I thrust out my coin and pointed to the meat case. She caught the drift of the sign language and, with a nod, mission accomplished. Buying a chicken meant a trip down Washington Street to the poultry market next to the telephone exchange building. The chicken had to be plucked and sometimes deboned. Purchasing a roast duck included reminding the clerk we wanted it chopped with added juice or gravy to keep it from drying out. I watched the scale carefully when asking for a quart or a pound of cooked food. To purchase authentic dry shark fin, I walked through Wentworth Alley to the import store. The pungent aroma of dried seafood guided my nose. For wonderful custard pies, it was venturing into Ross Alley and Uncle H's Café. In all cases, similar tactics applied – squeezing up to the front and competing with other buyers to grab attention. I dearly loved the sights, sounds and smell, for Chinatown was my neighborhood.

Not hindered by her bound feet and vision through only one eye Ah Pau and I went everywhere in Chinatown-- shopping, attending Chinese operas and Chinese theatres. The Chinese operas at Tai Mo

Toy (the Grand Theater on Grant Avenue) were usually four hours long. Long enough for me to play in the aisle and eat nuts and candy to while away my time. I didn't know the story line but knew that when the actor climbed a chair it meant the soldiers were climbing mountains or that when another actor had peacock feathers in his headdress and flags or pendants pinned to the back of his costume it meant he was a mighty general with many legions. Tai Koon, the theater on Jackson Street, featured modern movies – that is modern stories of romance, filial piety, and lots of gazing at the moon suggesting yearning or sadness. These movies were always in black and white. Seldom did we see any with martial arts but there was one time a historical story featured sword fighting and duels using magical power simply by raising their palms and thrusting energy forces against the enemy. This type of fantasy was very creative in those days but doesn't hold a candle to the kung fu and sword fighting in today's cinemas. Technology has made all the difference.

Ah Pau decided Chinese movies might be the key to motivate me in the Chinese language, particularly if I followed the bouncing ball on the words as the actors sang. I didn't really learn anything that way; and, unfortunately, I can still kick myself today for not being diligent. She loved television and American movies that had some Chinese elements. Among her favorite were *Blood Alley* with John Wayne, *Love Is A Many Splendored Thing* with William Holden and Jennifer Jones. She was a regular TV viewer of *Paladin* and *Dragnet* and, on the whole, was rather eclectic in her taste

Slices of Joy

Life with Ah Pau had its highlights. One was accompanying her to visit nearby relatives. I addressed mostly all the extended family members as "aunties" and "uncles" for they were of my mother's generation. I never figured out who were blood siblings and who were the adopted ones except her three sisters. But I was able to discern which relative belonged to Ah Pau's family line or that of grandfather Tom Foon. They were either "Ah Sook" (uncle on grandfather's side) or "Ah Kow" (uncle on grandmother's side).

Each of grandmother's sisters married into major family clans that were part of the powerful alliances within the Chinatown political structure. The most populous and influential were the Lees, Ah Pau's lineage. Dai Yee Pau (the oldest of grandma's sisters), married into the Chin clan, she lived on Washington Street just below Grant Avenue and across Portsmouth Square. Her family ran a parking lot and travel agency. Yee Pau, second grandaunt (grandma's second oldest sister) lived less than a block away on Washington Street. She married into the Ng-Yee clan. Her own building was income producing for it housed several flats. Sze Yee Pau (fourth grandaunt) married into the Lim family and had an apartment building on Grant Avenue. She was the most modern of the grandaunts and she was different in that her feet were not bound. She was much taller and weighed more. Unlike her sisters, Sze Yee Pau believed in Christianity and was a church-going Baptist. Of her five children two daughters were named after states: California and Virginia. Grandma's sisters were all very attractive, but I thought Grandma was the best looking of all. The first time I met Sze Yee Pau she asked me in Chinese what was my name and I blurted out, "*Sam Koo Ngerng*" meaning Third Princess. She busted out laughing as did Grandma and I didn't know why. That's what the servants called me in Bangkok and my folks never addressed me by a Chinese name. Ah Pau quickly let me know that no one in America is addressed as or is treated as royalty, I was, after all, her companion – her muy jey.

When we were with Au Pau's sisters or even alone we spoke strictly Cantonese and it was a good way to make me retain my mother tongue.

Chinese Language School – Hip Wo

Au Pau did send me to Chinese school, at Hip Wo housed upstairs at the Chinese Methodist Church (Washington at Stockton Streets). I attended from 3:00-6:00 PM during the weekdays but not on Saturdays (my apartment cleaning day). Teachers were strict and did not hesitate to whack students on the back side or hands for misbehaving. I played hooky often, Auntie Fran caught me playing outside on the sidewalk only once and she yanked me out of Chinese school. However, the most fun in Chinese school was marching in parades celebrating Chinese New Year or Nationalist Chinese Independence Day on October 10th. Sometimes we carried little lanterns or waved Nationalist Chinese and American flags. The most difficult part was straddling the street car tracks as we walked down Stockton Street and through the Stockton Tunnel to downtown. All the Chinese schools participated; the most impressive of the marching units was the St. Mary's Drum Corps. An all-girl band they wore gorgeous red and gold outfits and headgears. Everyone could hear the girls blocks away for they were the only group to play the familiar *Chinatown My Chinatown* or *California Here I Come* melodies on their xylophones. The marching route seldom varied and covered at least two miles often in the cold and even rain.

Venturing beyond San Francisco

When I was living with my parents they never took me anywhere. However my life with Ah Pau and Auntie Fran afford the opportunity to be included wherever they went. Very shortly after I came to San Francisco Ah Pau and I took a week's trip to Seattle and Vancouver. Uncle Charlie put us up at the Frye's Hotel in Seattle and the Colony Motel in Vancouver. He had not yet remarried and was living in a one room unit in the hotel which I thought looked very messy and dank. I remember I saw a gun in a holster laying on the table. Eventually I surmised that he needed it for protection since he was a high roller and belonged to a tong.

Auntie Fran took us for Sunday drives in her Studebaker. There was even a discussion once of selling the Powell Street apartment and buying a house in the avenues, way out on California Street. As Ah Paul and Auntie Fran debated the issue the conversation got a bit heated. It boiled down to the fact that Ah Pau needed the rent money and could she emotionally leave the Chinatown area after all those years. So to maintain peace the building was never sold.

One weekend Auntie Fran and I took a drive down to Carmel. Ah Pau did not want to come along, it was a long trip and we had planned to stay overnight. I was mesmerized by the beautiful La Playa Hotel, particularly our room. Dining outdoor was also spectacular with lots of twinkling lights on the patio. At the time the hotel was the crème de la crème, all pink and reeked of gentility. Valets and porters snapped to attention when we drove up. Today the cost may be prohibitive but one day I will return.

To my delight some summers we went to Lake Tahoe and Reno and I would spend time with my Seattle cousins, Cherk and Hwa-di, horseback riding or going to the movies. As I said, Ah Pau loved her Scotch and her Viceroy cigarettes; but most of all she loved to gamble. The dealers at CalNeva in Reno and on Lake Tahoe's north shore knew her as Mama Chew. Her small bound feet did not deter her from hoisting herself up to a blackjack table, crossing her legs and lighting a cigarette as the dealer dealt her cards. Ah Pau even acquired a dime slot machine that she stuck in the basement apartment. Elderly relatives often went down there to try their luck at the machine.

Ah Pau might have been considered a high roller, much like her husband; but she was also very frugal. That she did not waste was evident from her drying bok choy and dates. Even orange and grapefruit peels were sun dried, chopped and used in specialty dishes. An excellent cook, she seemed to do everything with speed and ease. I never saw her sweat over a hot stove or complain about endless hours of slicing, dicing and cleaning associated with Chinese food preparation. I dreaded it when Uncle Charlie came into town. Although he was a fantastic cook, his meals were much more elaborate and I spent hours picking and cleaning the shark fin as well as the bird's nest ingredients for his soup. It was tedious work with my fingers shriveling up because the ingredient was soaking in water all the time during the cleaning and plucking process. Uncle Charlie expected me to do all the work and he never said a word of thanks. When he was around I really felt like a servant or mui jey. He would preen from all the accolades he received from his cooking, and, admittedly, his food was even better than Ah Pau's.

Interactions and Holidays

As dutiful as I was to Ah Pau, my aunts and uncles' families were also part of my being. Auntie E gave birth to Paula in 1952. As Paula's first babysitter I was very apprehensive for she had epilepsy. I felt so helpless once when she had a convulsive attack. I watched as Auntie E bathed her in warm water to reduce the fever and convulsion.

Paula caused my second runaway experience. A relative died and Ah Pau, with her daughters, attended the wake as well as the funeral. Paula, then only a couple of months old, kept crying and I took to throwing a stuffed animal up in the air to entertain her. In one of the throws I hit the chandelier and it shattered. I told myself not to panic but I was so scared. After Auntie E came home I started back to the Powell Street apartment but the thought of Auntie E calling her mother made me high tail it out of there. Actually there was no thought of where to go or what to do, but to just keep walking. This was about 9:00 PM; I headed up hill on Clay Street. When I saw some people I quickly asked if they would like to hire me as a maid. Of course, there were no takers and people thought me strange. Nevertheless, at about 11:00 PM, I stumbled into a pharmacy on Broadway and Van Ness, some twelve blocks from Auntie E's apartment. I asked the pharmacist if I could work there; in response, he called the police and reported me as a runaway. Luckily, just as the police arrived, Auntie E's friend, Bill Fong, happened to walk into the pharmacy and said that he knew who I was and would drive me home. Whew! Now it was the matter of explaining my action to Ah Pau. It would be another seven years later before I would make my third and final runaway.

In 1952, Dida, at age sixteen, came back to the States and enrolled at Mills College in Oakland. She stayed at Mills Hall dormitory but joined the family on special occasions. Sometimes Dida invited me to stay with her at the dorm and I thoroughly enjoyed those visits, particularly meeting her friends and walking the campus. The Mills Hall was quite old and had an institutional charm including the high ceilings, wainscoting and banisters. Painted white in and out, the structure reminded me of an antebellum building.

Memories of Ah Pau's family gatherings during the holidays are quite pleasant. Every year I decorated the Christmas tree in apartment #1 and worked hard to make the bulbs with the percolating bubbles stand straight. It seemed neither Ah Pau nor Auntie Fran enjoyed the tree.. Ah Pau stayed upstairs in her apartment and Aunt Frances went from work to eat with her mother and then either out with her friends or Uncle George. It was rather perfunctory that we went through the routine of a Christmas tree or did they buy one just to have one or was it for my sake? If that was the case no one made mention.

The Chinese New Year meant lots of visits from relatives or we would make excursions to pay our respects. I received quite a bit of *lishee*, the little red envelope of lucky money. Opening the lishee in front of the giver was impolite, but fingering the envelope and feeling the diameter of the coin gave indication of the denomination. This money and the babysitting money that C.C. and Uncle Tim gave kept me in spending money all year. I babysat cousin Robyn at the hour rate of twenty-five cents an hour and C.C. marked the time on her calendar and paid at the end of the month. It wasn't much, usually about $5.00 and I never spent it all.

I was not paid to clean the apartment building, it was expected. On rare occasions Auntie Fran gave me a dime while I was in grammar school so that I could buy a small plate of spaghetti like the other children. Outside of that I did not have an allowance. By the time I was thirteen I was old enough to sling hash as summer work at the Chang's food booth at the San Mateo County Fair. I also spent another summer working as a receptionist at Uncle Tim's pharmaceutical plant on Clay Street. Working there gave me a first experience of clerical work and allowed me to test my newly-acquired typing skills. My mother was praised for her typing speed when in high school and I believed I inherited that same talent while in junior high school.

Annually, a bigger event than Christmas or Chinese New Year was Ah Pau's birthday in November. Each year the family invited numerous friends and relatives to a huge banquet in Chinatown. Attendance often numbered as many as a hundred or more. With tables of ten, there were at least 10 to 12 tables. I assumed Ah Pau or her children paid for the banquet that included gourmet dishes and lots of libations. Auntie E always provided Ah Pau with a huge orchid and smaller corsages for the female members of the immediate family from Podesta on lower Powell Street. One year Auntie E got me a tuberous begonia corsage and it was gorgeous. All the ladies wore their finest gold and jade jewelry, not one or two pieces but as many as they had, just layers and layers of gold chains with pendants encrusted with diamonds, jade, pearls or even rubies. Their wrists did not sport just a plain watch but bangles upon bangles. These jewelries had a lot of glitter and were beautifully crafted. These were "Fort Knox" affairs.

Banquets were common as sons and daughters used it as means to demonstrate their filial piety and to show the family's wealth. In due time, criminals took note of these types of birthdays for the elderly, children's weddings and other milestone celebrations. Eventually families began to hire security guards for these major events. Now that crime is so high I seldom see Chinese wearing a jade pendant on a gold chain as everyday wear. Ah Pau knew quality as well as value be it merchandise, food, clothing, jewelry, and even travel. From this I learned, if I can afford it get the best; if not, get whatever will give me the longest shelf life.

Ah Pau loved her parties and she loved the attention that came with it. The best part was that the party never stopped that night. One relative had a movie camera and filmed the entire affair from table to table and all the toasts that followed. When the film was ready, it was my job to show it to the relatives who stopped by weeks later. Each time we had visitors, I lugged out the heavy 8mm projector, propped it on the coffee table, set up the screen, threaded the reel, and waited for the signal from Ah Pau for the grand viewing. Sometimes the viewing continued well into Chinese New Year. Grandma re-lived her birthday with relish as did her visitors.

At Sze Yee Pau's birthday with her granddaughters. I am just to the left of Sze Yee Pau. Cousin Diane Wong is on the far right.

By 1955 the Changs moved to San Mateo and the family gathered there for special occasions. With a full stomach and the adults sufficiently libated Uncle Paul would break out in song. Then C.C. followed making it a duet and eventually I chimed in a three part harmony. We sang a lot of *You Are My Sunshine*. It was good fun.

Lonely Times

There were some quiet and lonely times. Although I did not get along well with my parents, I often wished to visit them during the summer or even anytime. When Dida married Larry in Taiwan I really wanted to be there and be part of the family gathering. I wrote almost pleading but did not get a response. I seldom heard from them except perhaps during Chinese New Year when Mom wrote a note reminding me to obey Ah Pau. She enclosed two dollars in the lishee; one from father and one from her. The short note was always the same. Of course, they never remembered me on my birthday or Christmas. I could never figure out why they did not make even a token gift of money to Ah Pau for keeping me. They only sent large framed portraits of themselves taken at professional studios. Dad in his tuxedo bedecked with numerous medals or in a Chinese jacket; Mom had glamour shots the type used for newspapers or magazines. On the matting of the picture my parents inscribed Ah Pau's name in Chinese as well as their message of love.

When I irritated Ah Pau she would remind me of the $400 airfare and that my parents never sent money for my room and board. I owed her. She never asked me to pay her back nor did she ever threaten to spend another $400 to send me back to my folks. She wanted me to be appreciative, and I was.

One very empty time for me was when I turned eleven. It was my birthday and it seemed, no one cared or made anything of that date. After school that day, I came home and discovered Auntie Fran left an unwrapped box on the kitchen table, with a note saying it was my birthday present. I needed a pair of school shoes badly. I guess it was at least something but I was filled with self-pity. This particular occasion has stuck with me.

Being sick also called for lots of lonely days, particularly when I caught the measles, followed by chicken pox, and then a relapse of the measles again. One home remedy to quicken and heal chicken pox was to soak fresh cilantro in boiling water and take a sponge bath with that water. It seemed to work for it stopped the itching and the scabs seemed to dry up and fall off faster without leaving much of a scar. All in all, Ah Pau believed in a100-day quarantine for each illness and she meant for me to be totally bedridden. The school administrators felt it was too long. I only stayed out 30 days in all. Staying in bed wasn't so bad when I discovered the joy of listening to the radio. A new world invaded my senses and captured the imagination, particularly the squeaky door that opened up *Inner*

Sanctum. I didn't know that *Amos and Andy* were Black characters. No one told me Charlie McCarthy was a dummy. I was the real dummy!

They say one's formative years are between one and five. I believe I had two sets of formative years. The first set provided the inner passion for specific food and flavors; the second, those seven years living on Powell Street with Ah Pau created the building blocks that set my character and personality. She brought me to America and gave me a safe and secured life. She taught me to be conservative, frugal, caring, and have great respect for the elderly. Without a doubt, my Powell Street years were some of the best years of my life.

Chew Family dinner at Grandma's Powell St. Apartment
Standing: Hank, Sylvia and Patricia
L to R: June w/Monica, Frances, CC, Grandma, Tim, Paul, Ethel w/Paula

Chapter 6

Silver and Gold

Make new friends but keep the old
One is silver the other gold

The longer I live the more silver friendships of yore have turned to gold. There were times when I had that orphan feeling sans parents and siblings. But given the circumstances, life with Ah Pau and her children along with school, classmates and friends, my teen years in the 50s were pretty normal. As the Chinese Argonauts of old discovered gold in California, I, too, found nuggets of gold with classmates and friends that have sustained through decades. They are, in essence, bridges which connected my past to present day.

Auntie Fran enrolled me in Jean Parker Elementary School in 1951. The school, on Broadway between Powell and Mason Streets, was four blocks from home. Commodore Stockton School was just around the corner on Washington Street but she chose the Parker school because her best friend, Auntie Jez's, daughter was going there. Her daughter, Donna, was the first person close to my age I called a friend and she's still very dear.

Jean Parker, built in 1912, was a typical three-story brick structure with the front entrance in the middle of the building and access to the upper floor was by sets of interior stairs from either end. The school was in the middle of the block; next door was Alfred's, an established Italian restaurant. The school was at the entrance of the Broadway Tunnel that connects the Chinatown and Broadway area to Van Ness Avenue and the nearby gateway to the Presidio. Cars whizzed by at record speed going through the tunnel, certainly not like today's need to crawl when near a school zone. If I stood on the sidewalk in front of the school, I could look downhill at luminating lights from Broadway's restaurants, nightclubs and stores; it suggests music, food and a world of entertainment. Only a block down was the Condor Club, one of the many burlesque places. This one featured the very buxom Carol Doda. I was fascinated with *Finocchio's* with its female impersonators and enjoyed watching folks at *Enrico's*, a sidewalk eatery. Ah Pau's favorite on that street was *New Joe's*, a family restaurant where we ate on more than one occasion. Almost all large communities now have a "Joes" restaurant. A quieter restaurant was *Elu* which featured Basque food. Yes, Ah Pau had an eclectic taste and I inherited that international palate.

Jean Parker Elementary School on Broadway bet. Powell & Mason

Fifth grade class, I am second from left in the front row

Educating the ABCs and FOBs

Enrolling late in the school semester, I was placed in the fifth grade. The following year I became more adaptive and immersed myself in the world of the ABCs – American Born Chinese, that is. Children can unknowingly offend. I was laughed at and asked if I was an FOB (Fresh off the Boat) like other immigrant children. Although I did not have a thick Chinese accent I did sound peculiarly "Brit." My English was British and not American. With a little more heckling I vowed that I would learn to speak American English so perfectly that there would be no trace of foreign sounds and, certainly, without a Chinatown accent. Consequently, now my Central Valley twang is recognizably unique.

Teachers, activities, and classmates make more lasting impressions than any classroom lesson. I felt I had learned more under the British Calvert System when in Bangkok. In this post war era we, students, wore dog tags, the thin metal, triangular identification tags for emergencies and we were taught to duck under desks for safety in case of earthquakes. At the time I did not know what an earthquake was but ducking was also good if a bomb was to drop – highly unlikely according to everyone. However, there were talks of people building bomb shelters, but in Chinatown such talk was nonsense. Who had the room?

Miss Adele Titus, the sixth grade teacher, had a striking resemblance to the picture of George Washington what with her white hair, hawkish nose and a defined semi-profile seen on today's dollar bill. Miss Titus looked old but was probably just over fifty years of age. She was quite a disciplinarian and made the students work at their studies. We were not allowed to speak Chinese in school and were severely chastised when caught doing so. One thing she said stuck in my mind, "You do not lend out your toothbrush, so don't lend out your fountain pen." We were then using bottles of ink and filling the ink reservoir by flipping the lever on Parker, Sheffield, or Waterman pens. Ballpoint pens had yet to be invented and owning a fountain pen gave students a certain aura of distinction. Miss Titus was good and earned my respect.

Curiously, one of the biggest school activities was conducted on May 1st. On this day girls made flower wreaths for their hair out of colorful crepe paper, similar to the Hawaiian Haiku leis. Part of the May Day celebration was to dance around a May Pole while wrapping it with colorful streamers. The country had just entered the Cold War and there we were Chinese children in the school celebrating like the Europeans and their holiday. The daily snack was also an issue; we were given a carton of milk and one graham cracker. I enjoyed the cracker but, like most, I was lactose intolerant. I tried every which way to pawn off my milk and dairy products are still not a part of my diet.

Elementary school was also the time when one was introduced to the breadth of American music such as the country western *Red River Valley* and *Oh Susanna,* Steven Foster's *Jeannie with the Light Brown Hair* and *My Old Kentucky Home.* In the 1980s I had an opportunity to visit Steven Foster's Kentucky plantation; the inspiration of his music and memories of Jean Parker Elementary drifted into my head as I toured the grounds. Our musical repertoire included learning folk dancing, but the *hokey pokey* movements made absolutely no sense to me. One shook the hands and the legs in and out of the circle followed by a full body hop in and out. The concluding line of the song was "…and that's what it's all about." I never understood, was there a point?

Old Jean Parker saw its demise in 1990 as a victim of the 1989 Loma Prieto Earthquake. The principal, Claudia Jeung, saw to the demolition and construction of a new Jean Parker School on the same site. Her thrill was to find a time capsule during its demolition.

Entering Junior High

By the seventh grade, I was at Francisco Junior High, a twelve-block walk to the North Beach area at Powell and Bay Streets. Caucasian old-timers often reminisced about walking miles to school. We Chinatown kids certainly did the same. While the cable car was available, who could afford to ride even though the student fare was a nickel? The Chinese and Italians were the majority in Francisco. Our class numbered about 110 in size. There was a slight competition between homerooms even though we all live the same neighborhood.

I was in Room 114 with Miss Virginia Hausman, the homeroom and English teacher. This redhead, who reeked of cigarettes, was quite thin and accented her waistline by wearing thick belts and billowing shirtsleeve dresses. Her expertise seemed to be diagramming sentences. We tore down full sentences into branches of adjectives and adverbs; however, I never saw the benefit of the exercises since we never put those components back or learned how to use this knowledge.

Even in our own homeroom we were predominantly Chinese and had few other nationalities. In hindsight what's striking was that we hardly communicated or socialized with the non-Chinese. We were that much into ourselves or our group. For instance two rows away from me sat a fair-complexioned, rather tall girl with braids, she often wore a Peter Pan-collared, white blouse and a pink and gray plaid skirt. We never spoke during all those school years. Some thirty years later we found ourselves living in the same town. I happened to go into her jewelry shop. She gave me a quizzical look and said she knew me from somewhere. I was baffled. We tried to reconnect making the usual stabs at neighborhoods, friends, and high school. Nothing fit. At 11:00 PM that night I woke and exclaimed to a sleepy husband, "I know her, she's Irene Silin from Francisco." I proceeded to rattle off my recollections as if he cared. Since that time Irene Sillin Borelli and I have become the best of friends. No one in our class would have known that Irene, of Russian heritage, was born in Harbin, China, and her family had lived there for at least three generations. During World War II they were merchants living in Shanghai and fairly wealthy. In those turbulent years of Mao Tse Tung's communist takeover, they fled leaving their possessions behind. Her grandma lost her large building to the government and was relegated to an assigned apartment to be shared with others. Irene's parents escaped to San Francisco and began as immigrants starting life anew within the Russian community. There were so many coincidences, mostly war associated, and our birthdays even fell on the same day.

Another classmate, who sat two seats behind Irene, also experienced similar childhood scars of war, dislocation, and eventually life in Chinatown. Wellman Chin, later to be my third husband, also suffered similar trauma and deprivation. I never spoke to him in the homeroom; he had all the bearings of a "*pachuco*"–baggy pants, a sauntering shuffle and a demeanor suggestive of a "bad boy." He was born in Hong Kong, the youngest of seven.

When he was a baby his father went off to war and never returned. His mother brought her children back to the village to survive and sit out the war. At age seven, Wellman's grandfather arranged for him to come to America as a son of an emigrating family, actually his married aunt's family. Life was not simple or idyllic for he was looked upon as another mouth to feed. His aunt's husband beat him often so he ran away and lived in the streets until his mother arrived. Even though he was under his mother's roof, she spent endless hours working in the sewing factory to support the family, so Wellman literally raised himself never knowing his father and receiving little attention from his mother. It seemed even at our young age some of us carried scars as a result of the war which we kept to ourselves unbeknownst to our more fortunate ABC friends born in America.

Rounding out my time at Francisco, across the hall from our homeroom was the typing room the domain of Miss Elvera Fusco, a young, energetic, pleasant Italian. The students adored her for she showed real interest in their progress. Once I watched her as she was watching two young boys playing around. Their curiosity was such that they took apart an old typewriter, removing the patent roller, stripping the casing that held the keys and other parts to see how far down they could strip the instrument. Rather than jumping up and reprimanding them, she pretended not to notice. Before the dismissal bell rang, the boys rebuilt the typewriter much to their satisfaction and that of Miss Fusco. I took two years of typing which became the mainstay of my working life. In the mid-1990s during a July 4th celebration I met up with Miss Fusco again at Tinsley Island on the San Joaquin Delta. She had not aged; she was still pleasant looking and charming.

Dr. Laurence Childress, the principal, gave me my first opportunity to see my name in print. I don't know why I was selected but I remember being called into his office. He asked if I was interested in writing a column on school activities for a local neighborhood Chinese newspaper that had an English section. Inspired by the thought of the mighty pen and my recent assignment, I ran for and was elected editor of the school paper in the last year of junior high. The previous year I served as the student body secretary. We campaigned by making 2x3 foot posters with catchy slogans. Incorporating the school colors of *Green & Gold* and using the school mascot, a ram, showed we demonstrated a high sense of school spirit.

I can't remember any of my slogans; most likely it was some type of jingle. Perhaps, these early gains in elected positions piqued my interest in civic affairs.

Some of us ate well at Francisco. Along with a few girlfriends we worked at the school cafeteria. Excused at 11:30 AM we ate quickly off of the daily menu, then put on the ugly hairnets and waited at the steam table for the students to arrive. Serving took less than thirty minutes including clean up and then we joined others at the playground for the rest of the lunch hour. Today's students want to eat off campus but during our school days we thought the cafeteria food was well balanced and flavorful. It certainly was a change from eating Chinese food all the time. Maybe we were not picky with our food but the food standards are so different today. We were never served fast food and never tasted a burrito.

I have to credit my time in Francisco with some curious firsts: I tasted pumpkin, as in pumpkin pie, in a home economics class. Until then I only knew custard and apple pies. The teacher thought it as an old American standard and got us preparing the pie near Thanksgiving. When we opened the canned pumpkin and dipped our fingers into the fruit the instant reaction was, "This is it? It tastes like sand." Some of the other girls had a similar reaction so I gathered pumpkin pies were not a Chinese American staple.

Our gym classes were also new to many of us; we wore blue gym suits similar to rompers and learned to shower with other girls – believe me, all of us had a very high level of modesty. Mrs. Stern, the gym teacher, wanted to teach us hygiene and asked that we purchase some deodorant. Although we did not know what that was and for what purpose since at that age our glands did not sweat much. I dutifully went to the dime store and bought a small dime-size can of Mum's deodorant (it was also the cheapest). After opening and seeing this white paste that smelled fairly nice I put a dab behind my ears. The next day when the teacher asked if we used deodorant I smiled and said "yes."

Auntie Fran provided a wonderful incentive to encourage good grades. Not only was making the honor roll a requirement but the A's had to out number the B's. The reward was tickets to light operas playing at the Curran Theater on Geary Street. It was wonderful to see the afternoon matinee original stage productions with Yul Brenner and Gertrude Lawrence in *Anna and the King*; Mary Martin in

Peter Pan and later *in South Pacific*. When the film *Gigi* made its debut, I fell in love with Louis Jordan.

Francisco Junior High 50th Reunion. I am second from the right on the couch.

A Full Blown Teenager

My social life began to blossom through church and scouting. My first experience with a local church was at the Chinese Congregational down on Brennan Street, now Walter U. Lum Place. The church was next door to Wing Sang Mortuary. The activities at the True Sunshine Episcopal Mission at Pacific and Mason Streets were more fulfilling. I sang in the adult choir for a spell. I can't carry a tune, but when I raised my voice along with ten other people, I went un-noticed. We also went to and taught Sunday school, but it took quite a bit of time. Ah Pau could understand disappearing for an hour or two but to be gone for the better part of Sunday meant that I couldn't be included in anything she had planned.

At True Sunshine we formed the three musketeers; Ernestine Lee and Claudia Jeung, the other two musketeers, lived across from each other on Clay Street.

We looked like stair steps, Ernestine was the tallest, Claudia the middle one and I was shorty. Our family life was also quite different in that Ernestine had parents and a younger brother. Claudia was the only child and I had neither. I had Ah Pau. Ernestine's mother volunteered at the elementary school; Claudia's mother, whom I called Auntie Rose, worked at the Rexall Drug Store on Mason Street. Both girls' mothers were very kind to me. I envied my friends' family life.

As the only child, Claudia had the prettiest clothes, particularly her flair skirts which accentuated her waistline. These were the days of multiple petticoats and wide cinch belts. I had a half-slip petticoat which didn't flare out much so I added two more straight half slips thinking that should have done the trick. But, all it did was accentuate larger and wider hips. I certainly was no fashion plate. Auntie Fran sewed most of my clothes. She was quite talented. From one Simplicity pattern she created three or four dresses -- one with collar, one without, short sleeves, or no sleeves.

Ernestine, Claudia and Sylvia

Scouting Days

We three musketeers were members of Girl Scout Troop 63 which met Tuesday nights at "The Rec," a city-sponsored recreational center on the corner of Mason and Washington Streets, just across from the cable car barn. This two-story building had a large, indoor basketball court, meeting rooms and a multi-use auditorium. Teens in the area took advantage of the facility. I even enjoyed the swings in the playground area up behind the building. The Rec has been totally rebuilt *in situ*, modernized, and renamed *The Betty Ong Center.* [4]

In the four years of scouting we had two leaders, one was Lorraine Leong and the other Shirley Sing nee Chin, Dai Yee Pau's granddaughter. (With Ah Pau's sixteen brothers and sisters, adopted or natural, I was related to almost everyone in Chinatown.) It was an almost all-Chinese troop except for Maxine Kaufman, a Jewish girl whose parents owned a car with a rumble seat. Mr. Kaufman was most generous in that he drove around the blocks endless times and gave each of the girls a chance to sit in that rumble seat. Maxine never appeared to feel out of place among her Asian friends. I thought she was just as Chinese as we were. Although our meetings lasted an hour, I stretched my night out another hour longer enjoying the camaraderie. My early taste of scouting in Bangkok compounded by this scouting experience reinforced my dedication to civic service. We earned merit badges, participated in Chinese New Year and Double Ten (Nationalist Chinese Independence Day) parades either riding on floats or marching. Quite often we had a choice of participating in the parades through the scouting program or by being part of the Chinese language school classes. Riding on a flatbed truck was far easier than marching two miles.

One day Claudia and Ernestine did some brainstorming and decided to enter the troop in a radio talk show contest to design "the perfect party." The troop won second prize thanks to this dual think-tank, the prize was a record player that got donated to the Ming Quong Orphanage.

For installation and other social gatherings the troop booked Friendly Garden, a piece of property owned by the Girl Scouts, in the middle of Clay Street between Powell and Mason. A six-foot, grape-stake fence shielded the garden from the neighbors. Within this secluded garden setting was a small building that housed a kitchen and a multi-purpose room with knotty pine walls -- giving the entire interior a rustic cabin feeling. For those of us who grew up in apartments and flats unaccustomed to yards, trees and plants, Friendly Garden was a delightful respite. In later years the parcel was sold and now holds a three-story condo building.

Troop #63 excelled in selling Girl Scout cookies. We were young entrepreneurs who set out to prove we could corner the market. Of course, we were the only troop in Chinatown and the financial district. Each year in preparation, the girls took pre-orders and overshot our initial estimates time after time. We scoped out marketing sites within our targeted area. Some girls sold at stores where their families worked. Auntie Fran allowed us a one-day set-up at the Bank of America on Grant Avenue. When we were through there, we hustled down to the bank's main branch at the corner of Montgomery and Clay Streets. There, after gifting the elderly elevator man a box of cookies, he suggested particular floors and offices where there were potential buyers. Afterwards, I trotted across the street and worked the Bank of Canton and then went upstairs to the Chinese Consulate. We did well, invariably selling numerous cases of cookies which increased our coffers and covered our expenses throughout the year.

Girl Scouts Troop 163 at Friendly Garden on Clay Street

Our troop was not big on camping. We did have an overnight at Camp Manor in Marin County. We slept on cots on the second floor in a sleeping porch. A bright, full moon, the sweet scented air from the pine trees and the silhouette of the trees gently swaying lent to the aura. I experienced another night similar to that within the walls of the L'Alhambra in Granada, Spain many decades later.

Our troop developed a friendship with a Concord troop; we took them to lunch in Chinatown and to the Chinese Temple on Pine Street. In return they took us to a dairy. I didn't know it would smell that bad. That was my first venture beyond the Oakland hills. Little did I realize that in less than seven years later I would live beyond the second set of hills, deep in the Central Valley where I have stayed.

Scouting also was a way to meet boys. We shared lots of social activities with Boy Scout Troop 211, a Chinatown boys' group.

Whenever there was an opportunity to include the opposite sex in an installation, special event or just hold a dance, we did not hesitate to plan, plot and plot again. Most of the boys were Chinese and were just as innocent as we. I did not date. I dared not because Ah Pau was strict; but that didn't stop me from enjoying boys at that social level. We did not wear lipstick, makeup, or exaggerated jewelry like today's teenagers. Cost and not wanting to look conspicuous were the main reasons. Thinking back, teenagers in the 1950s underwent an age of innocence. Perhaps it was the post-war era and we were influenced by family-type television programs the likes of *The Donna Reed Show*, *Happy Days* and *Leave It to Beaver*.

While I was absorbed in scouting and church there was another group of girls in the same homeroom that belonged to Cameron House. The namesake of the institution is legendary. A New Zealander, Ms. Donaldina Cameron immigrated to California in 1871 at the age of 2. She started as a sewing teacher at the Presbyterian Mission House at 920 Sacramento Street and became the superintendent by 1897. In the annals of San Francisco and Chinatown's history she is credited with rescuing young Chinese girls from prostitution and protecting them physically and while seeing them through the judicial system. In many cases she was awarded guardianship over these young ladies. Although the original mission house was destroyed in the 1906 San Francisco earthquake it was rebuilt two years later; it still stands today. In 1942 that the mission home was renamed "Donaldina Cameron House." Cameron House evolved into a youth center with many age-related clubs. My classmates belonged to the Chickadees. What a comparison! We were scouts and they were baby chickens. Although we were not competitive, it seemed that the Chickadees appeared clique-ish, or at least they talked more about their activities and hung around together more at school.

My introduction to a Chickadee living on Stone Street, Sandra Der, was most bizarre. I was on the roof of our apartment one day, enjoying the skyline of the city. Sandra was on her parents' roof that faced the back of Ah Pau's building. Although I didn't know who started it first, but we began to throw stones at each other. The stones were actually little pieces of gravel and pebbles that couldn't be thrown far but they could have broken other people's windows because our aim was not very good. It began as a silly little contact, but Sandra and I later shared several exploits such as taking our first smoke in the bathroom hoping Auntie Fran wouldn't catch us.

One New Year's Eve Sandra and I happened to be on Sze Yee Pau's fire escape on Grant Avenue with my cousin Diana (Sze Yee Pau's granddaughter) watching the revelry. The street was a mass of people saturated with confetti; it was great fun watching from above. Diana, who was visiting from Capitola, was quite brazen and attracted the attention of a couple of sailors down below. We were only about fourteen years old then and while it seemed safe to tease from above, it did not become a joke when the sailors said that they were willing to join us on the fire escape. At that suggestion we got scared and scrambled back into Sze Yee Pau's apartment, never saying a word as to what we had been up to. That was a good lesson in learning when and when not to tease.

Schooling Beyond Chinatown

When the class of 1955 graduated from Francisco Junior High, seven of us girls chose to go to Lowell High School. Lowell, well known as an academic preparatory school whose alumni were among the rich and famous, was open to students citywide and did not have the same boundary restrictions of district schools. A high grade point average was the key to admittance. I did not know that we were in an elite group-- all girls. The reason I chose this high school was because I did not want to attend Galileo where there were too many Chinese. Lowell, purportedly included a mixed population, but had a preponderance of Jewish kids. Little did I realize that natural selection played a role in choice of friends. Together we, seven, ate lunch and rode the bus home almost daily. Maybe our common geographic and ethnic backgrounds were the impetus for us to hang together. Mildred, Celia, Jo Ann, Leticia, Helen, and Sandra were part of the original Cameron House Chickadees and I was the sole scout. Studying was foremost in our minds and while we saw each other in school, I still did not socialize much with them outside of school. However there was the opportunity to mix with Japanese American girls and one, Louise Okubo, became a long time friend. The old World War II hatred between the Japanese and Chinese in the older generation surfaced when Ah Pau found out Louise was Japanese and Lou's family also was not pleased that I was Chinese. Maybe because of the older generations' steadfast opposition to our seeing each other, Lou and I worked much harder at retaining our friendship. Even at that age we were wise enough to transcend old prejudices. We are still each other's confidant.

Lowell sat on the corner of Hayes and Masonic Street quite far from Chinatown. I took the #30 Stockton bus, transferred to the #21 Hayes bus and got off on Masonic, or I would walk up to Clay Street, take the #55 Sacramento (southbound), transfer to the Fillmore or the Dividisaro and then take the Hayes bus. Either way, commuting required multiple transfers and early morning starts. This commute took at least an hour each way.

We arrived at Lowell just in time for the centennial celebration in 1956. The school doted over alumnus Carol Channing for she was a rising star as was Marty Links, the cartoonist of *Bobby Soxs.* There was a major rally and football game held at Kezar Stadium and the entire student body trotted to that facility. It was hard to explain to Ah Pau where I was going and why it was necessary to attend the football game.

Again, lessons didn't seem to stick in my memory as much as activities. Two years of Physiology under Mrs. Kellogg may have been the most useful for my adult life, particularly as we age; at least I know where the organs and muscles are located. In class I sat across from a couple of Jewish students. One in particular made a name for himself as head of the San Francisco Visitors and Convention Bureau. John Marks actually became the guru for the tourism industry in California. Peter Samuels, grandson of founder Samuels Jewelers, was a really jovial person. Five years after graduation, I decided to get my ears pierced and thought that he would be the best one to do it. So one day I walked into Samuel Jewelers on Market Street and asked for Pete. He had just come back from lunch; his persona suggested it was a two-martini one. Pete took aim at my left ear lobe and missed the center. He quickly dabbed some liquid antibiotic sealant. In a matter of minutes and a bit of small talk, he tried again while I shut my eyes and cursed myself for putting him and myself in such a predicament. Ah, this time it was painless and successful.

High school was not easy; at times I made the honor roll and at times I did not. One board of education requirement for graduation was to demonstrate the ability to swim. A test is given in the senior year. Oh, how I dreaded this since I had already had one near drowning experience in Bangkok. Bracing myself, I signed up for swimming at the YWCA down on Sutter Street as part of my gym program. In my junior year I stayed at the shallow end of the pool all semester. By the time the big test arrived, we lined up at the edge of the deep end and when it came my turn, I took a huge breath, pushed off as hard as possible, shut my eyes and kicked quickly and furiously towards the shallow end. Still holding my breath, never looking up, putting my arms straight ahead, and not cutting the water, I managed to reach the five-foot marker and then bobbled my way another foot. Now that I think about it that was the last time I was in a swimming pool. The year was 1958.

Most memorable were the after school bus rides. Not so much the ride itself but trying to get on the bus. Bus staff would be stationed at the rear end of the bus; the bus driver was in the front. Both men helped to get the students on board faster. Many of us jammed into the back entrance and held out our bus pass for punching. Frequently the pushing and shoveling made the conductor's ability to punch all the tickets impossible and resulted in hanging chads which looked as if the card was not punched at all and it afforded us another ride.

One day I talked Sandra Der into walking home from school at least once in our life. Since this was our senior year it was now or never. Yes, it was dear Sandra my conspirator in our first smoking session and the New Year's sailors incident. We checked our route making sure we avoided Fillmore and Divisadero for they were noted as the Black and "dangerous" neighborhoods. (Perhaps through local efforts these areas have improved.) It took us a good two to three hours. By the time we stopped at the little wayside shelter under the shadow of Grace Cathedral on California Street we were exhausted. But, by God, when we said we were going to do something, we did.

The Family Returns

My senior year was one big blur even though I paid my dues in the various before and after school organizations. I skipped a half semester and was due to graduate in June of 1958. What would have been a grand senior year became filled with tension and anxiety. Father was reassigned to San Francisco and the family arrived in March of 1958. That is, everyone except older sister, Dida, who graduated from Mills in 1956 and returned to the Orient to marry

Larry Gotuaco her long-time Manila sweetheart. In fact, of all the times I truly wanted to be with the family was at her wedding. I wrote repeatedly to Mom asking if that was possible; my parents' silence suggested I was *persona non grata.*

Father's new rank was Republic of China's Consul General to San Francisco. The office was still on Montgomery and Clay Street above the Bank of Canton. Auntie E, still at the consulate, served as father's

The old Lowell High at Hayes & Masonic, San Francisco

secretary. The family moved into Nob Hill's Stanford Court, a very exclusive apartment building on the corner of California and Powell Streets. The building faced the famous Fairmont Hotel and was next door to the Mark Hopkins Hotel. One good thing about Stanford Court's location was that Ah Pau's building was only three blocks away. With my family here I had to move back under father's roof. There was no way I could stay with Ah Pau even though I begged and begged for her to keep me. While she wanted me to stay with her, it looked inappropriate. With Auntie France's marriage the previous year and my return to the family fold, grandma no longer had a companion and in very short time her health took a turn and headed downhill. It wasn't much later that she became bedridden and stayed that way for many years before her death.

Stanford Court had all the appearance of "snob hill." The apartment, on the second floor, was a two bedroom, two bath with a huge living room and large dining room. Off of the pantry was a maid's quarter. Philip slept in the parents' bedroom on an easy chair that converted to a bed at night. Glo and I had twin beds in our own room. Our window faced the circular driveway of the court, giving us good view of cars entering and departing. My parents brought two service employees with them. Ung, a diminutive and kind maid and Ah Wang, the cook. I don't remember where he slept. He was a great cook and many years later opened his own restaurant in Los Angeles on the corner of Hollywood and Vine Streets. Ung was industrious and very caring to Ah Pau and Ah Pau's sisters. Eventually when she left my parents' employ she found other work in Chinatown to support herself and moved into one of the units in Sze Yee Pau's building on Grant Avenue.

My closest friends always thought my background was different from theirs. I never pushed the idea of being from high society or even bantered about my father's career except to say my parents were overseas. There was really nothing pleasant to say and it was better that I held my tongue. When the folks moved into Stanford Court I moved in with them -- from the friends' point of view -- I was definitely living high off the hog. Their gentle teasing belied a bit of envy; but they never realized I was unhappy and filled with trepidation.

Father knew Mr. Perino, the principal at Lowell, and personally went to the school to enroll my sister Glo. I was already a senior but the schools Glo attended in Taipei did not run on a parallel program, thus she was tested for a lower grade. Father did not want her placed in the class below mine, as a junior. As a result, we both were in the same grade. It really did not bother me because I had my set of friends and she quickly made some herself. And we did not hang around each other. Coming from overseas Glo already knew most of the hit songs and was very up on styles as well as teen interests. I felt like a country hick when it came to teen hot topics. Glo actually stayed in Lowell for three or four months prior to our graduation.

While living with the family I would slip down and visit Ah Pau whenever possible. Things had changed and I couldn't spend that much time with her nor could I again run her errands. It seemed a veil had begun to drop between us and our relationship was not as close. My mother and I never quite developed a bonding relationship, perhaps because her mother raised me and my traits were similar to her mother's. To my mother, it seemed, I acted like a younger sister rather than a long lost daughter. She felt I was old fashioned. In later years she even quipped that I was "rather dowdy."

Father never struck me again but the relationship remained strained. He did, however, discover I was useful in that I typed well. I typed his many speeches as he edited many renditions. Staying current with events, these speeches delved into activities occurring in Mainland China -- primarily the ongoing and changing policies of Mao Zedong's devastating Cultural Revolution. The subjective detection of traitors in Mao's *Thousand Flowers Bloom* pogrom was a way to seek out writers, artists, and even movie stars who lent voice against Communism. Mao's Red Guard Movement gave excuse for angry youths to destroy libraries, temples, and cultural and educational facilities. Intellects were beaten, killed, and/or sent to communes for rehabilitation. Father did an excellent job keeping the San Franciscan and Northern California Chinese apprised of the two Chinas situation. I absorbed what I typed but had many questions which I feared to ask as it might be construed as challenging his thoughts or authority. Much of the information needed some type of open dialogue before I could digest the knowledge. There was no one to talk to; my friends couldn't comprehend nor were they truly interested in international political affairs. Talking with relatives was no better. I did not know how deeply I was troubled by the information in father's speeches until twelve years later when I sought out counseling before getting a divorce. When the psychologist asked what were the things troubling me I found myself blurting out my confusion and the details about China's Cultural Revolution.

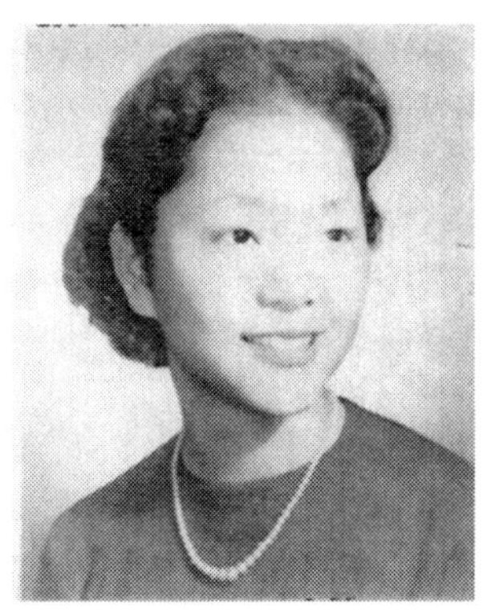

Living with the family created some memorable occasions. The first was meeting Madame Chiang Kai Shek as she came through San

Francisco in 1957. There was a reception for her held at the St. Francis Hotel. When we shook hands, I was captivated by her perfume and I remarked so, asking what brand was it. She told me but I cannot remember the brand. The Madame was very gracious and pleasant looking, very classy. The other eventful night was a dinner at the Forbidden City, a nightclub on Grant Avenue. The academy award cinematographer James Howe Wong, an old friend of father, was the guest. It was a double honor -- meeting a person connected to movies and going to my first night club. Jimmy (that's what Mom called him) was quite a gregarious person and he thoroughly enjoyed watching the Chinese dancers, particularly the one that danced semi-nude covering up with a big ball at appropriate moments.

Aside from attending the senior prom and the graduation ceremony at the War Memorial Opera House in the Civic Center, I did not cherish the memories of high school as much as that of Francisco Junior High. I have come to realize the friendships I had in junior high were much more enduring and sustaining. Perhaps it was because living with the family was more restricted than living with Ah Pau. I had less freedom and less self expression. No longer did I make quick trips down to Chinatown, church activities stopped, and my scout days ended with our vestiture into Senior Scouts. Shortly after the ceremony our scout troop disbanded.

Chapter 7

Moving On

In the late 1950s and early 60s the stereotypical goal of many girls was to attend college after high school and, while there, find and marry an eligible mate, one whose career allowed for children, house, and a station wagon. Television family sitcoms helped to push this notion. So did many Chinese families. To many the phrase "a white picket fence" was an image as well as an ideology. I, too, thought such a life would be great and uncomplicated. This was a clearly defined road map of life. But something went wrong and I took a turn shortly after high school that compromised this idyllic vision.

The Final Runaway

My sister Gloria applied to Mills College trying to follow in oldest sister Patricia's footsteps. Mills was quite costly and had the reputation of being a "finishing" school for the elites. Patricia (Dida) had proven herself well when she made Phi Beta Kappa, the national honor society. Instead of that institution Gloria landed up being accepted at Dominican College in San Rafael. Since we both graduated from Lowell at the same time I asked Father his thoughts regarding me. He said: "Gloria is older and she is to go to college first."

"But, I also want to go to college," I replied on my own behalf. At which point he replied: "Dominican is very expensive and I can afford to send only one child at a time.

Pressing the issue, I asked, "How long would that be?"

He quipped, "However long it takes."

I was aghast, I responded, "I received a partial scholarship to Lone Mountain College for Women here in the City and I can live at home."

In an offhanded manner he replied: "No one has ever heard of Lone Mountain. You just have to wait."

"Then I'll go out and get a job."

His curt response, "No, that is not appropriate."

"Then what do you want me to do?"

"I don't know, be quiet, and stay out of trouble." With that our conversation came to an abrupt end. I was furious and seething with rage. How unfair life had become again, I was relegated to the subhuman level while Glo remained father's little darling. The chip on my shoulder was getting heavier and heavier. From then on I seethed every time I saw father, resentful at his treatment or the lack of it towards me.

Okay, I said to myself, I'll wait. So I enrolled at City College and was there for only a couple of months. That Fall (1958) mother took a trip to New York and Washington, D.C. to attend a women's conference or something of that sort on behalf of the Chinese government. Before her departure she asked that I take care of Philip. Phil, age nine then, was attending Commodore School but was not exactly the model student. In fact he was down right spoiled and naughty. His teacher had several discussions with mother about his antics. While mother was gone, father was busy entertaining a visiting movie star. He always had an eye for beautiful women be they models, movie stars or even starlets. Mother knew about father's propensity, but I was ignorant to this fact. I did not know much about the birds and the bees when I left the family at age ten, but was quite aware of what was right and proper at age 17. The straw that literally broke the camel's back occurred when father brought a movie star to the house and he told me to go to my room, he meant disappear. By this time Glo was at Dominican and Phil and I shared the bedroom.

I had it! Quietly, I took out a small suitcase that I brought from Ah Pau's several months before, packed some bare essentials and took all the money I had saved. I slipped out the front door, got on the elevator, and as I walked out onto the cobblestone, circular driveway I turned and looked up. Phil was standing at the window looking at me in a very quizzical manner. I put my fingers to my lips to signal him to keep quiet and waved. He waved back.

I called Donald Chan, a friend whom I recently met at City College. Don was shocked but willingly found me a cheap hotel that night and then took me to some friends to stay for a week in Sacramento while I tried to sort out my situation.

My first concern was how to support myself. Quickly it came to me – assets? A high school diploma, something others never had but managed to do quite well. Work experience? I had babysat, slung hash for four summers working with the Changs at the San Mateo fairs, and briefly worked as a receptionist for Uncle Tim another summer. I could answer telephones even use a complex switchboard and I could type. With this type of bravado and self-assuredness I vowed then and there that I was never going to live under my father's roof again nor was I going to be under his thumb again. I had just executed my third and final run away.

Meanwhile the family noted I was missing and figured I ran away again. Although I finished high school at seventeen I was technically still a minor. Because of father's position, the Federal Bureau of Investigation (FBI) was called just in case something did happen to me that might possibly create a diplomatic incident. The FBI questioned many people including all the relatives and even some of my friends. No one at that point knew anything. There was speculation that I was pregnant or was in some other type of trouble. The family would never have considered that it was partially their fault that created this situation. The FBI even questioned Don. To throw off the scent, I wrote mother a short note stating I was fine. It was mailed from an obscure neighborhood in Vallejo.

More than a week passed and then I asked Don to take me to San Mateo to see Auntie E and Uncle Paul. I felt I needed some allies. After telling them why I left home, Uncle Paul agreed to drive me to Uncle Hank's in Redding until things cooled off. I still remember our night's travel. I hopped into the pickup. During the five hour drive Uncle Paul kept assuring me that everything was going to be okay. He said Auntie E would never say anything to father even though they worked together. It was also none of Auntie Fran or Uncle Tim's business. They both understood my circumstances and reasons I had to leave home. Uncle Paul never once even suggested that I return to the family fold. For that I was grateful. Eventually my weariness got the best of me and I was lulled to sleep by Uncle Paul singing to keep himself awake on the long drive in the dark. Ironically, one day Gloria looked directly at Auntie

E and said, "You know where Sylvia is." Auntie E never gave me away.

A Varitypist on a Varityper

I stayed in Redding for about a month then moved back down to the Peninsula, more specifically to San Mateo and found work in Burlingame at Tri-City Blueprint, a print shop. The job was entry level and the salary $1.25 an hour. This was fantastic for it was my first experience at being really self sufficient. I opened up a checking account and rented a studio apartment on Fifth Avenue in downtown San Mateo from a lady who operated a private exercise business in other parts of the house. Two airline pilots rented the upstairs for their short respites when they flew into town. Within a few months, the print shop owner realized that I had a knack for typing and an eye for creating print material. He sent me to varityping classes in San Francisco for a week. The varityper is a forerunner of our computer age of composition and justification. The machine had dual dials and a yard long wooden roller to hold and wind the paper tight enough to slip into the bowel of the machine. I would type the text on the left side and push a button and the machine would repeat the text on the right side fully justified. The trick was to keep an eye on the dials as I typed. This added skill gave me the confidence to leave the little print shop and find employment in San Francisco as a varitypist.

Stationers Price Service, a small stationary service company on Third and Mission Streets in the city, became my new employer. The company kept an enormous catalog of stationery products – from different sizes, colors, and weights of paper, pencil leads, assortments of envelopes, paper clips, ink and ink pads and so forth. It is amazing how many items are in a stationary store. My job was to type the price change, then bending over a light table, splice the change onto the original copy. These weekly price changes were mailed to their store subscribers. Yes, another technical skill learned that proved useful further down the road.

The company was housed on the second floor of a six-story, terra cotta brick building near the Convention Center. Surprisingly after some sixty years the building still stands but it does show it had better days. There was a small, greasy spoon café downstairs with two sets of counters but no tables. A Filipino husband-and-wife team operated the eating establishment and served a tasty bowl of chili which included a packet of saltines for only thirty-five cents. I found them fascinating with their tales of the Philippines, particularly during the war. Remi, the husband, had been, at one time, a cook for General Douglas MacArthur. It was a small world.

When I started work in San Francisco I moved in with a young Chinese Hawaiian nurse in training at St. Mary's Help Hospital. For a nurse she was rather lazy and sloppy. Moreover, her large family descended upon us for a long visit and I landed sleeping on the floor for a number of weeks. This was not a good situation. Thus, I met and moved in with Beverly Tang, a former Miss Chinatown contestant from Phoenix, Arizona. During the day Beverly worked as a receptionist in a patent law office and at night served as a hostess at the Imperial Palace Restaurant on Grant Avenue. She was down to earth, seemed to be at ease in any situation, and had a good head on her shoulders. Above all she was a hard worker and wise. Our one-bedroom apartment was on California Street near Polk. I liked that particular part of town. Many years later Beverly married Bill Lim of Sacramento. We had the good fortune to stay in touch. Sadly, they have both passed on.

An Attempt At Reconciliation

In August of 1959 my parents celebrated their 25th anniversary. Knowing this happy event I wanted to get them something special even though we were estranged. My feelings towards father had calmed considerably. I did not want the burden of bearing grudges and thought to extend the first olive branch by going to Macy's. I bought a crystal bowl and a nice, silver-etched anniversary platter. The store was to deliver it. A week later I heard footsteps by the front door of my apartment, but strange no one rang the bell. And just as quickly the footsteps ran away. Out of curiosity I opened the door and there were my Macy's gifts. My reaction was, "oh well, I tried." I learned later it was Uncle George who helped my parents return the packages to me.

It was about 1964 when my youngest daughter, Darcy was at that cute age of two when I felt it was time to take another crack at repairing my relationship with my parents. It had been five years since I last tried to connect with them. The parents had moved to a house in San Mateo across from Auntie E and Uncle Paul. I called saying I was going to visit Auntie E and wanted to drop by so they could see my children. Our visit went off quite pleasantly. Mother acted as if nothing was amissed. Clearly, it was my two daughters who helped rebuilt my relationship with my parents.

Chapter 8

Dreams and Realities

In the one and a half years since I left home, I became closer to Don Chan. There was something about him that made him seem more pathetic than me. He felt he had a more miserable childhood. His father, Wahso D. Chan, a young UC graduate artist, was killed in a car/pedestrian accident near the civic center one night on the way to work. Don was a baby then and Wahso's widow, Mary, was pregnant with her second child. After William (Bill) was born Mary married Thomas Kim, a local gym teacher at Francisco Junior High who had a passion for tennis. Mary and Tommy Kim had three other children, Roger, Richard, and Linda. Don always felt he was the outcast and by the time the Kim children arrived he was a belligerent teen who frequently got into trouble and was sent to reform school. He said he never felt he was loved. I learned much later that Don was officially adopted by Tommy, but Don did not want to recognize Tommy as his father or stepfather. Therefore, he kept the Chan surname rather than adopt Kim as his last name unlike his real brother, Bill. I actually got along with the Kims quite well and still enjoy Don's siblings to this day.

When we met, Don was 26 years old, fresh out of the Navy, working part time as a mail carrier and earning some credits at San Francisco City College. He purchased a tomato red 1957 Plymouth Fury with gold trim. The car was flashy and he dressed as if he was too. Girls flocked to the car and wanted to have their pictures taken with him and the car. I did not think the car or Don fascinating. Although fairly good looking, well built and 5' 11', he was not handsome in my book. I never liked hunks or body builders. Deep down Don was not flamboyant, he was soft hearted and just a real nice guy. I convinced him to replace the car with a 1960 white Pontiac Catalina, a four-door sedan – a family car. It was a sure sign that I was no longer running around with someone who thought he was still a playboy.

In December 1959 we decided to get married in Reno as I found out I was pregnant. Mary asked if I would like to have her old wedding ring, the one that she wore when married to Don's father, Wahso. What a wonderful gesture and I accepted. The white gold ring, a circle of hearts and flowers, was very popular in the mid-1930s. Both their initials and their wedding date were inscribed on the inside. Taking that ring was the worst mistake I ever made in my life and if it were possible to turn back the clock or change one thing in one's life I should have said, "No, thank you." Forty years later I paid heavily for accepting Mary's old wedding ring.

The day after Christmas we headed for Reno accompanied by Mary and Don's siblings Bill, Linda, and Richard. I should have known things were not going to be great. The civic ceremony did not take long and, for an unknown reason, I started to giggle which burst into tremendous laughter. Everyone didn't know what got into me. Was it a case of nerves? I was 18 and old enough to get married but not old enough to gamble. Somehow in my innocence, Don registered his two younger siblings and me in the children's section of the casino while he and his mother headed for the blackjack tables. He said he would be back shortly…he wasn't. What made matters worse was that I could not get out since an adult put us in there. In my heart I knew this was a bad sign. As I look back, I remember feeling quite disappointed then and having the premonition that our marriage was not going to last even though I held on to a strong vision of marriage and family.

Becoming a Family

Our daughter, Donna Kim Chan, arrived in mid-June. It was two days of hard labor and Donna stubbornly refused to make her entrance. Finally at Children's' Hospital my water bag broke. Quite a frightening sight to see the nurse put on a glove with something that looked like a sharp spike on the middle finger then she inserted into me without anything to deaden the pain. As soon as the warmth from the water gushed out the labor pains increased four-fold. The baby was not in the right position in the birth canal and had to be turned. Quite skillfully Dr. Marie Blehm delivered our beautiful baby. Donna weighed close to seven pounds and was larger than the doctor or I expected. No wonder there was such a long period of pain but she was so worth it -- healthy, a cherub face, and looked very much like her father and paternal grandmother. We were all delighted. These were the days when the government did not provide health insurance for employees; thus, my two weeks' stay in the hospital and delivery cost us over $900.00. There is something to be said about fringe benefits and amenities with federal civil service today. Thank goodness my employers held open my job for two weeks so I could recuperate. With mounting bills there was not even a discussion of my staying home, two incomes were necessary even though we lived frugally.

We moved into a two-bedroom apartment at 1664 Washington Street near Polk Street. It was an area that was quite familiar and within walking distance of my old apartments and former roommates. The rent was seventy-five dollars a month. We lived on the second floor in a back unit. The placed was furnished with donated furniture. Somewhere Don salvaged a four-panel screen, size 6'x 2' that depicted cranes, pine trees, and a mountainous background. The scenery was rather bold, each panel outlined by a thick black frame. Don's father, Wahso, painted the screen and while he was certainly gifted, I did not feel that it had the soft genre of ancient Chinese painters. The screen made a nice décor when pushed against the wall.

Donna's room was bright and sunny and had a Murphy bed. Donna's bassinet was a banana box camouflaged with contact paper on the outside and the mattress consisted of padding wrapped with a baby blanket. She then graduated to a drawer from a dresser with more padding and a larger blanket. Eventually we bought a used crib for $15.00 and painted it pink. I saved the banana box for practical reasons. It looked attractive and served as a perfect shelf to hold clean, folded diapers. I utilized this box until well after both babies were no longer wearing diapers. Sentimental? Absolutely and frugal.

Don was baptized Catholic at an early age but was not church going. Although I lived at Saint Paul's Convent in the Philippines I was not Catholic but remembered children of Catholics were instructed to follow in their parents' religion. When Donna was a month old the Reverend Bernard Morgan at St. Brigid's Church baptized her with Don's cousins, Terry and Spike, as her godparents. The church was on the corner of Broadway and Van Ness Streets. The Broadway-Van Ness intersection of San Francisco was fairly significant in my life. Just kitty-corner from the church was Dr. Blehm's medical office building where Donna and I went for checkups and directly across the street from the church was the pharmacy where I ventured into when I ran away after the chandelier-breaking episode while babysitting cousin Paula.

Don quit city college just six units short of getting his associate degree and became a full time mail carrier. Since he went to work very early in the morning it was up to me to pack up the baby, a day's worth of diapers, bottles and baby food in an oversize diaper bag and trudge some five block to the in-laws' flat on Jones and Jackson Streets so that grandma Mary could baby sit. Unfortunately, we could not afford a stroller and I must have looked like a pack mule carrying the baby and a stuffed diaper bag while walking up hill in high heels. Once we reached the Kims' flat, I raced down the hill to catch the Leavenworth bus and with one bus transfer arrive at Stationers Price Service by 8:30 AM. Don picked me up after work and we invariably went looking for Donna. It was not easy for we never knew where to find our daughter or Don's mother. Mary was a great school volunteer. Quite often we drove to different places searching, sometimes Mary visited friends or relatives, other times she was at the elementary school working on a project. Once I found Donna tucked in a corner in the mimeograph cubicle as Mary ran off newsletters. Other times Mary took her to the tennis court as she watched her husband, Tommy, play in a match. Mary loved her granddaughter but she was not the stay-at-home type. She was active and sociable. She certainly was no housekeeper; in fact, the amount of accumulated junk was incredible. A very narrow path led from the front door to the kitchen which was in the back of their flat.

When Donna reached six months old, Amy Mendoza, our downstairs neighbor, agreed to babysit. Amy and her husband, Fred, had six children of their own and they all lived in the same size two-bedroom unit as we. Donna was growing, her baby paraphernalia became heavier, and it was a relief not to climb the hill everyday. I had also suffered my first miscarriage by then. We really scrimped along with the $900 medical and hospital bills very much in our mind.

Donna never sat in an infant seat as we couldn't afford one. However, when she turned one year old she got a high chair as a gift. Finally, the hospital debt was paid off and I began to muse about suburbia and envisioning a white picket fence environment.

San Francisco has many good points, but a definite negative was the lack of parking spaces. Finding a place to park was as impossible as remembering where we did park the car. Quite often we stood at the front stoop and tried to recall, "Did we park the car on Larkin Street, or was it Hyde Street?" "Or was it the other direction on California, Jackson or even Pacific?" This query was a constant irritation, much less the fear of an early sign of dementia. I kept dropping hints of moving away from the city. Wouldn't it be nice to have a garage? Our children could learn to ride a bike, attend football games when they become older and do things that normal children do when they are raised in a smaller community.

Finally, Don became amenable to my dream. We began to look for affordable housing in the South Bay, but everything was too expensive. As we scouted around we ventured beyond the mountains of East Bay to the Central Valley. There, in Stockton, we visited his cousins, Frank and Pat Kim. Frank was a young attorney and Tommy Kim's nephew. Pat, his wife, was from Macao; I met her briefly when she was going to Stanford. We had all been married in the same year and Pat gave birth to their first daughter, Karen, two months after Donna was born. Aside from Pat and Frank, we also met Jimmy and Mary Lam. They were related to Beverly Tang, my former roommate. Mary taught school and Jimmy was in the grocery business.

There was something very appealing about Stockton's small town atmosphere – affordable housing headed the list followed by a cheaper cost of living, plenty of land and warmer weather. The downside was that Stockton's Chinatown was literally dying. We didn't know why and didn't care. It was time to make our move and Don applied for a transfer.

It was ten years to the month when I first arrived in San Francisco to live with Ah Pau. I was now leaving the City to begin a new stage in my life with a husband, daughter and another baby on the way. I thought I would return to live in City by the Bay again one day since our ties to relatives, friends and schoolmates were strong. Little did I realize how quickly I changed my mind once we established new roots in a community of my own choosing.

Stockton Bound

Stockton, lies ninety-six miles due east of San Francisco, about a two-hour drive. It is a Gold Rush city founded in 1849 as a staging area for gold miners to pick up supplies and head for the rich California southern mines. With early Chinese dreaming of making a fortune in the Gold Mountains, it was quite natural for them to come to Stockton, the gateway to the southern mother lode. Local history reveals the earliest Chinese came in 1850, the result of the great Gold Rush. Eventually, they developed three Chinese settlements - one in the center of town, a second just a little to the south became the largest, and a third near the Mormon Slough became a fishing village. Captain Charles Weber, the town's founder, had the foresight to lay out this city with adequate parks, cemeteries, and a wealth of churches. His legacy reaches deep into the history of this city. I had the pleasure of being acquainted with some of his descendants, specifically, great granddaughter Peggy Cahill, a benefactor of the San Joaquin County Museum. I also knew Weber's great, great grandson (Dr. Edward "Ned" Cahill) whose skills saved the full use of my hand after I broke it in a traumatic fall.

Stockton of the 1960s was undergoing an economic shift from its World War II reputation as a fine shipbuilding community into an agricultural center with terrific transportation lines. Civic leaders began the initial steps towards redevelopment, a new concept. They gave the Chinatown skid row area a "white wash" or, more colorfully, they sought to obliterate all the cockroaches. Stockton had other amenities such as an inland port, three municipal golf courses, and two hospitals - St. Joseph's and Dameron. We cared less about the positive attractions except for the affordable housing - a flat terrain and open space with lots of places to park the car. For these three reasons Don, Donna, and I added ourselves to the town's 86,321 population in 1961.

Weberstown – Claremont Avenue

Charles Weber III, grandson of Stockton's founder Charles Maria Weber, began building houses north of the Calaveras River. The first stage, Weberstown Phase I, bordered Pacific Avenue and Bianchi Road. With Phase I completed, Weber began the second phase in early 1960 of bungalow-type, stucco houses. Realtor Will Marsh had such patience when he showed all five models explaining that there were still many empty lots if we wanted to choose one or buy what had already been built. Although not my first choice, but being practical and within our budget, we selected the cheapest of the models, three-bedroom, one-bath unit, across the street from the model homes. The price was $15,250 a princely amount but the house was solidly built. We were reminded that this was just a basic house, no fence, no landscape, no dishwasher, but it had a garbage disposal. To us, however, this was far more luxurious than what we had in San Francisco. I believed we could make the house a home.

We barely qualified for the 5.25% GI loan and to pay the mortgage would require two incomes. My dream was becoming a reality. So in October 1961 and I expecting our second child, we packed up what little possessions we had and moved into 4838 Claremont Avenue, Stockton, California - my first real home.

The novelty of owning a house, one that sparkled with actual hardwood floors and turquoise color kitchen appliances, was exciting. Sears Roebuck became my favorite store as we racked up the bills, a Kenmore washer and dryer, a GE refrigerator, inexpensive curtains, and gardening tools - all on time payments. Purchasing other furniture increased our debt. But this and more were essentials for first time homeowners.

Our house was in the middle of other construction projects. A nearby mall was in the works. Trucks flew by with heavy loads, usually raising dust and spilling dirt onto the street. Field mice and other little critters scurried for cover, ducking into the nearby houses for shelter as the earthmovers eliminated their abode. Peat dust from the nearby asparagus fields added to the greasy grime on the windowsills. One day a city truck pulled up and started to plant a tree on our front easement, I flew out the front door not understanding what was happening and even after the man explained that it was the city's plan to add aesthetics to a new subdivision I insisted that they by pass our house. I was so adamant the poor fellow pulled away and muttered under his breath "She's a real banshee." Wow, I didn't know I could be that ferocious. My thought at that time was the city was going to send us a bill for the tree and we were responsible if something went wrong and, if it died, we had to replace it. I did not want any more expense than necessary.

Putting in a lawn was an immediate necessity both to hold down the dirt and to avoid a muddy mess when the winter rain arrives.

What a sight, eight months pregnant and my stomach was definitely sticking out; but, I was right behind Don in our attempt to level the yard and plant some grass. He turned the soil with the rototiller and I pushed the water roller to pack down the dirt before seeding. The water roller operated much like a mower except instead of blades it had a large drum when filled with water, gave the equipment the weight to compact the ground. I did a lot of grunting as I walked the length and width of the back and front yards. We were truly San Francisco Chinatown transplants and acted much like the couple in the television show *Green Acres* with Eva Gabor and Eddie Albert.

We had neither a plan nor any understanding which plants required shade or took full sun. We lacked creativity and money to make full use of the yard. Our entire lot was almost one third an acre, the house measured only 1500 square feet. Thus, the backyard seemed huge. A peach and a nectarine tree were the very first to be planted in the backyard. To prepare for the hot Stockton sun we added a mulberry tree. Mistake! It was fast growing, like a weed, the surface roots crept closer and closer to the house and threatened to rip up the foundation. Camellias were a nice touch and relatively easy to handle. Twenty or so were planted along the entire back length of the house. Slowly the neighbors on both sides put in fences. Our backyard remained open until in the middle of one night we heard footsteps run pass our bedroom window and shots fired – thief! This was our first encounter with crime in Stockton. The next day the back neighbors came over and said they were putting up a fence, we were grateful that we did not have to share the cost. Those neighbors turned into long time friends. We added a large concrete slab to increase the size of the patio and provided an area to put up a clothes line. Yet, the backyard looked sparse and unfinished. Don, grudgingly, had a friend frame and hang the side gate and I personally hammered in each fiberglass panel alternating the colors green and yellow. I called it my fence as, between the two of us, I felt more enthusiastic.

Baby Makes Four

To prepare for the baby, we found Dr. Ernest Weys, a fascinating individual with a clipped, white moustache, balding, and a friendly twinkle in his blue eyes that belied a sad personal history. He had a definite European accent although he also spoke Spanish,

Tagalog, and Czech. He was Czech and a Catholic. However, Hitler's investigation of Jewish lines reached back five generations and his whole family was sent to Auschwitz. His parents and sister died there but Ernie Weys and his brother, Martin, managed to escape the death camp, a rare feat. The identification tattoo on the inside of his arm bore out his hardship. Martin joined the French Foreign Legion which meant joining for life. It took quite some doing for Ernie Weys to help when Martin decided the foreign legion was not for him. Dr. Weys literally plotted his brother's escape. Dr. Weys and his wife, Zenka, themselves, fled Czechoslovakia to the Philippines and from there came to the United States. They eventually settled in Stockton where he had his private practice and served as the county coroner for a brief period. He stayed as our family physician until his death in the early 1980s. The Weys were wonderful friends.

Darcelle Wahsolynn (or Darcy) arrived a week before Christmas. As soon as my labor began, Don dropped me off at the steps of Dameron Hospital and took Donna to San Francisco to stay with his mother. A silly thought crossed my mind as I ascended those steps bowed over in pain, I said to myself – there's no turning back now is there? Unlike the first pregnancy, my labor took only twenty-four hours. Again the nurse broke my water bag and everything went into turbo speed; she held my legs together, literally throwing herself on top of me and using one foot she pedaled the gurney into the delivery room. It was a race to see who would be there first, the baby or the doctor. Like Donna's, Darcy's birth came just before dinnertime. There is nothing like working up an appetite. I ate soon and heartily. During my week's stay in the hospital I shared a room with Ruth Weaver, who also just had her daughter Katrina. It was going to be a small world; some thirty years later, Ruth's husband, Floyd Weaver and I served together on the Stockton City Council.

Darcy was five and one-half pounds at birth but dropped a few ounces when we brought her home. She was very tiny, about the size of a stewing hen. The kitchen sink was the ideal place to give her a bath. For this reason I have always been partial to single and not double sinks in the kitchen. After bathing the baby I slattered her with baby oil, it was like basting a chicken with a Q-tip. She smelled wonderful; there is something about the smell of newborns, something that no fancy perfume can duplicate. This baby, unfortunately, had a few early health issues - one being a projectile vomitter. When she burped her body expelled air and milk as far away as a foot or two. Once in a while, for no reason, she turned blue or seemed to quit breathing. Thank goodness for Dr. Weys, he was always available and made frequent house calls. Eventually as Darcy grew these incidents subsided.

Toddlers and Antics

It is said that the first born is the more responsible and Donna proved the case. One day in November before Darcy arrived, I showed Donna an empty wallet and said we didn't have any money to buy diapers for the baby and she needed to give up hers. At her tender age of seventeen months, she understood and literally potty trained herself within that month. I was amazed at her maturity. Donna took an early interest in her sister. She ran for the diapers every time I laid her sister on her back. Many, many years later when Darcy reached her late teens she complained that she had two mothers, Donna and me. Even at less than two years of age Donna helped around the house. Armed with a paper bag, she picked up dust balls when I couldn't get around to cleaning too well. It became a game, as when she found some she yelled "dust mouse" for dust mites and dumped it in the bag.

Darcy was baptized at St. Mary's Catholic Church on Washington Street in the heart of Chinatown. The church is very much a part of Stockton's history. Founder Captain Charles Weber deeded two parcels of land at Hunter and Washington Street to the Catholic Diocese so the Spanish, Mexicans, Chileans, and French faithful could have a place of worship. The existing brick building replaced the 1861 wood structure and is now designated a historic landmark. Father Clement Krause, a Franciscan, officiated at the baptism; however, he felt the middle name Wahsolynn (the pairing of Don's father Wahso and Aunt Frances' middle name) did not resemble or come close to a saint's name so she was baptized Darcelle Theresa Chan. My eldest sister Dida and her husband Larry became the godparents. The following month, in April of 1963, Don and I became man and wife in the eyes of the church, after much prodding by Father Clement.

Memories of raising my children during this period are ever so dear for it was truly a sweet time in my life. The daughters were a joy. On their second birthdays I gave each of them a pair of chopsticks and cooked Chinese food at every meal for the entire week. Through their own trial and error and the eventual need to put food in their mouth, they learned to manipulate the eating utensil skillfully. Many friends and relatives thought they were well behaved; what they did not know was that Don had implemented his own form of discipline.

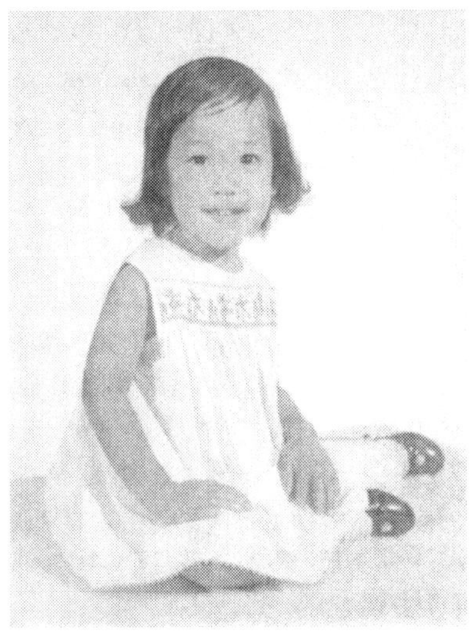

Darcelle Wahsolynn Chan

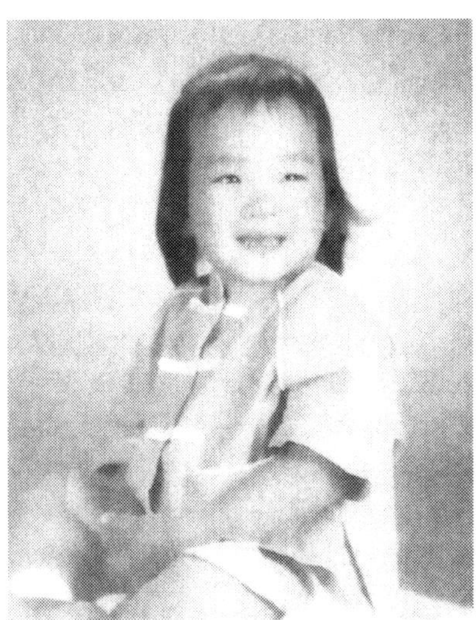

Donna Kim Chan

Sending the girls to the corner only resulted in their jiggling, singing, or dancing while facing the wall. Don added another component. They were to stand on their toes and extend their arms out like ballerinas. His thought was to strengthen their toes and increase their balance. Whether this accomplished his intent is questionable except it remains deep in Darcy's childhood memories.

Recollections of the girls' antics bring smiles to my face. Donna was about five. When Darcy dawdled too long in our only bathroom. Donna took her hairbrush and with one big slam she broke a hole through the hollow core door. You did not mess with Donna when she had a fit. Darcy, on the other hand, had so many trials and tribulations I learned the word "patience" quickly. She was a curious child. One day we rushed to vote before the polls closed in the neighborhood. We yelled for Darcy who was still a toddler to get into the car, but she didn't come. We called again several more times. Then we heard a "thump, thump, thump." Apparently she had been curious about a Venetian glass pitcher that I used as a décor; she wondered if her foot could fit into the pitcher. It did, but she then could not extract her foot. Our pressuring her to speed up didn't help. She then decided that perhaps we wouldn't notice the difference in her footwear so she thumped her way into the garage.

Both girls coincidentally had similar early childhood experiences as did I in my youth. Instead of jumping off the front porch and getting a scar in the middle of the forehead in Kuala Lumpur, Donna jumped off a low brick planter and broke her ankle. Darcy, however, at about age four, did jump off the front porch which resulted in two stitches just below her chin.

Cars and Animals

Don traded the Pontiac for a used Dodge station wagon. It was big enough so the girls could lie down in the back. That wagon didn't last long for the engine block cracked. A 1962 grey Corvair became the next mode of transportation. The car was one of the early compacts with the engine in the rear and the trunk in the front. It was so light several bricks and a one hundred pound sack of rice in the trunk gave the car a steady ride. This car was important as I learned to drive in it.

Surely everyone remembers their first driving experience. Mine was a bit frightening. Don taught me. He put Darcy in the front passenger side. Her car seat did not have any of today's safety features. Aside from the seat the metal brackets hooked on to the backrest. He climbed in the back with Donna, told me to turn on the engine, and said, "Go." He also indicated that if I got into an accident Darcy would fly out the window first. Through the years I retained a maternal habit of thrusting my right arm straight out to the side every time I came to a quick stop or made a sudden move. I envisioned it as an extra barrier or protection for anyone sitting in the front and a few adult passengers were surprised by a sudden jab in the stomach as they rode with me.

I sublimely noted that we bought or traded cars every two or three years. We also had a pickup truck; Don felt "every man needed" a truck – that was part of country living. We had been married only five years and had gone through three vehicles and, late in 1964, just before the General Motors' strike, we bought a 1965 F-85 Cutlass Supreme in Antioch. It was a beauty -- two-tone white and teale exterior with white leather upholstery and a 425-

horsepower engine. Payments were fairly steep and added to the other debts associated with the house. Yes, I felt the financial strain.

In the early 1960s pets rounded out our suburban lifestyle. Our dog, Bourbon, came to us when she jumped into Don's pickup somewhere on his route. With no tag, Don did not know where to return the dog. She was a cross between a poodle and a cocker spaniel, blond and very, very loveable. The children learned to love animals and Bourbon was very gentle with them. Bourbon was also a good mother. The dog had three litters, generally 7 or 8 per litter. To house the puppies we used a doughboy pool sans water. To give her some rest we pulled her out of the pen and when she was ready to feed her brood again she let us know. The runt of the last litter was my favorite who I named Scotty for Scotch. What a personality. Scotty learned to crawl under the fence to the next door neighbor's yard and gently tap on her sliding door. The neighbor, Margie Lee, would let the dog in with doggie treats in hand. Unfortunately, one day a car came around the corner and killed Scotty. It was a hit and run.

Our cats ranged from Manx to Siamese to Tabbies to Heinz's 57 and they, too, had several litters. As the animals grew older, it was interesting to watch as Bourbon and the cat sleep on the throw rug snuggled together. How did they communicate and develop such a close relationship? Bourbon died at 14 years. She just fell apart from old age. Two girls, two cars, cats, dogs, we are part of American suburbia.

Chinatown

Don went from a substitute carrier in the downtown main post office to obtaining a scheduled route in a very short time. Haye Chan, another carrier and no relation, took Don under his wing showing him the what and wherefore of the Chinese community and the nooks and crannies of Stockton.

For over a hundred years Stockton's Chinatown was a vibrant community filled with businesses, boarding houses, gambling institutions and family associations. But now the core of Chinatown shrunk to only one city block, mainly on Washington Street. Descriptively it was in the throes of arrested decay awaiting redevelopment and the wrecking ball. There were few business I remembered well. The two restaurants, On Lock Sam (began in 1895) and Canton Low on the southside of the street were the two frequented by the locals. The Lee family owned the oldest store Lee Yuen (1879), at the corner of El Dorado and Washington. It carried general merchandise. Rose Yip, a very pleasant widow, ran Marty's Shoe Store, a great place for children's shoes at reasonable prices. Foo Lung, a Chinese delicatessen and Quong Wah Yuen continued to provide community staples – roasted pig, roasted duck, and Chinese sausage (*lob cheong*). These businesses clung on desperately for economic survival. Haye's family ran Fook Chong, a soda fountain in the middle of the block. It also carried candies and tobacco products. Like his habit in San Francisco, Don rushed through his route and then searched for a hole-in-the-wall to kill time before returning to the post office to punch out. Fook Chong became Don's new hangout. I can't say that Don was a bad person but some of the things he did suggest that he did not put in an eight-hour work day. He was not opposed to "milking" the clock.

Telltale Signs

I needed to go back to work because of mounting bills. We could not afford to send the girls to pre-school and some of the neighbors agreed to help. The unspoken rule was that Don cared for them on his day off. He had added a new pastime – fishing. He loved to fish but did not like to eat fish and, much to my displeasure, did not want to clean his catch. Gutting and scaling strippers, black bass, or even trout were no problem; but, catfish was another issue. No matter how sweet its meat might taste, the thought of nailing the head down on a board then using a pair of pliers to pull the skin off of its entire body, ugh!

Along with fishing came camping; for most, it was the great American outdoor family fun. I'm a city girl and did not relish getting the children up at the wee hours of the morning, piling the four of us into the cab of the truck, and driving several hours to some remote area on the south fork of the American River or up by some rivulet not even close to any campsite with running water, toilets, or humans nearby. While he fished, I tried to cook with a portable Coleman stove, taught the girls to go toilet behind some rock, and kept the children occupied. On the way, either coming or going, Darcy would sit on my lap. Often motion sickness got the best of her, and her vomit would land on my clothes. I then spent the whole day with that sour smell on me. No, my form of camping was at a motel with a shower, television, a nearby McDonald's with a playland for the kiddies.

I tried working part-time for a temporary agency, but I felt guilty not being home with the children. Then there was the worry and resentment of Don's days off. The worry came when the children got sick or at times even got injured when they went off with their father. Two incidents, both dealing with Darcy, stick in my mind. Once Don took Darcy to see some Filipino friends on the outskirts of town. Darcy loves dogs and saw a big German shepherd. She toddled out to pet it not knowing the traits of a guard dog. As she turned around, the dog attacked her and sunk its teeth into the back of her skull. She was rushed to the City Emergency Hospital; the bill came to three dollars for the doctor's examination and minor stitching.

On a fishing trip in the delta Don placed Darcy at the rear of the boat under the shade of a tree while he sat forward. He cast out but his line snagged, he thought it got caught in the trees and broke, so he re-hooked and cast again. Soon Darcy gave out a meek call, "Dad." He did not answer and she called out again in her soft tone. He told this four-year old to be quiet and sit still for she might scare off the fish. She tried once more, this time he turned around ready to yell at her when he saw a piece of fishing line with the hook in the middle of her ear lobe and blood trickling down. It was not until they came home that we cut the hook and pulled it through. Don felt bad about the incident, but he would again just get carried away doing his own thing. To this day Darcy, as an adult, does not want to get her ears pierced, but she tells people she really enjoys fishing.

For all our hard work, cracks began to appear in our marriage. The signs were there. Was it complacency on Don's part or why was I not satisfied?

Chapter 9

On My Own

After a few temporary clerical jobs I underwent a retraining program offered by the State of California. It was a pilot program administered by the Department of Employment. Candidates who passed a test received eighteen months of training. What a deal, for free! The Manpower Development Training Act (MDTA) held at Humphreys College on California Street focused on shorthand and secretarial skills. The program had two wonderful teachers -- Mrs. Bernice Neugebauer headed the typing section and Mrs. Greer the shorthand. Mrs. Greer's shorthand penmanship was so good that a company asked that her penmanship be the model for their textbook. Mrs. Neugebauer gave me private coaching after the program ended. Like my mother many years earlier, I also earned a little trophy for my typing speed, clocking 75 words per minute on an old manual. I managed to get my shorthand up to 125 words per minute. The all-women class worked hard under the program and many excelled beyond the clerical field like my friends Sharon Kellogg and Peggy Terry.

A Marriage Unravels

Whenever I came home from work and tried to talk about my day it seemed Don wasn't interested. Along with fishing, he took up bowling. Initially I agreed to try this new game and we joined a bowling team at West Lane Bowl. It had a child care center. Bowling was not my forte, carrying a ball 11% of my weight and swinging it with enough inertia to hit bowling pins seemingly miles down a narrow alley exhausted the human body, at least mine. My average score was 125 which it was not good enough - such an embarrassment. I dropped out of the league. In addition to league night Don added another midweek night of bowling. Soon it was more visits to the bowling alley to keep score for the fellows. He reasoned that maybe, just maybe, he would earn a few dollars in tips. All this meant no family nights with the children.

I, too, had a desire – to go back to school. All my siblings had college degrees and I had only a limited education. By day I was mentally stimulated but by night I knew I was dissatisfied. We did not even have a single book in our house. I signed up for one evening course in English literature at the local San Joaquin Delta College. I was hooked. The thought of getting an associate of arts degree started to jell in my mind. I wanted more and also more for my daughters. Don pooh-poohed my evening class and made excuses on why he couldn't watch the children at night. He, himself, lacked six units to get his associate's degree but had no desire to finish. The signs were there, we weren't headed for a clash but each of us wanted to live in different worlds. There were a few arguments, a few shouting words; then, one day I proposed that we go our separate ways and part before animosity grew. I still wanted us to be friends and Don, surprisingly, did not object.

While the separation was amicable; Don convinced me that we should share the same divorce attorney to save money. He knew how to hit my weak spot – save money as in frugality. At the time it seemed to be reasonable since there was no great animosity. The attorney reasoned that since we were both working Don should be able to keep his federal retirement fund and I mine. In addition, he perceived that I could fend for myself and never mentioned alimony. Perhaps there was a sense of self pride and with my survivor attitude very much intact, I agreed. In retrospect I think I got screwed. I was naive. The attorney compared Don's seventeen years of retirement contributions to that of my three years - a full time postal carrier to that of a beginning clerk.

Together we moved Don into a decent apartment and he literally got half of everything from the house: blankets, sheets, and pots and pans. I got the children, all the bills including the house and car payments. He got his pickup truck which was free and clear; but he had to make a small child support payment of $75 per month. I knew I took the high road in this arrangement; however, I got the children and the house – that was all that mattered. The divorce became final the following year.

Don saw the children whenever he wanted; I never took back the house key. He was now free and able to play to his heart's content. Although we were married for a total of ten years; if I had any regret, it was that I would miss Don's mouth-watering, fluffy waffles and the way he cooked live crab. I will always be grateful that together we had two beautiful daughters. Don's stepfather, Tommy and his siblings were sympathetic; but, Mary, Don's mother, never spoke to me again.

The day of our divorce my mother remembered waking up sweating from a dream. She and father were back living in Manila. Father was now an ambassador for the Republic of China (Taiwan) and had returned to the Philippines after doing a stint in Jamaica. Mother called up older sister Patricia and said, "Something terrible is happening to Syl." Considering the time difference between Asia and Stockton, at the moment of Mother's dream I was in court making an important change to my life. Mother's premonition was the first indication of a spiritual or psychic bond between us. A decade later I would experience a similar feeling when she was dying.

As a Single Mom

There I was a divorcee and the single head of the household and ready to trash that picket fence dream. The girls were marvelous and accepted more responsibilities. Donna was now eight years old and Darcy almost seven. They rode the school bus to Woodrow Wilson Elementary School. Admittedly they were latchkey children. After school they called to check in. A number of times when someone rang the door bell, they quickly hid, dialed me at work whispering that the doorbell rang and Bourbon was barking. I told them to be quiet and maybe the caller would go away, figuring it was a door-to-door salesman.

Ralph Matsune, a very caring gardener also made sure the children were okay and, of course, Bourbon was there to give them a sense of security. Our neighbors pitched in to help. Across the street Rachael Kurita organized a bluebird troop; Vivian Rurup, at the corner, watched the girls after school. Their daughter, Kelly, played with Darcy while Donna was busy getting into arguments with their son Tom. The girls took readily to the neighbor on the left side as well. Jerry Lee, a house painter, had the patience of Job. The girls enjoyed watching him tinker. Our back neighbors, Evelyn and Jerry Egan, had two daughters Terry and Patty. Patty was just a few months younger than Darcy. Evelyn was a nurse and Jerry was the manager of the Stockton Country Club. Jerry built a dollhouse right at the property line and also had a kidney-shaped pool. My girls played there often and with someone yelling "Marco" and the response "Polo." I could hear the shriek, laughter and water splashing hours on end.

Quickly my daughters learned the old divorce trick pitting one parent against the other. They missed their father for he had become a hero since he took them to exciting places or to the movies. Living with me was rather mundane filled with homework and chores. I never said anything bad to the girls about their father and even encouraged them to remember to send him cards at Christmas and on his birthday. Don remarried but that marriage was short lived.

Darcy and I enjoying a light moment – 1967

A Necessary Revisit

Some six months after our divorce my father sent a telegram. It was short and cryptic. It stated: "You tried, now my turn." In other words while I got married my way and it failed, he now had arranged a marriage contract for me with someone he thought would be a good provider for us. Although I might now be considered damaged goods, he was thinking the best for his grandchildren.

There was no man in my life at that point. The audacity of father finding me a mate was appalling. How would he know my type? Or what attributes I would like? My independent streak kicked into gear. With a personal loan from the credit union I bought tickets to the Philippines, taking both girls on their first voyage overseas. Never mind that the loan was another expense added to my pile of other bills, but I needed to see father and tell him personally, "thanks, but no thanks."

A decade before, I vowed to never live under my parents' roof again; so we arranged for us to stay with Dida and Larry in Makati, a suburb of Manila. The folks lived in Forbes Park, another fairly close subdivision. Our visit to Manila actually turned out quite pleasant as it gave the girls the opportunity to meet their first cousins, the Gotuaco children. They were all close in age.

My discussion with father was not traumatic, he did not ask much. Our conversation wasn't exactly warm but it also was not hostile. It turned out his candidate was a banker in Taiwan. There was nothing father could do to force me and, since it was his idea he had to break the arrangement.

After twenty years absence from Manila, it was good to see the Tankiang family and visit St. Paul's Convent. I had a fleeting notion of relocating to the Philippines. I loved the people, food, and weather. Coincidentally, Sister Patrice who now headed the order in Rome was also visiting St. Paul's. Brother-in-law Larry convinced me that it would not be economically wise to move to the Philippines. He was right.

We spent the entire month of August 1969 in Manila and added another week's visit to Hong Kong. The two China issues reared its head in 1969 with Mainland China working for international recognition. Father was not sure how safe it was for me to bumble around Hong Kong; there were clues that both governments were well entrenched watching the comings and goings of each allegiance. Father asked Patricia and Larry to accompany us and strongly recommended that we check into the Fortuna Hotel. It was reasonably priced and safe. The children took to this new adventure with aplomb. They had much to tell their friends in Stockton. One incident told me how much I had changed. One day the girls and I hopped into a taxi and I spoke Cantonese to the driver giving him a particular address. He turned to me and said in reply, "Not bad Cantonese for a Japanese person."

I was stunned but then realized that my Cantonese was archaic. Grandma's San Francisco's Cantonese words were no longer in vogue in modern Hong Kong.

State Service - Caltrans

With added clerical skills learned from the MDTA program, I went to work, in 1965, as a junior stenographer with the State Division of Highways on Charter Way, more specifically in the Operations Department clerical pool. The salary was a wonderful $325 a month. In a few short months I became an intermediate stenographer. The clerical pool supervisor, Freda Winters, was unusual to say the least. Freda went to a teachers' college in Kansas but never taught. She was not attractive but loved to strut around thinking herself a knockout. She gushed over engineers who were willing to kid with her and stayed away from those who were gruff and no-nonsense. She had her favorites in the clerical pool and was quite a taskmaster to others. There were times when I resented her but at other times I thought she was decent. When she assigned me difficult tasks, I took it as a learning opportunity.

The ambience at work was stimulating though it made our own social circle lackluster. I loved my work and was absorbed in taking dictation from various engineers. One particular effort was working with the deputy district engineer, Frank Gregory, who dictated a long rebuttal letter to an eight million dollar claim by the Gordon T. Ball Company against the State of California for work the company did on the Merced Highway 152 project. The draft and re-write took over three weeks and resulted in a complex eight page letter and included many technical findings. I filled three full steno pads. In this, there was a sense of accomplishment. Another task was to set up instructional manuals for the newly-created nuclear compaction testing equipment and create a system to monitor the radiation level in the operators. Freda did not want to be bothered with such technical details and others in the pool preferred their own routine work. I loved these assignments. They were challenges and I was willing to take them on.

One year I accompanied the resident engineers (those who had assigned field projects) on their annual retreat to Bear Valley. It was an overnighter at the Bear Valley Lodge. Don came along since we had not yet divorced. He got talked into a poker game with a few of the fellows. I warned him that they were going to take him to the cleaners, but he was cocky and thought himself skillful enough. He did not know that many resident engineers working on projects away from home for weeks and months at a time would spend their nights at the bar or indulged in a friendly game. Sure enough when Don stumbled back to our room a little before midnight, he was cleaned out.

I truly believe engineers, be they construction, structural, electrical, or even mechanical, are different from common folks. They think in black-and-white terms, to them there is no gray. Engineers believe they can fix anything, build anything, and make the world more convenient and comfortable. They are earthmovers, tinkerers and, often, they assume the jack-of-all-trades role. They don't throw away anything, particularly if the salvaged item could be reused or was able to serve another function. Engineers exhibit confidence in their thinking, and they like to find solutions to technical problems. They can be hardheaded. Many are a bit macho. They also have many wonderful qualities in that they can envision the end result of a complex project and, at the same time, prioritize the minutest beginning steps. In other words, they contemplate, discuss, formulate, and calculate at the micro and macro levels. Cost was never an issue until confronted with budget constraints. When that occur some engineers resort to recalculation and even apply elements of value engineering – build for long term usage. God bless engineers and our freeway system.

Corrections – Deuel Vocational Institution

During our 1969 visit back to Manila (to decline father's potential marriage arrangement) Auntie Betty Tankiang insisted that we pay Mrs. Ledesma a visit to have my fortune updated. Her psychic reading suggested I would go through many doors – this actually came true upon our return to the States. I was offered a senior stenographer position at Deuel Vocational Institution (DVI) in Tracy, some twenty miles from Stockton. DVI is actually a state prison that houses violent young adults and the more difficult youth authority wards. To get into the prison one had to walk through several security gates and doors.

This promotion helped my financial status even though there was an additional cost associated with the commute. The Associate Superintendent of Education, John E. Hacker, my boss, was tall, thin, and bald. He had a shy smile and said he was a native of Indiana. During the interview he asked the usual employer questions and listed his expectations. He finished by saying, "Do you have anything you want to ask." That was my opening to decide should I or should I not work for him. Given the distance away from home I wondered if it would be worth it since my daughters would be by themselves for a longer period of time. All I could surmise he was a Hoosier and nothing else. So I asked him one question, "When is your birthday and how old are you?" My reasoning was to see if we were compatible astrologically both in the western and eastern horoscopes. He was taken aback but his answers assured me that we could work together quite well.

Working at Deuel was quite different than working for engineers at highways. It seems that the Department of Corrections had two missions and sometimes their goals are conflicting. Some of the staff believe their job is to guard the inmates and see to it that they serve their time as prescribed by law. The uniform gives the correctional officer a psychological boost of unquestionable authority. I would suggest, though, that a guard thinks about his job only eight hours a day, while the convict has 24 hours to come up with ideas to circumvent authority. Others feel what's needed during incarceration is education and rehabilitation, in other words remedial education and vocational training. There were two divisions in the educational system; regular curriculum to help inmates obtain a GED degree, and rehabilitation instructors taught skills such as carpentry, welding, arc welding, and sheet metal work.

John Hacker was quite open-minded when a vocational instructor suggested an incentive for the inmates – to allow them to build a flyable airplane. Hacker cleared the request with the director of Corrections in Sacramento and, of course, there was mild joking around the prison, "DVI inmates to build and fly airplanes." Uniform staff became leery but inmates were enthusiastic, even those who had no part in the actual project. In 1971, Tom Williams, the head of the vocational department bought plans for a Pitts Special, S-1C, a single seat biplane. The Pitts Special, named for Curtis Pitts who created the first of its type in 1945, became extremely popular in the 1960s and 70s as a versatile aircraft that dominated aerobatic competition in world championship events. The plane called for a 100-180 horsepower engine. The staff and inmates worked diligently for several months and when the plane was ready to be tested, the press was contacted. Can the plane be airborne? Who's going pilot the plane, an inmate? The big moment arrived when an instructor climbed into the cockpit, the plane took off and made several passes over the prison grounds and then touched down. This incident remains in my memory bank but it should also be part of the institution's history of accomplishments. The lack of funding and over-population at the prison inhibit creative ways to rehabilitate prisoners today.

Since I worked directly with the associate superintendent, I was not part of the clerical pool, I had other tasks besides being a secretary. One was the work furlough program which helped inmates adjust to society upon release. They were given opportunities to find work, get a car, and work in town at a bona- fide job. They lived in barracks outside the prison walls. If an inmate did not return at the end of the work day he was AWOL (Absent Without Leave) and a warrant issued for his arrest. It also meant more prison time and all privileges suspended.

Two incidents were memorable. Some prisoners took the rules to heart and tried not to violate the trust. One inmate working in Modesto, about 30 miles away, had a water pump problem with his car. He called the institution and I told him to go buy a pump and change it in a highly visible location and then come home. About half an hour later we got a call from the Modesto police department asking if we know so-and-so; my first thought was "oh no, he got himself in trouble." When I responded in the affirmative we were told the inmate wanted to let us know he was at the police station (a highly visible area); but, the police did not take too kindly to the inmate who pulled into the police station and proceeded to change his water pump blocking the entrance so no cars could neither go out nor come in.

In another incident a lustful inmate met a woman at a bar when he should have been working. We put out an APB (all points bulletin) when he didn't return. He called the institution and said they were on the way to Lake Tahoe to get married. He called again the following day and said they tied the knot and were on their honeymoon, on the third day he called again and said he was on the way back to the institution. He claimed he had a fairly wild 72 hours but changed his mind about marriage.

There were a few scary moments but these were overshadowed by my gaining the respect of some inmates and officers. Once I was working in the inner sanctum of the prison locked in a room with two minimum security inmates. We were working on a project that needed special printing equipment inside that room. The door had a glass window visible to people walking the "line." Soon a number of faces appeared at the window, gawking. By the third day one inmate asked if we could speed up the project as he had been threatened if he did not open the door. I had always been cognizant of my personal safety and was grateful that I had learned a few self-defense maneuvers. Unfortunately, an inmate did become very infatuated and started to send me correspondence. It was then my boss thought it best to transfer me out of DVI. I totally agreed. Although my time ended at the state prison, Mr. Hacker and I remained close friends until his death in the late 1980s.

The next job was working at the Cal Osha branch office in the State building in downtown Stockton. The parole office was on the ground floor. When parolees needed to check in with their parole agents and the agents were not in, rather than waiting there, some inmates who knew that I was on the third floor, would drop by to say, "Hi." Again, here was another potential safety concern. Thus, my stint at Cal Osha was short lived and I had no regret.

By now it was 1974 and I started a new life in a new marriage. Those ten years in state service was of great benefit. I was a vested member of CalPers, the state employee retirement system, I could look forward to a pension, albeit, based on a stenographer's salary.

Chapter 10

Warmth in an Old House

Marrying An Eastern Tennessean

People often asked, "How did you folks meet?" My answer invariably had been "over some dead orchids." Don gave me a large cymbidium plant for my birthday before we broke up. He knew nothing about orchids and neither did I. He thought it would impress me and it didn't. It took a while but after some neglect, the poor plant looked woeful. I felt guilty that the plant was dying and, yet, I didn't want to throw it out. Could the plant be rescued?

I looked around at the office for expert advice, or at least for someone who dabbled in raising orchids. Rumors led me to Richard Minnick, who then worked somewhere upstairs in the vast maze of offices in the district's transportation system. Our first encounter did not go well although he agreed to help. At the end of the workday, Richard asked: "Where's the plant?" His car was in the back lot and expected me to take it there. I suggested it seemed simpler if he brought his car around to the front lot to do the transfer. Reluctantly he did. I could not believe this guy really expected me to lug a fairly heavy plant from one end of the building to the other. He looked like a gentleman and logic would have dictated that my suggestion was the perfect solution. Wrong! Although he took the plant home, his first assessment of me was that I was a spoiled brat. To allay any hard feelings and to show gratitude I bought a huge bag of bark and other orchid related items he might need from Rod McClellan's orchid shop in South San Francisco.

Several months went by and one day Richard showed up with six pots, they came from the original plant. Our conversation went so much better this time, but the result was the same, all six plants also died.

Love This Engineer

Richard Shanklin Minnick, born in Wilcoe, West Virginia was a transplant by way of Virginia, Tennessee, Georgia, Florida, and Arizona before he landed in California in 1955. A true Heinz 57 -- German, English, Scot and Cherokee blood ran in his veins. He was a Masonic member of Nogales Lodge No 12, F & AM. He stood about 5'7", weighed about 155 pounds, had hazel eyes, brown hair, extremely pleasant voice, and one could tell he was a hard worker by the look of his hands; yet, his touch was surprisingly smooth. He loved to rub his hands over fine wood and appreciate the naturalness of it. As a civil engineer he received his training at the University Of Arizona School Of Engineering in Tucson. While in school he worked as a surveyor on a huge cattle ranch that straddled the US-Mexican border. His acute asthma and poor eyesight prevented him from entering the military which was his great ambition and saddest disappointment. He loved ROTC at the university. However, he did serve his country well by helping build the Marana Airbase about thirty-five miles west of Tucson. A stint at the Arizona Highway Department led him to believe California's highways and its civil service system an improvement over Arizona so he headed west. Thus, in 1955 he settled in at the District 10 Office at the Division of Highways in Stockton, California. With his construction background, Richard moved around the District working on various construction projects including those in Mariposa, Fairfield, and Sonora. In the later years he remained stationary in the district office with desk jobs in planning, design, and right-of-way utilities. That's where I found him.

Our friendship started with the orchid incident but it grew because we were novices in the employees' union activities. Apparently, Richard had spare time as his estranged wife and three sons were living in Spain and he developed an interest in the California State Employees Association (CSEA). I became active for financial reasons. The position of chapter secretary paid $25 a month. That little bit of extra cash was very much welcomed since I was a single mother of two and faced with the mortgage and car payments. I found that Richard and I shared similar philosophies. Quite often at the meetings when I became frustrated with the direction a particular issue was taking and spoke up, he played the devil's advocate to help me reach my desired goal, particularly when he felt I was not articulating well enough – what an ally. Both Donna and Darcy took to him immediately and he to them. It was so easy discussing various subjects including religion and politics. I often wondered if our 21 years difference resulted in a Pygmalion relationship; Richard knew the answers to satisfy my inquisitive nature.

Sometimes I felt bewildered. Richard was very intelligent but he created a situation that made him fortuneless. His wife and children preferred to live in Europe and left Stockton in 1963. Richard supported them but did not want to relocate himself for he was gainfully employed. He felt, in today's terms, linguistically challenged. Living in Spain opened the world to the children, at least the European world. They travelled; they absorbed the culture and today speak multi-languages. Eventually a family that lives apart leads to the parting of ways. Richard and Vera divorced after twenty seven years of marriage. In the settlement he faced a hefty alimony payment, child support, as well as financing his middle son's additional education. From a decent monthly salary of $1,295, his family got eighty percent leaving him only $285 to live on. This was unbelievable since Don and I divided everything in our household down to the last towel, frying pan, and pillow case. I have heard of fellows losing their shirts; however, Richard's generosity knew no bounds. He must have believed that he could always make it in life but was not sure about others.

With all his virtue, he was a bit dense. While we enjoyed each other's friendship, he did not notice that he started to occupy a lot of my time, thus, precluding me an opportunity to date others.

As latchkey children the girls were extremely good and knew not to open the door for strangers. It was not unusual to come home and find both Don and Richard in my house smoking, helping themselves to my liquor cabinet, and enjoying each other's company. Each came by to check on the children. The girls thought it would be fun and charitable to have Richard stay with us, but I indicated not unless we were married. Up until then Richard gave no indication as to the direction of our relationship. I may be accused of being impulsive but I am one who needs a map in my life. After almost a year of a no-suggestion or action on his part, one evening on the spur of the moment I slammed him up against the wall heater which had heated up quite nicely and asked:

"Richard, are you going to marry me or are you wasting my time?"

His eyes opened wide and gave me a dumbfounded look. After what seemed like hours he replied: "Never in my wildest dream would I think you would marry me given the difference in our age. So I never thought to ask." The twenty-one year difference never bothered me nor did marrying out of my race. He also had no qualm about inter-racial marriage.

As the proper thing to do, Richard wrote a letter to my parents, who were then in Taiwan, asking for my hand in marriage. There was no response; yet when he finally met my parents on their returned to the States for a visit, they were cordial and never mentioned the letter. I brought him to Auntie E's as well as to Gloria's house to introduce him. Auntie E and Uncle Paul were gracious. Even ex-husband Don approved. On November 7, 1970 we married at the Alice Ahern Chapel, connected to the First Congregational Church. Reverend Leon England, the Protestant Chaplain at DVI performed the ceremony. One advantage of working at the prison was the availability of other clergymen – Jewish or Catholic. All would have been willing. Claudia Jeung, my old Girl Scout and choir days friend, served as the maid of honor and Jerry Lee, our next door neighbor, was Richard's best man. Donna and Darcy were absolutely delighted for they played a part in the simple service.

The Minnick In-Laws

Although it seemed Richard's immediate family might be dysfunctional, his relatives were fantastic. His father Britton (Pop) and stepmother Natalie lived in Tucson, Arizona. Each had two previous marriages. Natalie Zook Minnick, a no-nonsense, thin-lipped, and short on words German, had a heart of gold. Coming from El Paso, Texas, Natalie had true grit. She suffered from a botched hip operation and shuffled on her walker to get around, even washing clothes by hand and hauling the wet laundry to the backyard to hang on the line.

On South Sixth Street, Pop and Natalie converted the garage into a hat shop. The sign at the door read: *Tucson Hatters.* She steam-cleaned the felt of the hat and changed the sweatbands of many cowboys who came off the range. Decades earlier Natalie owned another shop in El Paso and famed Norman Rockwell captured a portion of that store in a *Saturday Evening Post* cover of the theater right next door. From Natalie I learned to mash potatoes using mayonnaise and whipping it with a fork. For her there was none of that fancy cream, milk or butter and the fork worked better than an egg beater. Her salad dressing was simple – just sugar, a little oil and white vinegar. My rendition included a dash of garlic salt. Natalie was especially close to Darcy who spent a summer in Tucson with them. Darcy was nine when we put her on an airplane for a supposedly direct flight there; unbeknownst to us, she needed to change plane in Las Vegas and had the wherewithal to make the connecting flight. Since then her love for flying took off.

Natalie Minnick and Me

Richard's father, Pop, was okay but got mean when he drank. He frequently sneaked into the hat shop after dinner and indulged in Cream of Kentucky, real rot gut bourbon. Minutes later he was shouting and cussing at imaginary visitors.

Richard's mother, Eva, passed away a few years before we met; but Eva Strong Minnick Morse Morrison (also married three times) was a woman of substance. Eva's greatest love, however, was her son, Richard. She learned the real estate business and acquired property in Arizona, California, Florida, and Tennessee. Eva loved to travel and made it a point to keep track of her nieces and nephews, a total of twenty-six from far flung California to Puerto Rico. Her taste in décor, travel and general outlook on life seemed to parallel mine. The first time I visited the homestead in Johnson City, Tennessee, everyone spoke of Eva's vivacity and kindness. In fact, one cousin remarked that my sociability was very much like hers.

The girls and I loved East Tennessee and delighted in mimicking the southern-mountain drawl. In the early 1970s an Asian in the Appalachian country was a novelty. Often, as we sat rocking on a cousin's porch in the nearby town of Kingsport, cars drove slowly up the hill and reversed direction to take another glimpse at black hair and olive skin females a-rocking away and chattering up a storm in California twang.

In Johnson City, Tennessee with Richard's first cousins and families.

The cooking in that part of the country amazed me -- like magic green beans turned yellow, cabbage red, and they ate only the floret of the broccoli throwing away the stems that the Chinese would normally devour. They canned everything in sight for family consumption and to give away -- so practical and charitable. The ubiquitous country ham was cooked up into redeye gravy or used as part of white sop as in biscuit'n'gravy. The Chinese considered Virginia or country ham an expensive delicacy and used it sparingly in bird's nest soup or to garnish a West Lake duck dish. Our postman, Bob Ward, grinned when the cousins shipped us a whole country ham for the holidays. Bob knew that he would be recipient of several slices. We made it a point to visit Tucson at least twice a year and East Tennessee at least every other year. There were also opportunities to get acquainted with Richard's other first cousins living in Sebastopol, California and even those in Puerto Rico. Oddly enough many of those cousins had never ventured west of the Mississippi until we insisted. To this day I have remained close to the Tennessee folks and shared many a vacation with them.

This Old House

Fate can be a little funny, for in 1972 we moved from Claremont Street to an old Craftsman house on the corner of Commerce and Willow Streets. This 1905 beauty lay kitty-corner from our wedding chapel, a wonderful reminder of our new beginnings. Darcy and I dreamt about the house before we made an offer. While the house number did not sound lucky, it being 1404, the Chinese word for death is also four; but, its orientation on the southeast corner suggested its auspiciousness. I am not a fanatic but do practice Feng Shui when possible. Thus, we included wind chimes and painted the front door bright red. East met west and this house had a distinctive old world charm. In its day it boasted a state-of-the-art interior with high ceilings and indoor plumbing. For the most part indoor plumbing came into being around 1910 with a shed affixed to the side of the house similar to an attached lean-to.

The main floor consisted of our bedroom, full bath, and kitchen with adjoining laundry facilities. Two sets of double French doors separated the formal dining room, living room, and a twenty foot entry way. The latter became a semi-family room complete with an eight foot long bookcase, couch, and an electronic Yamaha organ. Upstairs, each girl had her own bedroom with a walk-in closet, a full bath and another complete kitchen. Off the small balcony was a set of back stairs that led down to the street. The girls were ecstatic; they had space and privacy unlike their shared bedroom on Claremont Street. We even had our own archaeological dig in the quarter basement. There had been a house on this property that suffered a fire, then another house built on the same location and eventually was lifted and moved to the empty lot just to the east. Our house became the third on the corner lot.

As Richard explored the basement area he discovered a dated 1860 Thornberry cane with slightly scorched markings. Clearly etched was the following inscription "*Suum cuique*" a Latin translation "To Each His Own." Other items reminded us of different tenants through the decades such as one lady's shoe, a wallet (no money), a perfect glass-blown, swirl design vase, a fragment page from a 1918 magazine, empty Chiclets wrapper and an abundance of empty liquor and wine bottles. Rather than disposing of these bottles, someone in the past wanted to savor the memories of his libation.

The basement belonged to Richard. It had a work bench on one side with a small closet for canned goods and stored wine. With his love of carpentry, Richard built Darcy a wooden box with a special lock for her forensic notes and night stands for Donna. On the other wall was a makeshift desk with shelves for books.

1404 North Commerce Street, Stockton, Ca.

I had always wanted a freezer and the unit above our regular refrigerator was not big enough. Richard did not want another freezer. He said we could always rent a meat locker. I shook my head but did not argue. One day at work a fellow engineer and I thought we could save on our respective food bill if we bought a cow, slaughtered it and split the largess. We bought a jersey that couldn't produce milk.

It was around Father's Day and I presented Richard with a card and indicated his gift was a half a cow. He thought it was a joke but I mentioned: "By the way, the cow will be killed in ten days; you need to figure how you want the meat cut, size of the packages, and where to put the meat." As the week ended, the vision of storing some four hundred plus pounds of meat weighed heavily on my husband. In desperation he purchased a second-hand, fairly large, upright freezer. Very soon thereafter he felt buying the freezer was the best decision he ever made. Since it was put in the basement it became his domain. Eventually he loved to buy sale items and the freezer became so stuffed we didn't know what was in there and threw out much when we moved.

The previous homeowner had converted the living room into an accordion studio with a soundproof acoustic ceiling. He also added a façade board to cover the recessed fluorescent lighting along the living room walls. It made the room brighter and cheerful. Green oriental rugs, white walls and light brown tone trim were the basic colors. We liked the tasteful combination of Richard's and my stuff as they blended and projected an inviting sense of comfort. Two pairs of Richard's swords graced the top of both French doors leading to the dining room as well as the living room. The swords crossed and formed an apex. If there was any displeasure about the house, it was with the wallpaper. Most were from the 1920s-30s era of large bold flowery prints, cutesy delicate blossoms and even repeated hunting scenes. They reminded Richard of his youth. I could only think of "yuck" followed by an "oh well…." The only decent wall covering was in the dining room, a mural depicting San Marco's Plaza, Venice.

Donna, Richard and Darcy in the entry way

For a junior high graduation gift we gave Donna a Pachinko machine which sat on a roaster stand in the kitchen. The Pachinko eventually moved upstairs to the girls' domain and was replaced by an

Atari game and, ultimately, a color television as kitchen entertainment. Our house was opened to the girls' friends. The children made our house their home. We often heard doors bang, rock 'n' roll music filtering from upstairs, an occasional dash down the stairs when the phone rang. We clanged a ship's bell at the foot of the stairwell when we wanted one of the girl's attention. The brass bell came from Natalie's hat shop. The girls' friends invariably hung out in the kitchen instead of up in their quarters. Many of them remembered learning how to use chopsticks and some learned to cook fried rice as well as other Chinese food.

In our early years of occupancy, we suspected the house was haunted. Rather than having visual encounters, each of us experienced a presence. Often the girls got a sense of someone walking up the stairs to the second floor. Of course all old houses creak. We were not afraid and thought if there were ghosts around, which surely there should have been given the age of the dwelling, these extra terrestrial presences must be friendly or, at least, considered us as co-conspirators. There was one time our resident spirit had the temerity to make itself known. One day some friends visited; their conversation turned to the subject of religion to the point of being didactic. I got bored with the topic. Suddenly the husband, who was sitting with his back to the entry way, turned around as though someone was standing behind him and his face blanched momentarily. I telepathized my thoughts to our spirit, "Oh you don't like him either, good." Our visitors quickly made their departure. Yes!

All the Good Memories

The Commerce house was our milestone home. It was here that any questions of familial difficulties associated with children and second marriages dissipated. The girls and Richard did everything typical of a biological family unit. At the Campfire Girl ceremony he tied the red scarf around Donna's neck, attended father-daughter dinners, and went to parent-teacher nights. In teaching Darcy to ride a bike the kick stand caught and tore his pants which he considered a badge of honor. As he helped her put on a coat one night she, inadvertently, punched him in the eye and popped out his contact lens at which time, all four of us got on our hands and knees looking for the lens. As Darcy stood up and started dancing around we heard a crunch…enough said. These are only a few comical moments raising our daughters.

Both girls walked to Commodore Stockton Middle School four blocks away. Darcy was in the last class before the school closed. Its buildings were deemed unsafe for earthquakes. However, when it came time to bulldoze those buildings it took more than a week with the wrecking ball to bring them down. They used to build sturdy structures at the turn of the century, not like today where cracks appear in the foundations and walls only after a few years. Both girls attended Stagg High School. Donna was interested in keeping stats for some of the school sports and Darcy excelled in forensics under the late Donovan Cummings, a renowned speech teacher who brought home years of state championships. In all, both girls got good grades, attended all the proms and even were homecoming princesses. In high school they took three additional courses: mechanical drawing, woodshop, and typing. These were not required by the school district but by us. We felt at the very least mechanical drawing gave another perspective both mentally and visually. Woodshop made the girls unafraid of using tools. Typing was another skill that guaranteed the girls could find a job in any field without resorting to being scullery maids.

The girls learned to drive as soon as each turned sixteen. Richard taught Donna in a Honda 500, stick shift with a two cylinders, two-seaters, midget-sized, green car. In today's world the car would have been praised for its size and economic savings. In those days, people scratched their heads and asked: "What is it?" There were times when Donna's friends played jokes on her and lifted the car from its parking stall and moved it elsewhere unbeknownst to her. She was extremely proficient shifting and tried to teach me in the Sears' parking lot. Again my short legs made it difficult to push the clutch down and we landed up yelling at each other. Since the girls worked while attending school they each anted up $20 a month into a kitty for car maintenance and insurance. Donna inherited the Honda 500 and Darcy got Richard's stepmother, Natalie's 1957 Mercury Comet. Thank goodness it was a fairly heavy car for she had her fair share of fender benders.

Both girls began their working career as babysitters and then, in their early teens, went to work at the summer fair circuits for Uncle Paul and Auntie E. They found it as hard work and, unfortunately, did not get along with their cousins. I heard their complaints but thought the experience was good for them. Donna began her Macy's career of twenty years at age 16 by restocking clothes from the dressing room. Macy's was a good employer. In her college years Donna entered the junior executive program. Although she started with the company in Stockton, she transferred to San Francisco and eventually Sacramento all the while learning various roles including being in security, a buyer, and a section manager. I was impressed that Macy's allowed her job schedule work around her college course studies.

Darcy found a clerical job at the army recruiting office and "slung hash" in the Gemco coffee shop. On holidays and Sundays they were substitute hostesses at Hoosier Inn, a renowned eating establishment in the 1970s and 80s on Wilson Way. By this time they were workaholics. They were driven not by the money, but the sense of accomplishment. Even in their adult careers their work ethic remained strong.

Our neighborhood had once been one of Stockton's best. But it began to deteriorate when many of the old, large houses turned into group homes or halfway houses for drug intervention and even homeless shelter programs. We had a break-in through the second story window outside Darcy's bedroom. The intruder came up the back steps and left foot prints on the window sill. Judging by the shoe size it seemed to be that of a youngster. Items taken included a portable radio, a camera and all our piggy banks and jars of coins. Not all the items were carted away immediately; some were lined up at the foot of the stairs. The thief must have been scared off for when he went into Richard's drawers he found a small brown bag and tore it open. The contents – short dark hair – scattered everywhere. This was supposed to be part of a family joke. Richard had decided to grow a beard. I liked his appearance for his portliness and coloring made him look very much like the actor Sebastian Cabot. The girls thought otherwise and their two votes outnumbered mine so Richard shaved it off and decided to save it to give to me as a future joke gift. But the joke was on the thief. We learned later that there was a foster home in the neighborhood in which the foster parents insisted the boys leave the house early and only could return when they brought home illicit gains.

A Thought About Cleveland School

When the girls were in high school I went back to college, first at San Joaquin Delta College and then California State University, Sacramento. One day, while studying, I heard helicopters swirling around and very shortly the television news broadcast a shooting at Cleveland School where five Cambodian children were killed and many wounded along with one teacher, Janet Geng. Patrick Purdy, the young deranged shooter was from Oregon. This became the spark that ignited anti-gun advocates to ban all guns with a primary focus on the AK-47s, a semi-automatic rifle. This highly publicized incident and the activities that followed in the ensuing months still haunt me to this day. Then mayor, Barbara Fass, took to testifying before Congress to ban guns; yet, she, being Jewish, adamantly supported guns in kibbutz to train youngsters. That type of thinking seemed to be incongruous.

As the weeks passed the school board and other educators resolved to eliminate all traces of the horrific event physically and in the minds of the young students: clean the area, paint out any evidence, and comfort the children. All these steps seemed obvious. I tried to talk to some of the folks involved to leave at last one bullet hole in the wall The look on the people's face told me that they thought I was all wrong. I am not a psychologist, I was not a teacher but I have lived through traumatic times. I questioned if those involved in leadership roles had ever experienced true trauma; I suspected not. If all the evidence was totally erased, then when the youngsters become adults and wanted to reflect on this incident they have nowhere to validate that moment in their life as unpleasant as it was. When veterans of war bring their families overseas to visit areas where they had served, they are remembering a traumatic time in their lives. Yes, their return was the validation they survived. Did we help to squash all the memories of the Cleveland youngsters by painting over the walls? Time will tell.

In the final analysis, the publicity generated and the outcry that followed forever tainted Stockton as a killing field. It could have been handled better.

In 1982 both daughters left home to further their education; one went north and the other south. Donna spent her first two years at San Joaquin Delta College and transferred to my alma mater where she received her degree in Social Studies. Darcy wanted a bit more distance and headed for Southern California, first to California State University at Fullerton then she finished her Anthropology degree at the University of California, Los Angeles.

When both girls left for college, Richard armed each with a bag of hand tools: two types of hammers, socket wrenches, tape measures, and miscellaneous screwdrivers. These were taken from his own workshop, something that a man would hand to his grown child. By now Darcy became adept at using carpentry tools and, in later life, built chairs and beds when she struck out on her own. Donna had learned to change the oil in the car much to the delight of her male friends.

Family portrait - 1979

Suddenly, Richard and I faced the empty nest. We were to stay at the Commerce Street house another fourteen years. My foray into politics was part of the reason for not moving. How I cherish the memories of that house; the roaring fire in the fireplace and Donna sitting on the living room floor leaning against Richard's legs as he sat in his easy chair -- both enjoying the television and their togetherness. I still envision Darcy pecking on the Yamaha organ in the entry hall and Bourbon, our cocker spaniel, sitting on the first landing of the back stairs watching people walk by. This old house had all the ingredients for raising a family and it embraced us with its warmth and charm.

Chapter 11

A Period of Grieving

The 1980s were a tremendous watershed decade. I was experiencing a subliminal feeling of abandonment. My girls leaving was a natural process; but other emotions came to fore when my mother died in 1981 and then father in 1986. In retrospect, my feelings towards the folks changed because of personal maturation, circumstances, and time. In 1973 Father retired as a diplomat for the Republic of China. His last post was a trade mission in Sydney, Australia, where they took up residence in Sydney's suburb of Rose Bay. Rather than a retirement income the Taiwan government gave him a one time retirement package which included a condominium in Taipei, capitol of Taiwan. Father quickly turned that real estate into cash as mother never liked living in Taiwan. She sensed, as an outsider (being American Chinese), there was a pecking order among Chinese diplomat wives. The Taiwanese women thought they were a notch above those from Mainland China, particular Shanghai and Beijing and even America. One can only imagine such shallowness.

A Generation Departs and the Heart Hangs Heavy

In less than a decade many of my relatives died. By the early 1960s, Grandma Chew was bedridden and remained so for the rest of her life. She still lived in the Powell Street building but occupied apartment no. 2 (this was the original apartment that Auntie Fran and I shared until she got married). Grandma, now totally blind, suffered from cancer of the esophagus and spine. She relied on a full time caregiver. In the early stages of her confinement she would listen to the radio but, slowly, she lost interest and retreated to a silent world. In this miserable state, Grandma's only pleasure was her scotch, Johnny Walker Black Label. A Rubbermaid tumbler with a straw inserted sat on the night stand within her reach and that was all she wanted. Visitors came but even those visits became infrequent and Grandma retreated even deeper into her depth of darkness. When I last saw her she asked if there was anyone else in the room other than myself and Richard. As soon as I replied no, she spoke to Richard in English. This startled him for he thought Cantonese was her only language. She wanted Richard to be part of the conversation and was accommodating, Ah Pau died in 1977, she was almost 88 years of age. The funeral was very much in keeping with tradition as it included a mournful band leading a procession down Grant Avenue. In spite of the sadness of the occasion, daughter Donna became very taken by my Reno, Nevada, cousin Cherk's midnight blue Corvette. He offered her ride to the cemetery. Somehow they ended up in line just behind the family limousine with the car's top down and rock'n'roll music blaring away. At 14, Donna was enjoying herself at her great grandmother's funeral.

The graves of Thomas Foon Chew and Lee Gum Ching at Ning Yeung Cemetery in Colma, Ca. By tradition the wife is on the left side and the husband on the right.

A few months before Ah Pau's death her middle son, Uncle Hank of Redding, died of emphysema. Auntie Fran who, along with Grandma, brought me to this country, succumbed to colon cancer in 1979 and her husband, Uncle George in 1984 from lung cancer. And dear Uncle Paul, who sang as he drove through the night taking me to Redding, died of a heart attack in 1982. These were my surrogate parents who, along with Grandma, gave me a stable family life.

Britton and Natalie Minnick

We relocated Richard's parents, Britton and Natalie Minnick, from Tucson, Arizona to Stockton in 1978. They were getting up there in age (Pop was 88 and Natalie 77) and the 14-hour drives to Tucson to check on them were taking a toll. We put them in an assisted living place not far from our house. The summer after Ah Pau's passing Richard and I decided to take a month's trip to England to places I wanted to visit for years. It was our first major trip together. Donna, being a very responsible person, thought she could look in on them, take care of Darcy, work, and still attend school as well as her other activities during our absences.

What an enjoyable trip driving through the English countryside, visiting museums and churches, staying in bed and breakfast inns, and sampling the local brew along the way. We visited my Anglican sponsor Mrs. Eagland and her daughter, Rosemary and family. Although we corresponded frequently our reunion brought back memories of early days in Bangkok. In that month we became very familiar with England's freeway system particularly the M1 and M6. Richard became quite an expert at driving on the opposite of the road and no longer sideswiped the tires on the roundabouts.

When the plane refueled in Goose Bay, Newfoundland, en route home we got the grim news that Richard's father, Pop, died of congestive heart failure. Donna took him to the hospital and stayed with him for several nights. She also looked in on his wife, Natalie, who was quite distressed. Not knowing exactly how to proceed Donna called all the funeral homes and actually shopped around. Her major question was the cost of storing the body not knowing how to contact us as we left no itinerary. Jim Soares, the owner of Chapel of the Palms on California Street near Gleason Park, was struck by her maturity given she was only 17. Donna did run into problems getting immediate care for Pop. In the ambulance and then in the hospital she said Pop was her grandfather and she the responsible party. Understandably the hospital staff was confused being that her last name was Chan and his Minnick. When Donna stood her ground the adults listened.

By the time we got home Pop's funeral was pretty well planned. Natalie had fallen and was in the hospital. While there Natalie became distended and the hospital staff did nothing to relieve her thus causing more complications. Richard suggested to the doctor that he not operate but, again, doctors think they know best. The doctor operated on Natalie the morning of Pop's funeral. Immediately after the service we went to the hospital to check on Natalie and learned that she died on the operating table. In our minds' eye we still feel the doctor cared more about getting paid for an operation and less about the patient. Richard called it murder, but there was nothing to gain by pursuing our belief. As soon as Jim Soares heard of her death and, without direction, he called the cemetery and got the burial plot right next to Pop. The following day we held Natalie's funeral. Although we mourned we were grateful that they enjoyed their move to Stockton even though their residence was short. The inscriptions on their singular headstone reads:

"The Gentleman from Virginia and the Yellow Rose of Texas"

My Parents Needed Attention

It seemed we couldn't escape from the mantle of illnesses and death. One late evening I got a call from mom saying something was wrong with dad and that he was acting strangely. Since my parents retirement they moved to an apartment in San Francisco's Diamond Heights area. Their two bedroom place afforded each their own space. Mom said dad got up went into the kitchen, opened the refrigerator and peed on the floor. She called Auntie Fran who was living up the hill. When Uncle George saw dad he surmised that dad was probably drunk but would be fine in the morning so they went home. Mom called Glo down in Palo Alto but Glo was out teaching that night. Mom was not clear in her message to us, was it an emergency or was it not, I didn't quite understand. The next morning while Richard was preparing for work I told him I had an uneasy feeling and asked if we could drive to San Francisco. We got to the folks' apartment around 10:00 AM. Dad was semi-comatose. The paramedics said he had suffered a massive stroke. I rode with him in the ambulance. Richard followed with mom. For several weeks dad remained in the hospital for evaluation. Initially his left side was paralyzed, his use of limbs returned after several months. The hospital staff also determined that he had lost much of his cognitive skills. I had my doubts and asked that they retest in my presence. The evaluator began to conduct the test by asking simple questions such as "where is the clock", or "what is the object on the table?" He pointed to the clock on the wall and the table object was a globe at which point he said: "le monde." This went on for a couple more questions. The technician was very professional and decided dad did not give correct answers. However, she was Chinese and spoke only English and Cantonese; whereas, dad, as a career diplomat, was fluent in many languages. He spoke English, Mandarin, Cantonese, French, Tagalog, some Thai and several other foreign words, phrases and expressions. The stroke caused a bit of scrambling in his thought process.

Patrick and Lonnie Sun in 1979

Once dad was able to go home my parents thought of seeking other treatments, such as looking for the physician who cared for Pui Yi, the last emperor of China. The doctor, although now quite elderly, was living in Hong Kong. They thought, Patricia (Dida) and her family might be helpful as they were living in Manila. The treatment in Hong Kong proved disappointing so they went and stayed with Larry and Patricia for eight months before returning to San Francisco. Meanwhile I took charge of their San Francisco apartment - their mail and bills. Yes, I had asked myself frequently why me? Why shouldn't Gloria do it? Phil was then living in Houston so I guess he was out of the question. But mother insisted and Richard relented. My resentment began to build when mom wrote almost weekly asking if the bank statements arrived, what about the stock portfolio report, or what bills had I paid. I drove to the city frequently in order to check their mail and to answer her. Her letters were short and crisp giving directions as if I was her secretary. She never asked about my children or Richard and least of all me. In retrospect I can understand her worries over their finances and realized her concerns were mostly about themselves. Things hadn't changed.

May Lan Chew Sun

When the folks returned to San Francisco dad's health improved greatly. He believed in regimen but mother took to bed frequently complaining of headaches. She took immeasurable amounts of aspirin and Tylenol. This went on for several months. She couldn't do any chores and they relied on microwave cooking or whatever food we brought. Donna also drove out to visit on her days off and took dad for rides. Mom always asked Donna to get ice cream. This should have been a warning. This was August of 1981.

Mom's tests showed she had nine tumors in her head, four on one side and five on the other. The oncologist never located the source of the cancer but we suspected it had metastasized to many areas. Mom had been a heavy smoker and a drinker. In addition she had a family history of cancer. Mom started treatment and soon lost all her hair. She kidded that she was now a "*wa shun*" a Chinese monk, but for all her vanity one could tell she was devastated, her beauty gone. Donna went out often to visit her grandparents and, on one particular visit, she called home and said she had driven mom to Children's Hospital. She cried and said it was not a good sign. Donna felt she had taken other grandparents to the hospital and they all seem to die on her.

Richard, Mom, Darcy and Dad - 1980

I was unfamiliar with the dynamics of cancer on the patient and family. My experience with those dying was congestive heart failure or operations. I will always remember my mother's last three months of life. While mom was never a deep thinker nor talked about current affairs, she was socially pleasant and had the tendency of making light of most topics. Admittedly we never really lived together for a decent period of time and I never saw her with a temper. But during her hospital stay she turned into a very angry person. Not at me but at almost everyone else. She was conscious but often her subconscious came to fore.

When she was admitted to the hospital she brought her purse and also the safe deposit key. She refused to surrender the key to the nurses and even to dad. She gave it to me and asked me not to give it to dad, she said he would give everything to his mistress. I wasn't surprised if he might have mistresses before because he was known to enjoy entertaining movie stars and starlets. Obviously Mom still held on to the past even though this was not his life at this point. I took the key and quietly passed it on to him without her knowledge. I heard mom scream at the nurses, the doctors and even my brother and sisters. When Dad tenderly tried to wipe her face she became quite violent and cursed him. It was truly a "why me" type of an anger. Most startling though was that when Mom saw me she cried, "I'm sorry, I'm sorry." This went on every time I saw her. I wondered if she was suffering from guilt because she never tried to protect me many decades ago. Had this feeling always been in her subconscious? I had read somewhere that some women don't interfere when they see abusive activity for the sake of personal safety

It is common that families gather, or rather hover, when death knocks. That we did in mom's hospital room. As a relief, we, individually, staggered down to the cafeteria for a change of scenery. On one occasion my siblings and I were sitting at a table and the topic turned to living with the parents. Gloria asked Pat if she remembered their days in Bangkok and various incidents there. Phil brought up the time when the parents took him to Sun Moon Lake in Taiwan. A few minutes into the rather pleasant conversation my siblings were clearly enjoying reminiscing, but I got up and left. Richard followed and I explained that it was very painful for me to hear them talk almost lovingly of their childhood with our parents – something I never shared. My memories were that of beatings, confinements, and other punishments. These were thoughts I tried to bury.

One day in late October I mentioned to Pat that I knew mom was going to die on November 12th. She was taken aback. Her first response was "Nah, it was the big Cal-Stanford weekend." I told her it did not matter because funerals are held generally several days or weeks later. There was a reason for my prediction – Grandma's birthday was November 12th. I had heard from someone years ago that Ah Pau had tremendous spiritual strength, stronger than her offsprings. When Uncle Hank, Grandma's second son, fell deathly ill in Redding, everyone wondered who would pass first, Grandma or Hank. That's when I learned of her spiritual strength. She outlived Uncle Hank by several months.

The morning of November 12th laid heavily on me. I had many things to do and many places to go. There was a deadline for turning in my paper in a graduate program; it meant personal delivery to the professor on campus in Sacramento. But first I wanted to drive to San Francisco and check on mom. Auntie E also came by to check up on her. By mid-afternoon mother lapsed into unconsciousness and began her death throes. Pat had a concern. She did not bring mom's false teeth to the hospital and wondered if they could get the dentures on after death or should she run home and get them immediately. The nurse said it would be a while before she passed. I looked at the clock and it was close to 5:00 PM, commute traffic had begun and so did the rain. I left the hospital, crossed the Bay Bridge and at about the Ashley exit on Interstate 80 near UC Berkeley traffic came to a standstill and the rain was torrential. I was bawling but didn't know why. Was it for Mom? Was I overtired? Was it stress? I pushed on and arrived on the Sacramento State University campus around 7:30 PM. By now I had composed myself and literally ran across campus to the professor's office. After a brief discussion I headed home to Stockton arriving at 9:15 PM. I called Pat immediately and said I know mom is still alive and will pass in an hour or so. She died before the night was over. I was exhausted and slept poorly; but strangely, woke up feeling good. That time by myself in the car with the tears streaming down my face proved to be a wonderful catharsis.

At the mortuary, three large flower arrangements in the shape of rectangular pillows surrounded the casket, one representing each of us daughters. The pillows, a symbolic gesture, were to comfort the deceased as she rested. Phil's arrangement was a large white cross. There was a beautiful orchid corsage pinned to mom's dress. Very fitting as her Chinese name was May Lan or Beautiful Orchid. Four thin scarves, representing blankets, were neatly folded and tucked just below her chest. These were to prepare her for the changing seasons in the after life.

For the funeral I volunteered to gather up black ties for the men in the family. We got the ties for under a dollar each from the Salvation Army thrift shop and from cleaners that had unclaimed ties. It is the custom for the men to throw their tie and women their veil into the grave after the casket is lowered. This was one of the final acts of the burial service. During Aunt Frances' burial Richard, not totally familiar with our custom, wore an expensive designer tie. I didn't want that to be thrown in the grave and I whispered to him to take off his tie when everyone else did and then slip it into his jacket pocket. By the time we got into the car, the tie had disappeared – strange.

Mom is buried near the rest of the Chew Family in the Ning Yeung Cemetery in Colma. The final memory of mom's burial was just before the grave diggers began to remove the wooden planks that supported the casket. We were told to throw some coins into the grave symbolically to give her travel money into the next world. As I began to throw a handful of coins a nickel landed on its edge and began to roll down the full length of a plank. Some heads turned to watch the coin and Donna, standing just behind me, whispered: "Mom, are you trying to pitch dimes at a carnival?" She walked away with a grin on her face. I wanted to bop her one but I too chuckled as I walked away.

I felt my mother's passing most strongly during full moons and would gaze upward with a strange longing. What a shame that we never developed a real mother-daughter relationship.

It took about four years before my baleful mood vanished.

Patrick Pichi Sun

Dad stayed in the San Francisco apartment only a few months. By then his only interest was looking at the Chinese newspaper particularly for advertisements on new restaurants. We invariably sought them out when I visited. One day I asked if he would like to live with me since our daughters were gone and we had plenty of room. He said it would be inappropriate for he was going to leave for Houston and stay with Philip and his wife Chen. Dad even brought a set of everyday rice bowls; symbolically he was going to share rice with them. As we packed up the apartment and his belongings I found it strange that he had been issued an Australian passport. I knew he had an American green card but assumed all along that he was still a Taiwan citizen. He could not articulate well enough to discuss this matter with me and it left me wondering about his allegiance to his former country.

Father tried to adjust to life in Houston. His brief letters were frequent. He wrote well for someone who had disabilities from a major stroke. The one page letters were continual efforts toward conversation and memory retention. A one liner would say: "You were born on April 26, 1941. Love, Dad" or "We were three brothers: Patrick, George and Sam. Love Dad." Father felt the depth of loneliness for his wife, the ambiance of San Francisco, and having other family around. Chen and Phillip were childless and unaccustomed to caring for the needs of an elderly, particularly one with disabilities. Dinner hours were customarily late because of their busy schedule. Dad made a concerted effort to keep up with my brother's lifestyle but it was hard and his health declined further.

The Chinese who relocated to Houston from Taiwan visited him, particularly his old friends Peter and Amparo Wong. As kind as they were, long conversations proved difficult. It was only a matter of a few years before he suffered another stroke and entered an assisted living facility. A Filipina caregiver, Ida, stayed with him during the day to give him personal attention and she wrote often about his progress.

We flew to Houston a number of times; we even stopped by on our way home from visiting Tennessee or from cruising the Caribbean. The last time we visited, Dad had really deteriorated. He laid in a fetal position most of the time. He recognized both of us but could not give verbal responses. As we began to leave he grabbed both our hands with amazing strength and gazed into our eyes. His were bright as if he was talking through them and he hung on to our hands for the longest time, not wanting to let go. Tears came to all our eyes, his included. His was the most pitiful, almost pleading, and we knew we would never see him alive again. What angst we felt when we left. Richard said he would never forget that look as long as he lived. Surprisingly, none of my childhood memories of the man flooded my psyche. Instead, his eyes were those of a man who tried to reach out to me in recent years as if to form some type of bond. Yet, he knew it was too late. He knew I had returned to school and was working on my degrees. He wanted to know about my writings but couldn't articulate. He thought by giving me some awareness of my past in those one page, one line letters might help. He also knew that I was the type of person who was not spiteful and I did all I could to help him and even offer our home to him. But out of tradition and because it was not appropriate, he could not accept. Fate is cruel. We never achieved the father-daughter bonding that my daughters experienced. In the end we did try to bridge a relationship.

In February 1986, Ambassador Patrick Pichi Sun died in Houston, Texas. The announcement of his death was in the Chinese and English newspapers in Houston and San Francisco. His service at the Green Street Mortuary on Green Street in San Francisco was very similar to his wife's. Reverend T.T. Taam of the Chinese Methodist Church on Washington Street conducted the service as he did for mom. Reverend Taam was not only an old family friend, but also cousin Joan's father-in-law. My brother, Philip, did a spectacular job creating and organizing large portraits depicting Patrick Sun's life. Some of the pictures showed dad in dress uniform, bedecked with a multitude of various medals and awards; some with mother and various notable international leaders and other segments of his diplomatic life. Dad's medals and his one sword that he had made for the King of Siam's funeral laid on top of the casket. All this was as impressive as Ambassador Chieh Liu who gave the eulogy:

"...I may perhaps recapitulate the highlights of his career. Patrick graduated In 1929 from Tsing Hua University, one of the most prestigious institution of learning from which hailed many leaders of China.

"He began working as a statistician first in the Legislative Yuan and later at the Salt Gabelle of the Ministry of Finance...then joined the Ministry of Foreign Affairs. He was sent to San Francisco as chancellor of the Consulate General which, by his own description, was the lowest ranking officer in the Chinese Diplomatic and Consular Service...in his spare time he earned a Master's Degree at Stanford...promoted as e'leve-consult and vice consul until transferred to Kuala Lumpur.

"Soon after Pearl Harbor, when the Japanese war machine was sweeping through Southeast Asia, he made his way by a hazardous route to Chungking, the wartime capitol...promptly posted again to San Francisco as Consul...during the San Francisco Conference in 1945 he took an active part in drafting the Chinese text of the United Nations Charter which was no mean accomplishment.

"When the Republic of the Philippines came into being after V.J. Day, he was transferred to Manila as First Secretary of the newly established legation...years later he returned as Ambassador...January 1950 he was promoted to Bangkok as Counselor of the Embassy in Thailand...he was recalled to the Ministry of Foreign Affairs in Taipei...after several months of studies at the Yangmingshan Institute where Senior Government officers underwent advanced training, he was assigned for the third time to San Francisco, this time as Consul General with the rank of Minister Plenipotentiary.

"He then headed the Department of Information at the Ministry of Foreign Affairs in Taipei...after three years he became the first Ambassador to the newly independent state of Jamaica and subsequently in a concurrent capacity, Ambassador to Barbados...in 1966 in New York he attended the 22nd Session of the General Assembly of the United Nations. His assignment with the delegation was all too brief, but thanks to his island-hopping activities, he succeeded in rallying the Caribbean nations to vote in support of the position of the Republic of China in the world organization.

"He was in Kingston less than two years before he moved to Manila which was considered for the Republic of China strategically and politically more important than the Caribbean. His accomplishment and his popularity as Ambassador in the Philippines may be summed up...by Foreign Minister Carlos Romulo...I quote: 'I consider you one of the best ambassadors in our Diplomatic Corps in Manila. You have represented the interests of the Republic of China with dignity and unexcelled competence and you have won my respect and admiration....

"Indeed, everywhere he went, he left behind unforgettable marks of friendship and goodwill. He knew particularly well the countries of Southeast Asia...yet I think it was in San Francisco that he left his heart...."

As the ambassador spoke of Dad's role on the international scene I realized Dad saw the strength of powerful countries. As such he gave his three daughters the following names: Patricia - *Lai Wah* (Beautiful China), Gloria - *Lai Mei* (Beautiful America), and mine *Lai Ying* (Beautiful England). It was not meaningful to me when I was a child, but in my adult years I was in awe to think this man had so much stature and this man was my father. I, too, am humbled and regretted that I bore such early feelings. Yet there are many regrets in each human's life and I do understand the frailty of the man and the lack of understanding of youth.

Neither Dad's nor Mom's funerals included the burning of incense, joss sticks, or gold-patched paper money or even a marching band down Grant Avenue similar to Grandma Chew's. My parents were Christian and we had moved another step away from Chinese tradition. Yet on the way to the cemetery, as we all piled into the limousine following the hearse, no one said much until the driver of the hearse reached out of the window and threw out shreds of paper symbolizing money. We all looked at each other immediately thinking of the extra cost and someone asked: "Who ordered that?" It turned out it was part of the funeral package. The scattering of paper money enroute to the cemetery was to deter evil spirits or bribing them not to harm the deceased. If there was one humorous memory of Dad's funeral it was when Steve Tom, an old family friend, after making his three kowtows (bows) went up to the coffin and slipped a pint of Cutty Sark down to the hallow bottom of the casket. What a nice gesture, Dad had scotch for his journey. After the service we filed outside and lined up in the hall waiting for the casket to be placed into the hearse. As the pall bearers lifted and carried the coffin down several steps of the first and second landings one could hear the "klack kung, klack khung" as the pint bottle pitched back and forth on the sides of the coffin.

The graves of Ambassador and Mrs. Patrick Sun at Ning Yeung Cemetery. At the upper right corner the Masonic emblem grave is that of Tom Foon Chew and Lee Gum Ching (my mother's parents).

We were now four orphans, even though adults. Our parents were married for forty seven years, bore four children and travelled the world. Yet it was for a very short period, less than two years that all four children were together under one roof. Patricia went off to college by 16, Gloria to boarding school in Taiwan, Philip stayed with them the longest and me the shortest since I joined the family at age 7 and left by 10. All of us were never together for a family Christmas nor any other family holiday. As we now have our own families, we have no memory or history of holidays past as a nuclear family.

Chapter 12

The Many Roads of Samfow

Beginnings of the Road

While my daughters were still at home I completed the Associate of Arts degree at San Joaquin Delta College. Then when they both entered college, I commuted to CSU-Sacramento for my Bachelor of Arts degree, majoring in history. I have always been curious about people, their families and their ancestors who had the foresight to stakeout a place in the great American dream. Fortunately, my timing was good as other historians began to take greater interest in ethnographic stories of early American communities. My search for community history began in earnest in 1982 during my Masters program. I felt I struck gold. For five months I traipsed off to the Stockton Rural Cemetery and pored over the original death records dating back to the cemetery's beginnings in 1862.

Tucked in the thick, yellow pages of four volumes were 1,296 names of Chinese whose original burials took place in the northwest corner of the cemetery. The ledger entries, once written clearly with black ink, had faded to a light brown; regardless, the information jumped out at me. It screamed for me to hurry as if the entries were going to disappear into oblivion. The extrapolated information for the years of 1863 to 1936 became a virtual recreation of an entire community. For seventy three years Chinese remains were buried, exhumed after seven years, repacked, then transported and reburied in their native village in China. This practice ended when the Japanese invaded China in 1936 and never resumed because of the chaos of World War II followed by the Communist takeover. My research had a definitive start and stop period of accumulated data. In front of me was fantastic evidence of a people who breathed, worked, reclaimed the delta land, farmed the rich soil of the central valley, and gave birth to the second and third generations of Chinese Americans. They were not just coolies and day laborers. They were not just a statistical number. They had names; they were married; some died of old age; others met unfortunate circumstances of tong warfare. They were my Chinese.

I just couldn't stop researching the Chinese community. Questions lead to further exploration: how did the Chinese dovetail into the larger history of Stockton and the San Joaquin county communities of Lodi, Tracy, and even into the smaller hamlets? How did they deal with education, religion, and more importantly, discrimination? How did the Chinese Exclusion Law of 1882 or the Alien Land Act of 1913, affect the Chinese locally? These two federal laws were road blocks that many Chinese families faced for generations. The first prohibited the emigration of Chinese workers and the second prohibited Chinese immigrants from owning land.

Notecards, shoe boxes, and bits and pieces stuffed in envelopes began to accumulate in the dining room and my upstairs study, formerly Darcy's bedroom. One day Richard quipped: "When does research stop?" I thought, good question! I always assumed NEVER. The cold realization was that I had spent eight years researching and had a fairly good grasp of Stockton's community in the nineteen and twentieth centuries geographically, socially, and politically. For me a vision of the Chinese community during this period came into focus, it had a sense of virtual reality. So what now? I never intended to write a book, much less a magazine article. But being dutiful in nature I began to sort the accumulated pearls and disciplined myself to writing. From 11:00 PM to 5:00 AM I commandeered the dining room table. The house was absolutely quiet, no phone, no doorbell, no television and Richard was asleep. My intent was to describe the evolution of a Chinese community only a mountain (meaning the Altamont) away from the San Francisco and the Bay Area experience.

After two years of writing, I sent the manuscript to fifteen friends in various sectors of history and local communities for comments. The suggestions, interjections and critical remarks led me to believe it was worth going to the next step – asking for pre-review comments. Among the many I selected: California Secretary of State March Fong Eu; Thomas W. Chinn, the founding president of the Chinese Historical Society in San Francisco; Beulah Quo from Stockton and a recognized Southern California community leader and actress; Dr. Alexander Saxton of University of California-Berkeley; and Dr. James Deetz, professor of anthropology of UC-Berkeley. Dr. Deetz was on a dig in Africa. My heart thumped rapidly when he readily agreed to send comments as soon as he received my manuscript. The content of his work, *Small Things Forgotten*, 1977, was poignant to my writings. This was a reminder to me that small stuff has equal importance in history.

Like many aspiring authors, my list of inquiries to publishing houses grew and the rejection letters followed. My work did not conform to the traditional ethnohistory. It did not belabor all the immigration laws; it was neither fish nor fowl. How could they market this work; was it too risky? I promoted that it had value; it offered gems of authenticated new information. Several university presses took the tried and true, and rather staid, position of sorry – "but we wish you luck."

A university imprint is prestigious but there are some downsides. Traditionally the book would be sent off for review into a narrow academic niche. This strategy generally takes about eighteen months. Sometimes it may be over a year before a review is written. Absolutely glowing reviews are difficult to come by. Typically, kind comments also are accompanied by a few disparaging remarks. This may seem unkind but it allows a reviewer to make a counter point. Even then the book's shelf life is short, one year at most. If after two years without an all out push by the university the book slips into that dark abyss of the academic world.

About eight months after sending out queries, two publishing houses showed interest and each had a history of producing local and regional works – one in Franklin, Tennessee and the other in Fresno, California. Panorama West of Fresno was the obvious choice. Its proximity meant the ability to work directly with their staff only one hundred miles down the road. Owner Charles Clough had many years of publishing experience.

Thus, in the spring of 1988 *SAMFOW: The San Joaquin Chinese Legacy* was born.

Unintentionally, but characteristically Chinese, the book was introduced first to the Stockton Chinese, then to the San Joaquin County residents at the county museum in Micke Grove and finally to the Chinese American history community in San Francisco. All the book signing parties were well attended. The Stockton Chinese community was elated; this was their story and their party. At one point City Clerk Frances Hong commented that they were selling a book a minute. Members of the San Joaquin County Historical Society and Museum also laid claim to that part of history that

Signing books – red banner displays attendees' signatures

mentioned contributions of the early Chinese in all parts of the county. There was now considerably more history about the local Chinese than ever before. In the next two years I traveled, gave many presentations, and signed books. For the most part newspapers, historical journals, and magazines were gracious in their reviews. However, time and time again, it was the average reader who told me he found SAMFOW the most interesting and pleasurable. Many local families purchased numerous copies for their children and grandchildren. Little did I realize that this one book would lead to other activities, interests, and passions. My world opened in large and small ways.

Highways and By Ways

In the next several years I traveled up and down California making presentations at events for large Chinese historical organizations. Visits to Los Angeles, San Diego, Oakland, San Francisco, and Sacramento seemed like reunions with old friends. Faces, places, banquet halls, back rooms of coffee shops reminded me of years ago when I traversed California organizing for California's state clerical employees. The Central Valley, Central Coast, mining communities of the Mother Lode, the foothills of the Sierra, and along the Oregon border all became familiar once again as I spoke at these venues. The smaller communities offered distinct locations: the historic armory in Copperopolis, the quaint hundred-plus year Harmony church in Lockeford, and even a wine cave in Murphys at the Ironstone Winery. Often times I stayed in charming bed and breakfast inns, a historic hotel in Groveland, and even an Arabian-themed hotel room in Reedley. I made new friends and learned of Chinese in the far reaches of California having the same experience as my Stockton Chinese.

The Academic Byway – Papers, Conferences and Classroom

One method of introducing SAMFOW to the academic world was to present papers at conferences and symposiums. While keeping with the theme of the Chinese in California, I appeared at universities and colleges speaking to topics on the environment, Asian American studies, and women's history. Some of the places included University of San Diego, UC-Santa Cruz, Mills College, University of Washington, UC-Davis, CSU-Long Beach, CSU-Sacramento, University of the Pacific and numerous community colleges. I argued that because of the energy the Chinese put forth in the making of California they should be considered a major contributor in the opening of the West. I emphasized this thinking at the annual conferences of the Western History Association and the Oregon-California Trail Association. Rubbing elbows with cowboy-like historians was as much fun as talking to the Sons of the Golden West. While remaining a non-stereotypical, female, Asian historian, I pounded home my point. Thanks to two friends, Clarence Louie and Richard Luevano, I managed to squeeze in five years (1990-95) teaching Asian American Studies at CSU-Stanislaus, a part of a team focusing on minority experiences that also included Hispanic and

Black histories. These upper division courses were held at the Turlock and Delta campuses.

A Larger Audience

Consulting became another unexpected outcome. Contacted on a variety of issues from excavation sites to purported "Chinese tunnels", to burial site discoveries by archaeologists, cultural anthropologists and even once by the Army Corps of Engineers, I looked in nooks and crannies in the most remote of places. Once, in the repair of Main Street in Walnut Grove (a small town in the Delta), workers found a large safe. The digging opened up into a passage way and a subterranean room below a gambling house. The safe was locked and great speculation ensued. When asked my opinion, I suggested that there was nothing inside the safe. Knowing Chinese habits, if my countrymen had to flee for whatever reason, they would have emptied the safe first and foremost. My logic prevailed, the safe was empty.

I consulted on several television documentaries: a half-hour documentary of STOCKTON-CITY OF IMMIGRANTS produced by the local CBS station and the Wells Fargo-sponsored *THE GOLD RUSH*, which has been shown numerous times on Public Broadcasting Stations (PBS). A LAND BETWEEN RIVERS, a documentary of Central California between the San Joaquin and Kings' River and BITTERSWEET SOIL, the Delta communities including the town of Locke, initially seen in public broadcasting stations, became available CDs sold in bookstores. My name appeared in the credits of other Asian American documentaries. The late Huell Howser, noted for his CALIFORNIA GOLD television series tapped me for a segment when he filmed highlights of Stockton. My reward for being in front the camera was the opportunity to work with the best and brightest historians such as State Librarian Kevin Starr and author, Dr. Jim Holliday (*The World Rushed In*).

As documentaries appeared in the media, the same information also occurred in print. Some of my appearances at conferences led to invitations to publish articles in historical society quarterly journals and anthologies such as *ORIGINS AND DESTINATION: 41 Essays on Chinese America* published by the Chinese Historical Society of Southern California. This effort included a chapter in *RICHES FOR*

ALL: The California Gold Rush and the World, University of Nebraska Press. Written during California's sesquicentennial, this latter publication, edited by Dr. Kenneth Owens, was a scholarly analysis of the residual effects of the Gold Rush.

Recognized Effort

SAMFOW was definitely the catalyst as I found myself evolving with new experiences and contacts. I continued to take interest in and help organizations wanting to highlight their own Chinese pioneering histories: Hanford, Oroville, Folsom. In helping them I was helping myself and validating my thesis that the Chinese and Caucasians established symbiotic relationships during the early founding of many California communities. By now, as a research historian, I was included in other people's activities. Then recognition came. The Consul General for the Republic of China presented me a distinguish-looking citation for SAMFOW. I earned the title of Elder Advisor for the Weaverville Joss House. The Captain Weber Award for Historic Preservation recognized my leadership on Stockton's Cultural Heritage Board as well as for other efforts in the name of history for the city of Stockton. One of the most prestigious awards, however, was being inducted in the International Educators' Hall of Fame. I received a framed Chinese calligraphy gift from my late friend, Mr. Gong Lee. In bold strokes Mr. Lee wrote: "The higher one climbs the clearer one sees." He was sagacious. My critical thinking skills had sharpened and my interests now stretched beyond Asian American Studies.

Birth of a Company

Sadly my relationship with my publisher, Charles and Carmen Clough, was short lived. The Cloughs were getting on in years. He proposed that Richard and I buy Panorama West, his company. This would have entailed our relocating to Fresno, California. Fresno, as well as Bakersfield, is in the southern part of the Central Valley with no evening delta breeze to cool off hot summer nights. In addition the area is blanketed by an inverted air layer, meaning the air that drifts south from the northern part of the valley slams into the Grapevine mountains and settles back over those communities. Richard had emphysema. For these environmental reasons alone, we did not want to relocate.

My wheels were turning; if someone else bought the publishing house how well would they market my book? Not short on proactive ideas, I bought the rest of the stock and decided to market it as if it was self published. I did not know the first thing about marketing, but how difficult could it be? It seemed logical that instead of being a Chinese peddler hawking only one book, handling a few more would draw much more attention. In quick time I was marketing and selling four titles, the other three were from self-publishers. Two, *Heart of Iron* by Colonel Harley Heib and *Never Too Late* by Margaret Smith, told of personal experiences in World War II. Both authors wrote well; their writings were delightful. Mrs. Smith also was a former teacher at Lowell High School, my alma mater.

In 1989, my company, Heritage West Books, was born. There were a few bumps along the way -- storage and money. It seemed the most logical place for a small startup company was to apply to the Small Business Administration (SBA). A visit to the local agency soured any hope of ever crossing the doors of bureaucracy. I brought forth the company's prospectus that included a business plan and other required information. Much to my disappointment the head of the local office sat across from me in his three-piece brown suit and without the courtesy of even giving the prospectus a cursory glance he said: "If Stockton never had a publishing house, it was because it never needed one." Was he implying that the reading standard in Stockton was so low no one read? Was he correct? This kind of thought had never entered my mind. Our circle of friends read, my children read, and where have I been all these years not to recognize this failure in our schools. His next statement was another stab to the chest. He indicated the SBA funds were already allocated to certain designated minority groups as it always had been. Asians, however, were not one of them. I was furious but did not say a word for it would not have done any good. Here was prejudice in the coldest form. I thought I was part of a minority group, but obviously not the right group. This was 1989, was this a common practice or only in Stockton? I had noticed Asians never expected much out of government, now I knew why.

In spite of the disappointing SBA experience, I was determined that Heritage West Books succeed. What was I going to do with cases of books? A hunt for space brought me to a two-room office on the Pacific Avenue Miracle Mile. The Tuxedo Post Office was only a few doors away making it handy for shipping books. I focused on being a niche-publisher, specializing in regional biography, ethnography, and local history. A part time helper answered the phone and packed the books for shipping. Cold calls to bookstores generated sales and, when time allowed, I took to visiting stores both locally and in the surrounding area.

A year later the company moved across the street to Regent Court. The new location was a 600-square foot office that included a storeroom, enough space for production and staff, and my own office. We shared one half of a former fraternity house with two dentists: Drs. Frank Rossi and David McCann. These wonderful gentlemen never raised the rent in eleven years nor did they do any improvements. At times friends who frequented the dentists popped in. In the twelve years of operation, Heritage West Books produced nine titles bearing the company imprint: *Nevada Newspaper Days* by Jake Highton; *Wagons West* by Robert Shellenberger, *Yesteryear's Child: Summer Days and Golden Nights* by Dr. Richard Rohrbacher, *Weber* by Dr. Jim Shebl, *From The Ohio to the San Joaquin* by Olive Davis, *Vineyards In the Sky: The Life of Legendary Vintner Martin Ray* by Eleanor Ray and Barbara Marinacci, and *California's Chinese Heritage: A Legacy of Places* by Dr. Thomas McDannold. Some books were cooperative agreements whereby the author helped augment the printing costs while the company handled the production and marketing. Other titles were fully funded by the company. The books were attractive and their assembly showed they were of high quality. Most importantly, they were a good read.

Our customer base grew to over two hundred retail and wholesale outlets. Unsolicited manuscripts came across my desk and as the years passed those numbers increased appreciably. My heart went out to the writers and it was difficult to write rejection letters for I, too, at one time had mailed unsolicited manuscript. The primary stabilizing factor for the company rested on one person's shoulder, Marian Vieira, a very faithful employee. She ran the company when I was on the City Council, worked at my state appointed position in Sacramento or when I made sales calls to bookstores. I depended on her to prepare invoices, handle accounting, pack and ship out orders and field inquiries. For ten years Marian did it all. A personal tragedy and the pressure of "too much" forced me to close the company at the end of 2000.

Still the Writer

It was fourteen years before I authored another book. An agent from Arcadia Publishing asked if I would do a pictorial as part of that company's *"Images of America"* series. He had read SAMFOW and this was to be Arcadia's first venture focusing on a Chinese community. The idea was to amass photographs and provide captions. Sounded simple enough and it gave me a chance to create a sequel to bring the Chinese story to the present. I put out a request to the Chinese community, spelling out the types of photos needed; very shortly the length of our fireplace hearth was stacked three feet high with photo albums, shoeboxes, and bags filled with old photos that friends dug from the recesses of their drawers, trunks, and attics. It took less than four months to put *The Chinese of Stockton* together. It was printed in 2002 and is now in its third reprint.

Three years later, in 2005, the Friends of the Fox, a local theater support organization, commemorated the 75th anniversary of the theater. The theater had undergone an eight-plus million dollar renovation and changed the theater's name from the California Fox to the Bob Hope Theater. They asked if I would do a brochure, but I said I only do books. Eight months later *Stockton Crown Jewel: The Bob Hope/Fox California* came off the press.

This coffee table book was truly a "jewel" in itself. It has stories of old theaters in Stockton, the architectural changes to the Fox, movies and stage shows, past management and employees, major films shot in and around the county, visiting movie stars, testimonials, and a wealth of color photos. I wrote the bulk of the content and served as the production manager. Five other friends (Tom Bowe, Bob Shellenberger, Don Geiger, Bob Hartzell and Marian Vieira) contributed separate chapters ranging from the history of the theater's pipe organ, the theater's legal relationship between the city and previous theater's owners, and the theater's occasional usage by small defunct thespian groups. Snyder Lithograph, a local print company, did the final layout before it was sent to a Canadian press. I was very pleased with this product. It told me that I can research and write beyond the Chinese American genre and, even with passing years, I retained the wherewithal to put a book together.

Chapter 13

Community Activism

The Genesis

Just as writing a book and creating a publishing house were natural progressions, my foray into community activism followed the same direction and was again unintentional. Was it because I didn't know how to say no or was it taking those baby steps and not knowing where they were going to lead? Did my interest start in junior high school when I was elected the school secretary and then school editor? Was it a dormant interest? Did "getting involved" occur during my Division of Highway days when I accepted the local California State Employees (CSEA) chapter's secretary job? Or was I proactive by nature and as one of my college professors remarked: "Minnick, you seem to be the first to always jump into the trench." It seemed I had an instinctive urge to lend a hand and maybe to prove to myself that there was a reason for my survival during the war years. I do know that I get energized when I can do things that are positive and when such actions affect people and goals.

There were times in my thirties during which I got ideas late at night and would remain sleepless until I put them to paper even if it took all night. In those throes of passion, I formulated responses to articles I'd read and disagreed with; I would write and send off my thoughts to whomever initiated the article. I didn't particularly expect a response but got my say off my chest. Other times when an idea hit me I theorized, strategized concepts, and introduced to fellow workers one of my "Wouldn't it be nice if …." For example, back in the early 1970s while working at DVI, the newly-elected Assemblyman Willie Brown announced he was initiating a fact-finding mission to assess conditions at the DVI state prison. He planned to tape testimony from inmates as well as staff. It seemed to me that while correctional officers were getting a 5% hazardous pay, clericals working inside the prison should also. Being female in an all-male environment was hazardous. Women had to pass through the same gates -- some interfaced with inmates be they trustees or deemed “low risk” prisoners. I questioned if these women were considered vulnerable. I thought they were much more vulnerable than the officer in the watch tower. These females were at ground level. For days I worked on my proposal and tested my thoughts with other administrators and a superintendent at a youth authority facility. Then I asked for five minutes at the end of the scheduled meeting with Assemblyman Brown. It was getting mid-afternoon when my turn arrived. As I read my statement, I glanced often at Mr. Brown who had nodded off momentarily. I remembered that the culinary staff prepared a gourmet lunch for him. I was so disappointed I stopped speaking. There was dead silence for about a minute, then I whispered quietly in the microphone, “Are you sleeping, Mr. Brown?” He snapped to. I finished my delivery and left. All the testimonies went to Sacramento and, I suspect, were shelved for nothing came out of that hearing. Surprisingly, some clericals were not supportive for they feared calling attention to this type of inequity might cost them their job. At least I planted a thought that some day the idea might take hold among others who cared about equity pay in a hazardous environment.

Developing a Network

While participating at the local and regional chapter level of the California State Employees Association (CSEA), there were opportunities to rub elbows with clericals and other professionals at statewide meetings. In the 1970s, state employees began to talk more openly about collective bargaining after a group of employees attempted to strike at the Castaic water power plant in Southern California. CSEA leadership believed there were other ways to achieve greater employee benefits by reorganizing or re-tweaking its internal structure. A new union vocabulary appeared in many people’s dialogue such as “shop stewards” and “occupational councils.” I even attended a job steward workshop led by the radical union organizer Saul Alinsky of UC-Berkeley fame. It was a very strident type of organizing and not my forte.

I was one of the first to embrace a new method to help state clericals, one that would help address the great disparity among clerical classifications. A new grouping called occupational councils separated job classifications into bargaining units. Thus, the Office and Allied Council (OAC), geographically carved into seven regions, was charged with representing some 90,000 clerical employees in work-related issues and heard grievances at the local level. For reasons I couldn't fathom, bridge toll collectors were thrown into our occupational council. I guess they were the "allied" part of our OAC. I ran and was elected to represent District D, the central valley area that stretched from Stockton to Fresno. I thought all clerical work was alike: typing, answering phones, dictation, and general office practices. Not so. The OAC encouraged appointing shop stewards in large institutions and facilities. Through them, clericals would have someone to hear their individual grievances.

In its first year the OAC spent time establishing procedures, getting to know their own geographic area, and networking with each other. Two clerical council members worked at state hospitals, one was a legal secretary from Los Angeles, and another worked for the Department of Motor Vehicle. Geographically, Noby lived in Los Angeles, Paul in San Francisco, Mary in Napa, Armenta in Redding, Fran in Pomona, Karyn in San Diego, and me in Stockton. The following year, 1972, I was elected chairperson. Staff created a monthly newsletter that disseminated information on legislative bills going through Sacramento, changes statewide that directly benefitted clericals, and happenings in the various regions. The newsletter had a moniker, WRTOA; it stood for *Who's Running This Office Anyway.* I wrote a column to boost morale and call for greater cooperation among clerical units. It was positive, uplifting and added a bit of tongue-in-check humor. It was great fun, much like writing for a junior high school newspaper. What struck me even in the early 1970s was the large number of clericals who were single parents. It only seemed natural that the OAC offered SPICE (Special Paycheck Insurance for Clerical Employees) an income protection policy exclusively for clericals with a payment plan as low as $1.15 a month.

There was a greater need besides a newsletter to tie the regions together into a more unified voice. With Richard's blessings and also that of John Hacker, my boss at the state prison in Tracy, I took a six months' leave of absence and travelled the state visiting and speaking to clerical groups in state hospitals, DMV, consumer affairs and other various units. In my travels I was discovering parts of California and state services that I did not know existed. It was an eye-opener and even though I incurred personal loss of wages that affected my overall retirement compensation. I was not paid by either the state government or CSEA - I was a volunteer. Again, there was no regret for I truly believed many of the clericals appreciated the ear that I lent to hear their grievances. I had the easy part as my reports were turned over to Dick Gleed, our assigned staff, to deal with the issues. When I left state employment due to health issues, my activities with CSEA and OAC also ended. By now I had a satchel of tools to understand bigger and smaller issues while dealing with people and organizations. Little did I know that some twenty years later, I would travel the length of the state again and work as an organizer at another state job.

Involvement at the Home Front

While *SAMFOW* received wide approval in the Stockton community, in my heart there was another voice that found it difficult to reconcile what was in my book and present day reality. I had come to Stockton in 1960 and thirty years later I saw the city with more discerning eyes. The downtown was dying. The never-completed local redevelopment and Crosstown freeway projects cut through the heart of what had been Chinatown. Drug dealers, prostitutes and the homeless wandered wantonly everywhere. Pavements were falling apart, some streets even had no sidewalks, crime was up, and police presence was down. Even the local newspaper tiptoed around the idea of getting tough. If the average citizen read the newspapers of the 1880s clear into even sixty years ago, he or she would not have tolerated the conditions of the 1980s. While civic leaders feigned concern and community organizers wrung their hands, their pussy-footing reeked of political correctness. Council members and even school board members were elected based on ethnicity rather than qualification or experience. The City Council was a circus and there was no decorum.

Having a momentary fear that I might have misconstrued the past in my book, I began to ask questions and voiced my concerns about the neighborhood, crime, and the dilapidated appearance of the city core. Because of my ranting a friend said: “If you are so dissatisfied with the conditions in the city, why don’t you run for City Council?” Even without any experience I was told I couldn’t do any worse up at the dais. Until then my only association with city government was to serve on Stockton's Cultural Heritage Board while going to graduate school. But, being a city board member did not constitute a desire to venture into the field of politics.

The Stockton City Council… yes, here was an opportunity to put my foot in my mouth. Philosophically I believe that people who seek political office for the first time have truly good intentions. They want to do good for the community and it is after becoming seasoned that other factors come into play -- often compromising good intentions.

In the summer of 1989 I started my publishing house but I also found myself taking out candidate papers for the District 5 seat on the Stockton City Council. There's that familiar "District 5" designation so reminiscent of my CSEA days. Rather than paying the $2,000 filing fee I opted to gather twenty signatures for my application. It was quick and there were plenty of well wishers. Then the campaign kick off began with a series of fundraisers -- and they were "fun-raisers"! The Asian community was enthusiastic to get the first Asian onto the City Council. The major support came from the Chinese community and, more particularly, some of my best Chinese friends in the City Clerk's Office. Bankers and developers were skeptical but assessed me from a distance until they ran their own polls. My opponents were a Latino lawyer and a white gambler. I wanted to show that this contest was not about competition and even suggested to Tony Gutierrez, my opponent, "Let's carpool to the debates to show that we are concerned about the environment."

One day I agreed to meet Patsy Noble, a former neighbor and also a retired police sergeant. She was sitting with a rather scruffy, unshaven, collar-length, white haired man. He looked questionable but when he smiled he gave off a warm Portuguese glow. All Pat said to him was, "Rudy, take care of her, she is running for City Council." And with that Rudy Monte became my bodyguard, my protector, and one of my best friends. What a gift! Rudy, a career retired former narcotic police sergeant, made sure I worked (with a capital W) to gain the people's trust.

District 5

The district was in the very core of downtown - north to Harding Way, west to Interstate 5, east to Highway 99 and south to Hazelton and the Mormon Slough. Strange enough it took the shape of an AK-47. It was the most diverse section of the city. It was beautiful, it was ugly. It had history, landmark buildings, and early churches: the First Baptist, First Congregational, First Presbyterian, St. John's (Episcopal), St. Mary's (Catholic), and it had all the mortuaries. It was home to both St. Joseph's and Dameron, the only private hospitals in the city. The downtown housed major banks and businesses. There was midtown with small bungalow and craftsman houses, some neglected neighborhoods where the sidewalks were never repaired, and rundown Victorians chopped up into apartments. The Latinos laid claim to the eastern part of the district with businesses and homes that stretched from East Main Street to Highway 99. Nearby were the rail yard and Stribley Park and other low income areas.

The Haggin Museum and the Fox Theater were the cultural landmarks. The Crosstown freeway served as a barrier dividing the respectable part of downtown from that of the forgotten and underserved. The Sonora Street filth and litter discouraged the more stellar citizens from driving through. Drug dealers and denizens staked out their territories. Often drug dealers hid their supplies in upside down Styrofoam cups or crumbled paper bags while they stood nearby. They even used the heavy concrete lids of public utility meters to hide their drugs for safekeeping until a buyer came in sight. The homeless used alcoves to relieve themselves. It was here that the older Chinese lived, those who did not want to experience the flight to other neighborhoods. I became angry at these sights. As often as possible I would ask to "ride along" in patrol cars to gain more knowledge of what was there and what could be done to improve the areas, particularly if I were to be the council member of the district.

Of the twenty precincts in District 5, Rudy and I walked a full sixteen. We walked and walked, house to house - in the heat from early morning to late afternoon. On weekends I literally followed the ball games on television and the ongoing scores. I developed a real disdain for dirty doorbells and took to using a pen to push the buzzer. It did not matter if there was no sign of life at a particular house I still had to ring the bell and leave campaign literature. More often Rudy stopped at the sidewalk and even hid behind a tree. We didn't want to look like missionaries or solicitors. If it were friends of Rudy's he did not spend time chatting. He wanted them to focus on my message. Rudy knew the town; he knew the political landscape and had worked various divisions in the police department. He was a good narc. He was an excellent conduit for those curious about me. I would drag home after a 5-mile day clutching precinct lists, maybe a small bag of homemade cookies, a cutting from someone's yard, and always an appreciation of Rudy.

I got to know the areas and remembered those who stepped forward to help my campaign: from the south and eastside – Sachus Orosco, founder of the CalMex Baseball League and barber Buster Gray; the central and west area – Minnie Infleise, the Wallaces, John and Wayne Louie (they are twins and their mother was fascinated

A drug bust, my smaller hand was able to reach the drug hidden between the cab and truck bed.

with John Wayne), and Art Johns. The small business owners in downtown such as Paul Mariani and Dan Dixon of the Mariani's clothing store that served the farm workers and ran a bank for the Mexicans to send money home; Jun Agari and George Tabuchi of Tabuchi's on Main Street, Tom Migliori and his Riteway Cleaners, Harry and Evelyn Sasaki of Star Market; Jim Soares and his Chapel of the Palms Mortuary, Mike Heffernan of DeYoung's Mortuary, and that list went on. I needed these individuals' support; they were the key to persuade the downtown workers and residents we needed change. I cannot forget two former mayors, Dean De Carli and

Chuck Bott who served with dignity and honor on the city council during their tenure; they willingly endorsed my candidacy which drew many other supporters. Dean De Carli, who started out delivering milk to households landed up quite a successful entrepreneur, he had much advice. The best was: "When you get into the ring have no regret." Chuck Bott, an accountant, had very crisp answers and never beat around the bush when it came to figures. He was definitely a financial guru. The bankruptcy of Stockton would not have happened on his watch.

In the heart of any campaign there is always a core of friends candidates use to bounce off ideas. I was grateful for mine; they were my campaign's brain trust: Don Geiger, Terry Hull and the late Larry Lopez.

The Fair Political Practice Commission is a bane on all elections campaigns. This Sacramento-based state agency served as a watchdog and financial clearing house for all election campaigns; the paperwork they required was incredible. We ran our campaign as if it was a business but under the ominous shadow of this "big brother."

Official Council picture

Nevertheless, we pushed on. Lawn signs sprung up on many a street, some even appeared in the corner windows of Chinese restaurants. Fundraisers and in-kind donations filled the coffers. I worried about my height and ethnicity as a hindrance but others felt it might have really been an advantage. I used my full name on the ballot and in printed material so there was no contention about my ethnicity.

Del McComb, teaching at San Joaquin Delta College, tried to persuade a neighbor to vote for me. Several days later the neighbor came back to Del and said, "Your Asian friend sounds like a good candidate but I think I am going to go ahead and vote for Minnick."

I won! It was unbelievable and I felt so grateful to so many. The morning following election night I remember distinctly that I staggered into the kitchen. Richard handed me a cup of coffee and I responded: "Good grief what have I gotten us into." If we ever had an idea to move, we couldn't. If we thought of going on an extended vacation, we couldn't. If we thought we had a private life, we didn't. For the next six years it was tough; however, it did have rewards and they came from friends who believed in me.

While political campaigning was a continuation of community activism, little did I realize serving in office required an even greater effort.

Chapter 14

The Power of Politics

The election results came in and I won by 59.4% in the citywide election. Many friends, volunteers and residents of District 5 were jubilant. Stockton heralded a new city council under a new policy of district primary and citywide general election for all council seats and the mayor's post. I did not know the other council members, not even a nodding acquaintance except for Floyd Weaver whose wife was my roommate at Dameron Hospital when Darcey was born. That was thirty some years ago.

The word "politics" I thought was a give-and-take activity associated with diplomacy. My optimism reasoned that things were going to improve since this new council was perhaps the most educated in Stockton's history. All of us had bachelor's degrees and three a master's degree. As to occupations, Joan Darrah had a public relations firm, Floyd Weaver was a principal of a middle school, Nick Rust worked for a bank as a trainer, Mel Panizza ran a landscape maintenance company, Beverly McCarthy was a counselor at Delta College, and Loralee McGaughey. We were all in our fifties and there was only an eight-year spread between the youngest and oldest. This was also the first time women were in the majority. Three council members were native Stocktonians, the rest long-time transplants.

The swearing-in ceremony on February 25, 1990 was quite a production held at the Civic Auditorium. Orchestrated by Mayor Joan Darrah, we each selected our own judge to swear us in personally but simultaneously. Superior Court Judge Frank Kim did the honors for me. On stage our assigned positions were marked with large white tapes and a second row for the judges. After the last musical note by a trumpeter we marched into position. It was a night filled with dignity and decorum, supposedly a far cry from that of the previous council who had been accused of being "clowns in a three-ring circus." The fanfare more descriptively suggests the mayor was high on pageantry. I was especially proud that the leaders of the Chinese community attended this event. Normally the Chinese shied away from such functions.

I quietly swore to do the best for the residents of the city and to render aid and improve the conditions in my district. This new career didn't seem very difficult. After all, I am a people-person, I like to solve problems, and I know how to seek out volunteer help. Unfortunately, it did not take long for me to realize I was not quite in step with my new colleagues. Their approach to governing was entirely different than mine. While the office of city councilmember is non-partisan philosophically, five of the council members were Democrats and the one other councilmember, while registered as a Republican, hung around and voted with the rest of the council members. Clearly, my fiscal conservative nature proved I was a square peg in a round hole.

Stockton City Council – 1990
Sitting: Floyd Weaver, Mayor Joan Darrah, Loralee McGaughey
Standing: Sylvia, Nick Rust, Beverly McCarthy, and Mel Panizza

A Quality of Life

At the first council meeting Mayor Darrah formed a nine-member citizen, police-funding committee that included herself and me. Mike Heffernan of De Young Mortuary was chairman. The city was severely understaffed by 42 uniformed personnel and considered in a "code blue" state indicating it was much below state average. This committee was charged with studying financing options to increase police officers. Six weeks of meetings led the committee to recommend a graduated increase on the utility tax for the next three years to pay for 62 police officers and use a portion of the transient occupancy tax (TOT) from hotel/motel tax to fund their equipment. Bart Thiltgen, an attorney in the City Attorney's Office, and I wrote the final white paper.

My immediate attention turned to things around my district given the crime, drugs, failing infrastructures, and the safety of the residents. My plan was to find people in certain sectors of the district enthusiastic enough to take back their neighborhoods from reprobates and undesirables – specifically the areas around Gleason Park, Stribley Park, Wilson Way, Flora Street, Weber Park, the Magnolia Historic District, and Chinatown. The Crosstown Freeway and Downtown Redevelopment projects moved the folks living in Chinatown farther south. The July 1, 1990 editorial of the *Stockton Record* reported that the block on El Dorado between Lafayette and Sonora was *"...the worst in Stockton. That one block is so dangerous that it is not uncommon for motorists on El Dorado to give the red light at Lafayette the CRS (California Rolling Stop) treatment and speed on. It is no place to stop unless you are looking for trouble."* Even former county supervisor Victor Mow said his mother's house *"...is like a fortress, wrought iron on all the doors and windows and a reinforced cellar. She's locked in as well as locked people out."*

I begged City Manager Alan Harvey to do something and do it quickly. He came up with a 60-day pilot program to physically cleanup a ten-square block that bordered Lafayette, California, Church, and Center Street. Daily street sweeping occurred starting as early as 5:00 AM, early enough to rouse those sleeping in alcoves and street corners. The overturned Styrofoam cups hiding small packets of drugs got caught up in the whirl of the street cleaning brushes, glass from broken bottles and tossed garbage were shoved into the waste management bins. Tow trucks made their rounds moving stalled or semi-dismantled cars and then any vehicle parked within the 24-hour tow away zone. It was strident but necessary. Even the sidewalks were cleaned and ruts in the streets repaired. The physical shakeup included increased police enforcement and undercover operations. Dealers began to stuff their stash in recessed water meters, window sills and other cracks and crevices. Meter readers for utility companies were alerted to spot new hiding places for drugs.

There were a few complaints from some business owners fearing that customers could not park in front of their businesses, but they were told to encourage patrons to park around the corner where parking was available. The owner of Emerald restaurant on Hunter Street was the most vocal and down-right angry. But we stood firm with no exceptions. In time when he saw that the area was truly getting cleaned up and the restaurant clientele changed for the better he too bought into the concept. Only Wayne Osborg, an apartment owner, sued the city stating the parking issue created a hardship for his tenants. After being subpoenaed I gave a deposition which included my knowing Mr. Osborg and had even gotten the key for his backyard to share with the police when they chased criminals onto his property. I was trying to level the playing field between cops and robbers. By 1994 Judge William Giffen ruled in the city's favor stating the parking ban was needed to help clean up the area "*...and has advanced the public interest which it motivated.*"

In a few short months the undercover operations led to 85 felony arrests, 117 misdemeanor arrests and 163 drunken arrests. There were large quantities of confiscated narcotics as well as $1,803 in cash. Illegal parking, jaywalking, traffic infractions, and 106 cars towed accounted for another 361 citations. Parking received the greatest number of complaints and we promised to look towards a modified plan by September. I was quoted to say: "*This was a declaration of war to bring back the quality of life for people south of the Crosstown Freeway.*" [5]

In Phase II of the project we turned to residents for help. Thus far the city's crew and police department had done the heavy lifting. Two strategies occurred simultaneously: the first a need for garbage cans, heavy duty waste receptacles that could be bolted two feet down into the sidewalk; the second was an all volunteer graffiti paint out. There was no money in the budget for any of these needs. Eight garbage cans cost $4,000. Zelda Costa, a senior citizen on social security sent in the first donation, a check for $500. Philanthropist Thelma Stewart and a few developers also contributed. Large and small checks arrived and were quickly deposited into a small miscellaneous account buried deep within the Public Works budget. No city funds were expended for the garbage cans. We planted one can in front of a grocery store in the middle of San Joaquin Street where denizens consumed their cheap Thunderbird or Red Bull and tossed the containers onto the street. Albert Garcia, an elderly Hispanic, often stood outside the store (more like leaning against the wall) after being satiated. In a persuasive tone I called upon Mr. Garcia to do his civic duty by making sure people used the can instead of littering. Weeks later on my routine drive-bys he yelled: "See Mrs. Minnick, clean sidewalk." Even though he was a little tipsy, he did his job. With the excess donation and some monies from my election campaign coffer I bought a 4,000 psi high pressure washer for the merchants' use in that area. The washer, housed at the Mariani store on El Dorado Street, served the area well. Once in a while I could see Dan Dixon, Paul Mariani's son-in-law, pressure washing down the entire block.

Two months to the day when we started our project, I organized the first graffiti paint out south of the Crosstown. The call for volunteers went out through the newspaper and radio stations KWIN and KJOY. Volunteers came from the Gospel Rescue Mission, St. Mark's Methodist Church, California Conservation Corps (CCC), city employees, and even teachers. Arlan Williams, owner of the Main Street Velvacon paint store for 26 years, provided paint and brushes that we warehoused at the Port of Stockton. Paul Mariani threw in other supplies and refreshments came from CentroMart, Bow Bow, Gan Chy, Sun Wong Kee, and even McDonald's. Many of the Chinese associations' buildings that were heavily grafittied got a healthy dose of paint. Mae Lee, living on El Dorado Street, whom we considered godmother of the area, busily swept off the sidewalk so volunteers had a clean area to sit for lunch. The cost for this worthwhile project – zilch; the fellowship – worth millions. At the end Zelda Costa sent a little note and concluded: "We are grateful, we are hopeful." By mid-September the ten block sweep extended another four blocks.

Providing Other Resources

Other people asked for help in their neighborhoods. Comments included: "Come see the hypo needles strewn on the grass at Stribley" and in Gleason Park "There's broken glass in the sandbox," or the litter at Victory Park. "Our street is quite dark. How about putting in lights?" These types of requests were prevalent. Thank goodness for the city staff who quietly helped to resolve some of the problems.

Before cell phones, drug dealers monopolized public pay phones which were scattered throughout the downtown area. These became their offices. How else would they make contacts and deliveries? Many of the pay phones were individually owned and service was contracted to the phone company. Gary Tsutsumi, the city traffic engineer, held the record for removing the most pay phones. Phone booths had nothing to do with traffic. But people loitering at corner near phone booths did hinder sight. And, they increase criminal activity. A few friendly conversations between Tsutsumi and the right persons at the phone company and these telephone booths disappeared. In one case a phone booth just outside a corner store on California Street near Flora Street attracted a lot of vagrants. The store owners, Desmond and Josephine Li, did not know how to eliminate this unpleasant condition. They did not know me, but one day they noticed the booth was gone. It was many years later that they realized I had something to do with its removal. From my entry hall window I used to monitor the activities around the phone booth up the street at the corner of Harding and Commerce. I was so pleased when Tsutsumi removed the phone. Customers no longer worried about their safety or their cars when patronizing the Mexican restaurant at that corner.

Stribley Park, south of east Main Street, was another area that needed attention. One of the biggest gripes was the railroad track that ran down B Street. Trains no longer used the track and the railroad company had abandoned them. Drivers were forced to straddle the tracks as they went down the street. This made driving difficult. Public Works tried hard to find a solution and, if I remember correctly, there was a 19th century requirement that trains traversing through a town required a cow catcher affixed to the front of the engine. Even though cows no longer wandered through town, trains without cow catchers did. The city could have enforced the antiquated regulation on all engines but the railroad company found it easier and cheaper to remove the tracks totally. In another situation Sacchus Orosco got volunteers to dig narrow trenches and laid conduits bringing electricity to the baseball field in Stribley Park. Since they were working to improve the city park it was only right that they tapped into the city's electrical supply. Their volunteer efforts looked rather primitive but served an instant purpose without a public works work order or use of city staff.

Little did I realize that in 1990, our first year, I created tension between my fellow council colleagues and me. Admittedly, I enjoyed the publicity our neighborhoods received and always remembered to applaud various volunteers. No one took me aside to say that each time I used city resources such as police and street sweepers I needed to get council permission. I did not know it was protocol or was this a way to rein me in? I thought we were all equal and could tap into staff's help and advice. I had seen the mayor ask staff for favors often; council members reported on nuisances in their area. None were presented as needing a council action vote. And none were as pressing and serious as in my district. Thus, my colleagues perceived me as making a mountain out of a mole hill. I really did not think so.

It was 1991, my second year and I had won a full four year term by 80% of votes cast. Previously in the 1989 election all the council seats needed to be readjusted with alternate election cycles. I had drawn a short straw indicating my first term was only for two years. Now I had much more time to work for my district. A number of the downtown businesses and residents took interest in a new crime fighting strategy. Setting a precedent, Molly Wetzel, a resident of Berkeley, sued reprobates in her neighborhood in small claims court and she won. The State Attorney General encouraged this novel idea. Our enthusiasm created two citizens groups. Their acronyms were: SCUMLORDS (Stockton's Crime Unit Members to Let Our Redevelopment Downtown Succeed) and SMAC (Stanislaus and Main Action Committee).

The members of the SCUMLORDS included Sheriff Baxter Dunn, Dr. Howard Abrams and his staff, Sergeant D.R. "Buzz" Mazzoula, head of Stockton's Police Department's street crime unit, attorney Don Geiger, Meleta McEntire who managed the Medical-Dental Building, and me. Eleven plaintiffs sued M Jawald Aktar owner of Diego's Deli at the corner of California and Weber, the owners of the St. Leo Hotel at 39 North California, and Dayarum Patel owner of the Steve Hotel. McEntire was a powerhouse when it came to collecting evidence. She videotaped the goings-on at these locations and compiled police reports to show that these areas were havens for undesirables. It cost each of us just the filing fee and the small claim suits of $5,000 amounted to $55,000. We planned to donate our winnings to the police street crime unit for equipment, erect "no trespassing" signs, and set up funds for future cleanup. Two months later the judge ordered the defendants to pay $50,280 for operating public nuisances. [6]

Being sworn in for my second term on the City Council – 1991

SMAC, headed by Tom Migliori of Riteway Cleaners, targeted Hotel Bronx, the Stanislaus Apartments, and La Verta Hotel. These seedy hotels had prostitutes and drug dealers hanging around soliciting and dealing. They were nuisances to the nearby businesses. There were ten people involved in this suit. I have endearing memories of this particular corner of California and Stanislaus. Not so many months before I had just met downtown lawyer Don Geiger in the back of a patrol car. We were both doing a night ride. The squad was doing a bust and Geiger had charge of the camera. I felt he was a bit slow getting out of the car and I gave him a push to speed him up so that I could also get in with the action. Once out we started to look for hidden drugs around the hotel, between the dirty window sills and the wrought iron bars, and other accessible nooks and crannies. SMAC was awarded $15,000 as rendered from a 16-page decision because of graphic testimonies by witnesses. The judge excluded Sheriff Dunn and me since we did not suffer any direct damage. We were ecstatic that suing through small claims worked. Here was another tool to help clean up downtown – empowerment.

A Gathering Storm

I could not thank city manager Alan Harvey enough for the support he gave the downtown cleanup. I was riding high but political alienation was on its way. In late October of 1990 a South African entrepreneur, Norm Jarrett, came to town and proposed a Gold Rush City theme park similar to one he built in South Africa. He sold it before he came to California. His design, a 400-acre amusement park resort coupled with a life-size recreation of a gold rush town, would need both sides of the downtown Stockton Channel, portions of the unincorporated area of Boggs Tract and other blighted areas south and west of the city center. As a newcomer to the area, Jarrett teamed up with two other local developers, Howard Arnaiz and John Verner. Their preliminary proposal caught my breath and I thought: "Wow." I was then the chairman of the Central Stockton Revitalization Ad Hoc Committee and thought this was an exciting project and could have a very positive effect. Jarrett had already pitched his idea to other neighboring communities such as Fairfield, Rio Vista, and the farmland area of Mossdale between Lathrop and Tracy.

Since Gold Rush City dealt with the heart of my district I wanted to sit in when staff began preliminary talks to discuss its feasibility. This very complex project would involve major issues such as assembling over 500 parcels of land currently occupied by operating industries, traffic considerations and access to the Port and the port's growth. It obviously would be "*...a huge job. Politically tough and financially tough...*" according to Deputy City Manager Lyn Krieger. [7]

Jarrett wanted a moratorium on all development downtown for 18 months and exclusive rights to negotiate an all-encompassing redevelopment contract. City Manager Harvey prepared a resolution for the council's adoption supporting the project and agreeing to the negotiation period. He held firm in asking for $750,000 be put into an escrow account for the city's preliminary title search and consultant fees and for obtaining more detailed information. In less than a week the developers pulled their plan accusing Harvey of "bad blood" or rather bad faith negotiation. My attitude was, "Huh?" What happened? Did Jarrett expect the city to do all this work without any effort or upfront monies on his part?

It was a very difficult council meeting with the developers saying the city manager scuttled their project and that the city was being overly cautious. I believed what was asked of them was reasonable and the city manager was applying due diligence on behalf of the city. However, a number of council members feigned surprise that the project was pulled even before it had been aired at a public hearing.

Rumors began to surface as several council members vented their frustration. They claimed what was perceived as a potential benefit to the city had been muddled and stalled. Allegations of secret meetings, bad faith negotiations and the general lack of council involvement in the project shrouded the proposal in controversy. On a four to three vote the majority wanted me to write a letter asking Jarrett and his partners to return to the table. This renewed interest was to gave city staff and Jarrett's people until February 1, 1991 to see if there were any grounds for discussion. Jarrett also reminded the council he was also revisiting his proposal for the Mossdale area while continuing his discussion with Stockton. It seemed Jarrett was leveraging one city against the other to see which would give him the better deal.

Today I believe the Gold Rush project was a "straw that broke the camel's back" and in this case it was Alan Harvey's. The mayor called for a semi-annual evaluation of the city manager on November 13, 1990. There were innuendos, rumors but no specific allegation against Harvey. On the docket for November 19th the city council adopted a resolution to strip Alan Harvey of his authority to hire and fire the finance director who, according to contract, answers directly to the city manager. I became suspicious when the council overstepped its boundaries and into the city manager's realm. There was no report from Harvey regarding a negative or positive relationship with the finance director and suddenly the council vote was almost unanimous. I was puzzled particularly when there was no specific misstep on Harvey's part except a dubious $205 question on a car expense for an official trip to St Petersburg, Florida. Given the minor amount of money, wasn't this action unduly harsh?

Mayor Joan Darrah recalled in her memoir: "*He (Harvey) hired an attorney to negotiate a good severance package, and the council hired its own attorney to get off as cheaply as possible.*" At the January 28, 1991 meeting the council took a public vote to dismiss Alan Harvey and the vote was six to one, I being the lone dissenter. I had always saw myself a team player; but, this was a case of my conscience versus politics. It was also the first of several gut-wrenching votes where I took a public stand against my colleagues. These were my words to support my stand:

> *"It is difficult to stand up and be the only dissenting vote, but as an elected official I feel I must state for the record the reasons for casting this vote. I owe you, fellow council members and my constituents an explanation. I fully support the fact that we should not renew Mr. Harvey's contract. However, there are three reasons I believe his termination at this time is inappropriate.*
>
> *1. Based on the evaluation process that we conducted on Mr. Harvey I do not believe there was sufficient cause to prohibit the City Manager from completing his contract.*
>
> *2. The reason that some council members believe as justification to terminate...seems to be as a result of an unfortunate miscommunication between two city departments.*
>
> *3. We inherited the responsibility of Harvey's contract from the previous council and we should have either honor the severance requirement or negotiate a good faith buy out.*
>
> *Again, I cast this "no" vote because of my concern that this action is not in the best interest of the city."*

I later learned from Darrah's memoirs that there had been rumors that a majority of council members wanted to fire Harvey possibly as early as April of 1990 but wanted to wait until after the November election as three council members were running for re-election and they wanted to make sure they had the votes. If the rumors were true then there were other backroom dealings going on long before Harvey's dismissal.

By January 31, 1991 Alan Harvey was gone and, uh-oh, the mayor and council members found out that I had a backbone and was not be afraid to speak up. I didn't know, however, my action was a crack which began to widen between the council and myself. My thought then was okay the vote was taken and the deed done. Now let's move forward. But it was not to be.

The Nail That Sticks Up Gets Hammered Down

In the new year of 1991, the mayor assigned committee membership and committee chairmen. Unfortunately of the five standing committees and four ad hoc committees I did not chair a single committee. A number of council members were given two or three chairmanships. Publicly I questioned why and even threw in the query that maybe they did not like the color of my hair or my eyes. The question I asked myself was how far back did this alienation go? Apparently it began with the downtown cleanup when I bypassed the council and, as the mayor wrote, "*we (the council) were not happy about it.*" They honed into the expense of the six full-time officers regardless of the many arrests, the use of public works staff and, more importantly, the amount of press. As she wrote: "*The Record ran several stories that praised the project and Sylvia personally, the council was angry about the expense, the non-inclusion, and the parking complaints.*"

I never knew that whatever I wanted to do in my district required council approval even though I used volunteers and there were no city funds or staff involved. The same applied when I first spoke about the Gold Rush City project. As Harvey recalled a meeting was set up with Councilmen Panizza and Minnick to meet with the developers but Panizza did not come to the meeting and Minnick did. Again, I knew too much and maybe said too much. The mayor then justified her decision by thinking I was considered not qualified or effective to serve as a chairperson of a committee; moreover, I was not a team member.

So again in the mayor's words:

"*Since I anticipated that no council member would come to Sylvia's defense and I had an excellent alternative nominee, Councilmember Beverly Fitch McCarthy….. Sylvia was extremely upset and hurt. Instead of accepting this outcome as I had anticipated she would, Sylvia went on the offensive and attacked the council at its meeting January 28….*"

The Stockton Record editorial headline for January 30, 1991, read: "*Still playing those games in City Hall*" and noted "… *Minnick alluded to some other problems: 'Master manipulators'…using committee assignments as part of a reward and punishment system...The pragmatic appeasement policy of the mayor toward the majority.*" The article concluded: "*The saving grace may be that Minnick is just starting a full four-year term, as she said "I plan to continue to represent both my district and the citizens at large and to participate on the council as a voice of reason."* A few people spoke on my behalf but nothing came of it.

Okay, I admit I was angry and disappointed at the blatant actions by my colleagues. I swallowed my feelings and accepted the situation. My reasons being: I did not need this skirmish, my plate was full with my publishing house, District 5 problems, and I had a family life.

In March 1991 the *Stockton Record* suggested, "*Now, much of the optimism that enveloped the council has dissipated. Many observers believe this council like previous ones has gotten bogged down with petty politics, meddled in administrative affairs....*" It was time; the newspaper staff thought that citizens, city hall watchers and city staff should evaluate the council members. They developed eight categories: personal integrity, grasp of city issues, ability to communicate effectively, ability to work with others, responsiveness to constituents, accessibility, overall effectiveness, and leadership vision.

The public had a chance to rate us and we rated ourselves on a scale of 1-5, five being the top score.

Three months later the results were tallied. It was quite telling on how council members saw themselves. Mayor Darrah, Mel Panizza and Beverly McCarthy gave themselves all 5's in all categories. I gave myself one 5 (personal integrity) and the rest 4's and even two 3.75. Readers saw it differently and felt the council as a whole was low in all categories. Totaling the seven categories by the individual averages were:

Mayor Joan Darrah	2.42	Nick Rust	2.57
Beverly McCarthy	2.14	Floyd Weaver	2.57
Loralee McGaughey	2.00	Mel Panizza	2.57
Sylvia Minnick	4.42		

Some of the comments made by city hall watchers suggest: "*... the emphasis of decorum and efficiency has gone too far. The council has become enamored of its own procedures, confusing activities such as hiring consultants, drafting studies and appointing committees....*" [8]

The scrutiny we came under from time to time was unbelievable. In some way it was understandable, as the *Stockton Record* reported on how many meetings we missed, where we traveled and how much we spent on city business, how much money we raised from developers and union members, and even how much water we consumed in our own household. In all those surveys I was neither at the top nor the bottom in ranking except for monies from developers and unions. I was at the bottom on both as well as water usage.

In 1992 at the next go-around for committee assignments the mayor again was pressured into making sure I did not receive a chairmanship. This time, as she recalled in her memoirs, she was literally blackmailed. The dynamics leading up to the decision and its afterthought was quite clear, again from her book: [9]

> *"Just before I announced the new committee chairs, a council member came to my office and solemnly informed me that several members did not want Sylvia to be chair of either the planning and development or the downtown revitalization committee. They felt Sylvia could not be trusted. She not only supported Frank Fargo for mayor, but she had also publicly spoken against me. 'She's a Republican.' I was reminded. "Look Joan...politics is not Junior Aid. Politics is playing hardball." said this council member. It was also made clear that they would oppose renewing our membership in the U.S. Conference of Mayors if I appointed Sylvia to any standing committee. This visit suggested that Sylvia had by now forfeited the respect of her council colleagues and that, as a result, her nomination would never be approved. Moreover, without council support, a chair could not effectively perform a job. Because of these attitudes toward Sylvia and my intense desire to rejoin the U.S. Conference of Mayors, I did not appoint Sylvia as chair of one of the five standing committees, nor did I give her one of the four ad hoc committees, for various reasons. In consequence, there was no committee chairmanship for Sylvia.*
>
> *"I thought then and do now that it would have been the fair thing to do to make Sylvia the chair of the planning and development committee, as I originally intended. In retrospect, part of me wishes I had told that particular council member to go to hell and threatened at the council meeting to accuse the group of four of bullying both me and Sylvia. But as I have said often enough, confrontation was not my style...."*

No, I did not turn the other cheek nor did I slink under the desk. Again I asked quite emphatically "why?" I was not alone. Many sectors of the Stockton community watched the council meeting in their living room, others took part also in asking why and where was the equity. For at least four consecutive weeks citizens came to the podium during the citizens' comment segments. Some spoke extemporaneously and others read their well-written words. Several Chinese, Japanese, Filipino community leaders raised the question of prejudice and asked the council to reconsider. Among the leaders were Richard Gacer, Nelson Nagai, Elena Mangahas, Clarence Louie, Aeko Yoshikawa, and former county supervisor Richard Yoshikawa in his last comment, he whispered into the microphone: *"Joan, your slip is showing."*

The people who spoke were not just Asians but a cross section of Stocktonians who saw the unfairness of the situation. The Hispanic and Black community leaders joined in as did former elected officials, educators and business leaders. There were letters written to the *Stockton Record* expressing similar views. Even Rev. Barry Means, the aging pastor of the White Rose Church whom the mayor greatly respected, lumbered to the podium and said:

> *"A seventy-four year old black man of the deep South knows how it is to be passed over. It's far better that you change. How do you think the person feels when she walks among people and they say she is unqualified? Correct this and let the city go forward."*

With his words the mayor asked Council member Panizza for reconciliation and he gave up his chair of the building/space planning committee which I assumed. Without a doubt regardless of ethnicity - many believed the unfairness was an affront to their view of how government should be. As Filipina Joan Singson said, "The upside is that it brought political awareness to many people, crossing racial, ethnic, social and religious lines. Everyone questions the current distributions of power at the City Council. It's not about racism, it's about inequity, imbalance and politics." [10]

I had by now gone through some soul searching, self-deprecating feelings of shame, low self esteem, hurt and had shed buckets of tears half believing maybe my colleagues were right. But then I had an epiphany similar to that when I was a child and abandoned by my parents. Being ostracized by my peers could turn into something positive. Even though I was supposed to feel shackled, I emerged with a sense of freedom.

A Stronger Me

Without fear of intimidation I spoke out against issues that seemed wrong. When the council raised the property transfer tax from $1.10 to $3.00 per $1,000 to help balance the budget I voted no. "It's really not fair. When an owner gets ready to sell does the seller pay or does the buyer." I was thinking of senior citizens who would sell and were ready for the rest home. This fee would cut into money they could use in their limited future. Another issue I opposed was eminent domain, the taking of people's property purportedly for the public good. In one particular case, a proposal to build a library on Thornton Road came before the council; it required several pieces of properties. Again the vote was six to one; my negative vote stemmed from the fact there was no monies budgeted for building the library but only acquiring the properties. What was to guarantee that new monies would be forthcoming to erect the building?

In May of 1992 the council voted unanimously to allow St. Mary's Interfaith Dining Room and the Homeless Shelter to remain under the Crosstown Freeway until the year 2036. I wanted these organizations to move outside of central Stockton and accused my colleagues of a "slam dunk" approving the motion without a detailed study, public hearing, or input from council's own Downtown Revitalization Committee. I got "dinged" in an editorial because they thought the Homeless Shelter was a good thing. My thoughts concerned the fragile nature of downtown.

It was most irksome to see the council shift the time for citizens' comments, from the first part of the agenda to the end of the meeting and people had to stay to the bitter end so that they could have they say. In addition the mayor reduced the allotted minutes for each speaker from five to three minutes. Even when citizens spoke on certain agenda items the time allotted varied, sometimes it was based on who was speaking. Admittedly no one wants to be harangued, but everyone needs to have the same allotted time. Often the council and mayor sat stone-faced when they heard something unpleasant. Often Councilmembers Rust and Panizza got confrontational with speakers or just walked out. My demeanor was to be courteous and showed I was truly listening.

Another distressing sight to witness was the mayor's treatment of Thi To Can Nguyen, a 59-year old Vietnamese refugee. Nguyen, a regular at the council meeting took great interest in city, county, and board of education affairs. There was something a bit unbalanced about Nguyen, but she was smart. When she came to this country she earned two bachelor's degrees in Texas – English and Math. She, invariably, needed to say or opine her thoughts even though she lacked the agenda's background information. Quite often I sat quietly and watched the dynamics and thought we were helping fuel her passion and what's the harm in her vocalizing her thoughts. They were harmless. It was downright rude to cut her off midsentence. Yes, she called almost everyone "criminal" but she made me the exception.

The mayor particularly tried to come off as being genteel and a notch above upper-middle class. She was, after all, married to a superior court judge. I often described her as being quasi-royalty and I even kiddingly referred to myself as "Her Majesty's Loyal Opposition" which was taken from a tongue-and-cheek comment. Interestingly, she never disputed that characterization.

A Little Panache

One day the Consul General of China paid the city a visit and we met in the Mayor's Office. As we sat in a circle Mayor Darrah, in polite Junior Aid fashion, poured tea into Styrofoam cups in front of each visitor. But in my mind's eye I was shaking my head and thought – "this was not good." Several things bothered me; the obvious one was those Styrofoam cups. Even though the city was on a tight budget, surely, it could afford decent china rather than paper cups, even if we had to buy them from Kmart. I mentioned this thought to the mayor and the city manager days later, nothing came of that suggestion.

Most importantly, my early years growing up in Asia and being part of a diplomat's household had ingrained in me the proprieties of Asian culture. The mayor should not be pouring as if she was a typical housewife. Staff should have done the job or it could have been poured earlier and placed on a tray and passed around by staff. Her posture as she poured meant she leaned forward in a serving position but her back side was aimed at some other person's face across the way and this continued around the room. Not acceptable in Asian culture. Truly, City Hall was lacking in certain cultural finesse and begged a smattering of diplomatic savoir faire. So I pushed to hold an International Business Etiquette seminar. The reasoning being Stockton is part of the Pacific Rim and we need to prepare ourselves if we believe in foreign economic development in our city. A little panache never hurt anyone.

Local business leaders who worked in the international field came forward, such as port director Alex Krygsman, Sumiden Corporation Bob Olson and Kiyoshi Arakawa of United Bank. They helped plan the day-long seminar held on the University of Pacific campus. The Port of Stockton played a major role providing guidelines, materials, books, and even gift baskets for the speakers. Professors Bruce La Brack, Jim Goodrich and Mark Plovnick from the Pacific School of Business were among the speakers who spoke on cultural expectations in countries such as Japan, Korea, Taiwan, Thailand and Singapore. The day spent was entertaining and well attended.

A gun control issue catapulted our city into national news in February 1994. Mayor Darrah wanted an ordinance to regulate guns and gun sellers. Councilmember Nick Rust recommended a ten-member panel that would include gun shop owners and members of the National Rifle Association. After a heated discussion we agreed to a seven member task force with each of us naming a candidate to the task force. Six months went by and the Mayor and Council member Panizza had yet to name their candidates. Rust was getting antsy for his term on the council was getting close to the end as was mine. I took a shot at the mayor and said: *"She (the mayor) doesn't take orders from us very well. She talks about this big teamwork. Well, team work is only when we do what she wants to be done."* Panizza, in her defense, said: "... *it may not be fair but it is politics….*" By September 7th the task force panel had a short two months to deliberate and to report back to the council in November at which date the council expected to take action. While this was in the works Rust threw out a red herring and suggested that whoever wants should be able to get a concealed weapon permit only after a testing and background check. When I indicated I would support the measure, the media frenzy fanned by both the mayor and Rust was incredible. I was dogged by the *LA Times, SF Chronicle, Orange County. Register,* KPIX, all the Sacramento television stations and CNN. The internet and Paul Revere link (national internet) also flashed my name, address, and other information. All this happened when the local paper called me a "*pistol-packin' mama.*" I had a concealed permit for a number of years and did not think it necessary to go public. The police chief also was tight lipped. Months following my first election to the council I received a few death threats, some stupid enough to leave it on the answering machine at my office. One person, after watching the first televised council meeting, realized I was Asian and made some threatening remarks. I turned the tape over to the police department. In addition to crazy calls I travelled alone with considerable cash when working book sales. In conclusion, Rust's resolution was shot down.

Peace did not come between the council and me. A very painful reminder occurred at an annual League of Cities' conference in which each of the cities was to present their city's flag at the closing ceremonies. I was sitting by myself on the left at the aisle and saw my colleagues seated together when the program started. Then as various cities marched down the aisle with their flags here came the mayor, all five council members, city manager and assistance city manager each holding a tip of our flag passing me going down the aisle towards the stage. I know some of them saw me sitting there but no one beckoned or suggested that I join them in this flag display.

Other Recognized Efforts

It was unfortunate that during my years on the council I did not get the opportunity to prove my leadership skills because of personality clashes. However, I was privileged to have other adventures and accolades. The League of Cities' presidents appointed me to serve on the statewide Transportation and Public Works Policy Committee, Subcommittee on Alternative Fuel and the Immigration Taskforce. This latter committee assignment was an eye-opener. I gathered with a small number of council members from other cities at the Mexico/California border near San Ysidero. Very late in the evening we were assigned to patrol cars. We drove to a slight rise and the patrol cars fanned out, seemingly, miles apart. The tall, corrugated-metal fence loomed in front of us about a half mile away. No trees or hills blocked our vision. Using a night scope, we scanned the horizon looking for movement in the vast empty land below. The naked eye might spot rustling bushes but pointing the scope in that direction enabled me to see vague figures darting from one bush to another. Sometimes the illegals scaled the fence and when they reached the top, waited for the right moment, then they jumped down on the American side and ran. Watching the dynamics was similar to being on a ride-along with the Stockton Police.

During my two terms on the council there were many other high points. I was a California delegate to the Republican Convention held in Houston in 1992. Many extraneous committees and boards took my time such as the advisory board for CSU-Sacramento's Center for California Studies, and the CSU-Stanislaus Advisory Board-Stockton Center. I squeezed those meetings in with other obligations. Whatever time was left I balanced it among Heritage West Books (my publishing house), District 5 constituents' interests, and family life.

In 1993 Governor Pete Wilson appointed me Deputy Assistant Director-Community Liaison for California State Parks. I became a full-time state employee again. The appointment was a godsend; it provided me a salary that I needed to keep the publishing house running and it allowed me to accumulate additional years towards my pension.

Even though I had a very responsible state job and commuted daily to Sacramento, I continued to do due diligence serving the District 5 constituents and kept up with the many issues brought before the City Council.

My term on the Stockton City Council ended in December of 1995. My friends affectionately referred to my time in office as the "outsider who ruffles feathers." I made friends and enemies. A person could not pay enough in college tuition to experience the lessons I had learned. There's a saying: "If you want to get anything done, find a busy person." Yes, I was certainly busy. The Tierra Del Oro Girl Scouts Council awarded me the 1991 Female Role Model for the World of Community Service and my alma mater CSU-Sacramento gave me the prestigious Distinguished Service Award. In retrospect, I enjoyed being a policy maker but did not enjoy the political games that went with that role.

It has been twenty some years since I was on the Stockton City Council. This city is now the largest in California to file for bankruptcy. Mistakes have been made along the way with some traced back to the early 1990s. I can't help but feel sad at the conditions that have led to this point. However, my conscience is clear and I feel vindicated by my actions and votes while in office.

Chapter 15

Footprints

One's footprints may appear fleeting such as footprints in the sand; but when left on wet cement they endure. Admittedly some of my experiences and contributions were fleeting and others sustaining; yet, each activity remains etched in my mind and heart. Governor Pete Wilson's appointment in 1993 came as a blessing and it catapulted my spirit. I was emotionally drained from my weekly dealings with colleagues on the Stockton City Council. I could not walk away from unpleasant people nor could I resign. My tenacity and fighting spirit to do battle came from the support of those who elected me to office.

Many wrote letters to appointment secretary Chuck Poochigian at the Governor's Office suggesting that I be considered for an administrative appointment. Some letters detailed my working relationships, others opined as to my character and integrity. Friends such as the late Matt Fong who was then on the Board of Equalization, Lawyer Don Geiger, County Assessor Robert Shellenberger, Superior Court Judge Frank Kim, and many others in the business community as well as private citizens pleaded my case. While all were supporters, I believe, my strongest ally was Alex Spanos, Stockton's foremost developer, philanthropist, and strong Republican advocate. I never publicized any relationship with the Spanos Family. I have always held them in high esteem for their contributions to the Stockton community. Their daughter Dea Berberian and I became better acquainted during the 1992 Republican Convention and, I believe, they admired my feistiness. It is known that many political candidates and developers form symbiotic relationships. I can say honestly that the Spanos Company never influenced unduly nor asked for favor on land use issues.

A deputy assistant was not high enough to be on the director's cabinet but I was the highest ranking Asian in a department that oversaw 250-plus parks, beaches, historical sites, wilderness, and off-highway vehicle facilities. Of the various state departments in which I have been involved, it is clear the state park employees are the most dedicated to preserving California's natural and cultural resources. Educating the public is secondary in their mission. It seemed in the 1990s the department was working towards increasing their control of public lands. Their land acquisitions required additional public funds just to maintain and operate. And, yet, there were areas where they had not done well in maintaining what they already had.

Sylvia with Governor Pete Wilson - 1996

Coming Home to Pio Pico

My first thought was to familiarize myself with some of the parks' holdings; of course, historic sites were of particular interest. Would there be a chance for a "hands-on" effort? It did not take long and there it was – Pio Pico State Historic Park, nestled in the corner of Interstate 605 and Whittier Boulevard in Southern California. The park, acquired by the State of California in 1917, was home to the last governor of Alta California, Pio Pico.

Pio Pico was born at San Gabriel Mission in Los Angeles on May 5, 1801. He was of Spanish, Black, Native American, and Italian descent and rose from humble beginnings to wealth but later died in poverty. His life exemplified a family man, politician, and a businessman. He used his wealth and influence in the field of education, banking, and town development. Few realize that Pico pioneered California's first oil venture (in Santa Fe Springs), which eventually grew to become Standard Oil of California. He was twice governor of Alta California and his legacy is reflected with his name in many areas of Southern California.

There are better reasons to celebrate Cinco de Mayo in Californian than focusing on a battle in far away Mexico between the French and the Mexican government. That battle had no relevancy to California's history. Cities and counties do point to early pioneers and immigrants who founded specific communities, but no leader has covered the breadth and depth of our economic, social, political, and ethnic psyche as Pio Pico. Three strong reasons - date and place of birth, his multi-ethnic background and his accomplishments - are enough to recognize this man on May 5th of every year. This we have not done; and now, his house was in arrested decay. I had a crusade – Pio Pico State Historic Park.

When I visited the park there was a chain link fence surrounding the governor's adobe home. It was damaged in 1987 by the Whittier Narrow earthquake and further ruined during the 1994 Northridge earthquake. The three-acre parcel is surrounded by the cities of Whittier, Pico Rivera, Montebello and Santa Fe Springs. All the incorporated lands had once been part of his estate. I saw a few old men quietly talking at a picnic table but no one else was in sight. Even though there was a freeway on-ramp a few hundred feet away and one can hear muffled roadway sounds, I was instantly drawn to the tranquility. Rumor had it that the park had a certain sense of sanctity. Within the boundaries of the four cities, Latino gangs were pervasive; however much they caused damage to each other's territories, the grounds at Pio Pico was off limit. An unspoken creed existed not to trespass, not to damage – and, basically, to leave the park alone.

Jean Ekstrom, an interpretative specialist, lived on the grounds as caretaker; her salary and minimal maintenance were about all the expenditure the Sacramento office was willing to spend. I also learned there was no money for restoration nor was any going to be allocated in the near future. Talking it up in Sacramento went for naught. Most Park staff saw me just as a political appointee - the big talk no action type. They did not know me. To my advantage I was unencumbered with duties and was pretty much left to my own devices. I now had a cause and needed a plan. Jack Shu, the regional interpretation specialist for Southern California, listened and we quickly became co-conspirators. Jack was a Park Ranger III with peace officer status; his interest was really in education and curriculum. He and his counterpart, Carole Nelson in the north, were assigned to the Deputy Director of Community Relations. I never figured out what their supervisor did. Jack and Carole, along with Donna Pozzi, head of the Interpretive Services, guided me through some of the inner workings of the department.

I took my title "community liaison" literally and used it as part of my plan. I met with the city managers and/or city council members privately in each of the cities. Because I, too, was still a sitting council member, they showed me professional courtesy. While I assured them that there were absolutely no funds at State Parks to renovate Pio Pico, weren't they (the individual cities) angry that the State was creating an eye sore by not repairing Pico's house? Couldn't it be a tourist attraction that would benefit the cities? With that thought planted, I suggested that all the cities come together and hold a multi-city commemoration on Cinco de Mayo day right on the grounds of the state park. I gave the same pitch to the LA County Supervisor, Dean Dana whose area fell in his jurisdiction. This particular year coincided with the one hundredth anniversary of Pico's death. I secured a small McDonald's grant and built a triptych panel on Pico's life and Jack arranged for it to be displayed in various elementary schools in the four-city area.

Santa Fe Spring hosted the first organizational meeting at its Heritage Park with all the cities sending a representative from their own parks department. It was a constructive and enthusiastic session with promises of cooperation. Supervisor Dana sent a staff member, Angie Valenzuela. She was a dynamite of an organizer and her leadership showed. Ekstrom ran the control center. Jack Shu was good at keeping Sacramento abreast and telling the department to get on board. They knew something was abuzz but did not know to what degree. The event was on a fast track with only three months to pull together various organizations, local leaders, and other government representatives. How else could we bring politicos from these cities, nearby neighborhoods, and Latinos, together to show the park's state of disrepair and also its potentials? Reluctantly, about three weeks before the event the ranger who oversaw the region removed the chain link fencing and brought in a few potted plants for the front porch.

Almost every other week I spent two days down in Los Angeles to check on progress. As Ekstrom filled me in, I could tell there was an anticipated celebratory feeling in the air. Montebello's zoo was to bring bales of hay for the seating area; Whittier was constructing the stage; Santa Fe Spring was donating the sound system; and Pico Rivera was setting up booths for the non-profit organizations to sell food. All the parks were to rotate that day's entertainment.

One particular late afternoon when the area was deserted and near dusk, I sat quietly on the steps of the adobe home absorbed in thought. All of the sudden from a nearby bush a black rabbit hopped out. We stared at each other for what seemed like an eternity and then he retreated back into the bush. His appearance was a good omen. I read somewhere that while Pico was alive he was fond of rabbits. I took this as a blessing.

The weather was beautiful on Cinco De Mayo day in 1994. Volunteers began to gather early, crowds streamed in and temporarily-assigned parks personnel directed traffic. There were some nice touches to the event: it began when color guards dressed as vaqueros in shiny-buttoned pants and embroidered jackets rode in on mounted horses and stayed stationary for the salute of the flag and the national anthem. Local citizens over a hundred years old received commendations from their respective cities and descendants of the Pico family came and were recognized. The park, itself, received over 20 commendations and resolutions from various federal, state and local office holders. While all the presenters and recipients were in proper attire, the director of Parks showed up a little too casual in an open-collar shirt and a windbreaker. I shook my head, no class.

A video created by Parks staff on the life of Pio Pico played continually in one of many rooms. Mariachis and folklorico dancers took turns on the stage. School children who participated in their own city park's activities also performed. I gave the planners tremendous credit for their cooperation and organizational abilities. To me, that day was an example of how historic parks in urban areas should be, not just for tourists, but also for local use. The next day before I flew back north I swung by Pico's park and did a short walk on the grounds. To my surprise there was the black rabbit again; this time he was surrounded by a few smaller rabbits. He looked at me for a moment and then with his charge scampered back into the bushes. I just smiled.

Because of the Cinco de Mayo event, all four cities felt a responsibility to restore Pio Pico State Historic Park. In the 1996's election cycle there was a countywide recreation bond measure. Normally this type of bond when passed generally got divided among the cities and county parks departments. In this case $2.5 million was pledged towards restoration of Pio Pico State Park. While State Parks did the actual renovation, the monies came from the local bond measure. Seven years later, on September 20, 2003 Pio Pico State Parks celebrated the completed project. I drove down and sat as a quiet observer of the event. With a new Parks director, new leaders in all the cities and new employees, none knew who I was. I ran into Angie Valenzuela now a mother pushing a baby stroller, we chatted a bit and I returned to Northern California contented.

A Failed Sesquicentennial

A few weeks after the Pio Pico event the Parks Director called me into his office and asked if I would take on a new project: creating the framework for the upcoming California Sesquicentennial. I immediately jumped at an opportunity to highlight California's Gold Rush to Statehood commemoration. He already assigned some staff to the project: Gail Kulhavy, an executive secretary, actually the director's own factotum; Dahlynn Shiflet his publicist; Marilyn Olson who just returned to Parks from another agency; Ken McKuen an analyst from within the depth of the Parks bureaucracy and student intern Jeanne Shabbir recommended by my old mentor, Ken Owens. I wondered why the director gave me two of his personal staff unless he was "tired" of them…hmmm. As it turned out these employees were extremely energetic and not short on visions and ideas. We bolstered each other up and called ourselves the "motley crew."

Logistics plagued us from the very beginning. My office was on the 14th floor of the Resource Building at 9th and O Street and staff worked on the 9th floor, this meant we were constantly in the elevators. Our logistics got worst several months later when our entire unit was shuffled from Parks to the State Library. They were now housed in one building and I in the State Librarian's complex.

Marilyn, as a staff service analyst, had the longest tenure in state service, supervised the group. She tried to get a handle on my type of supervision and asked, "Are you a process or project person?" This question was quite telling and my answer was quick. I am definitely "project" as it connotes fairly short term, excitement, and one can see end results; whereas "process" is very typical for most government employees. I saw it as a process of crossing "Ts", dotting "Is," filling out forms until the day of one's retirement. I am not the hovering type and prefer to mentor and encourage employees to use their imagination.

Our motley crew had a mission; "they" envisioned the Sesquicentennial years of 1998 to 2000 filled with celebratory activities statewide. In our mind California's Gold Rush is very much alive. We easily listed many of California's accomplishments in the last 150 years. These pertained to more than the coarse ore. California's "gold rushes" included Hollywood and the entertainment industry, science and aerospace industry, and even birth of the high tech companies in Silicon Valley, just to name a few.

During this period staff was undergoing a metamorphosis. In short order, Gail began to contact museums, volunteer groups, nonprofits, and local organizations statewide to create or include activities that would coincide with the sesquicentennial years. Her "to-do" items included coordinating with the tall ships and wagon trains, linking two historic modes of transportation. The events occurred in three cities, one being Stockton. Gail encouraged quilting groups to create one huge commemorative quilt. I thought her to be an energized bunny who even spent weekends on the road. Dahlynn developed contacts with states that had already celebrated their sesquicentennial, fitting their ideas into our bucket list. She also tapped into entertainment industries and worked to solicit funds from them.

For me getting a commemorative postage stamp meant dealing with the enormous postal institution; unfortunately, it would have taken at least three years to work through the system. An artist created artwork for a commemorative license plate; but, getting approval involved legislation (a bill to this effect passed the Assembly by 72 to 1, but my successor never took it to the Senate floor). We received pro bono services from legal and accounting companies and even those in the business sector. They designed Sesquicentennial logos and paraphernalia associated with marketing. My main concentration was creating a nonprofit foundation, purposely to fund all the major activities. Three friends agreed to be the original signers when we processed the tax-exempt paperwork: John Moorlach, treasurer of Orange County; Art Takahara, president of De Anza Manufacturing and former mayor of Mountain View; and Don Geiger, an attorney in Stockton, my friend and cohort when we sued to clean up Stockton's downtown.

We had energy, we had vision; however, the Sesquicentennial was ill-fated. I had a political interruption, rather a call for duty, by the powers-to-be at the Governor's Office. More about this later. After I left the Sesquicentennial office complex issues surfaced among which was, arguably, the overlapping duties between a newly-appointed Sesquicentennial commission and the foundation. My successor, now given the title of Executive Director, should have had more clout since my title was only Executive Coordinator. Unfortunately, he lacked initiative and did not seek legislators' support as funding was so crucial.

His new underlings decided rather than allowing staff to continue their work they wanted to reinvent the wheel even though there were time constraints. One by one the original staff was dismissed and death came to the Sesquicentennial office. As an aside, I must give kudos to one particular commissioner, actress and writer Beulah Quo. She put forth major effort for she believed in the California story. Through her contacts the Asian sector created and produced a musical production entitled "Heading East" complete with veteran actors and singers. The storyline was that of the Chinese and the Gold Rush. It was very successful and the funding came strictly from Quo's effort as did a traveling exhibit that reached major California museums and schools.

Aside from highlights of Pio Pico and the Sesquicentennial, there were other smaller Parks incidents where I lent a hand. In Los Angeles local leaders wanted to build a museum in the Garnier Building in the El Pueblo Plaza in downtown Los Angeles. My first visit and first impression was a roofless building with pigeons flying between rafters; yet, the enthusiasm of the volunteers and dreamers was infectious. The end result became the Chinese American

Museum. Today the museum is a "must see" for students, educators and, definitely, the Chinese.

And then there was the Railtown Museum in the Mother Lode community of Jamestown. Once a large highway sign stood on the highway directing tourists to the museum; but, a car going around the bend eliminated it. The volunteer group wanted their large directional sign replaced. Caltrans thought a small sign was sufficient. However the sign was so small it was not noticeable even when travelling at 30 miles per hour. Their effort to get an equal replacement went for naught at the local Caltrans district office. This was a case for me to be "at the right place at the right time." I arranged a meeting with the District 10 deputy director, Randy Iwasaki, in charge of maintenance. My Park volunteers and I set the meeting to take place in a boxcar, no window just the small sliding door. We (about ten of us) sat on one side of a long table and the three representatives from Caltrans sat across. Did we look intimidating? Yes. Did the Railtown Museum get an adequate replacement sign? Yes.

Sesquicentennial Foundation founderss:
John Moorlach, Don Geiger, and Art Takahara

A Fleeting Assembly Attempt

At the start of the 1996 election year the Governor's Office called and asked that I throw my name into the race for the

Assembly. The Republican Party's poll showed that I had positive name recognition. They needed me to run. I knew I was a sacrificial lamb since my opponent, Mike Machado, was the incumbent and the district was heavily Democrat. I was in a difficult situation. To say "no" would be going against my boss, the governor.

It is always tough to run against an incumbent. The 1996 election was no different. I gave it my best shot; however, his ability to raise dollars far outweighed mine. One cannot compete with lobbyists' backing and union dollars. On the positive side, I drove through many a country road, and even learned to sit on a tractor. I lost the race by four points (meaning four thousand votes).

There were some shenanigans. We sent out campaign literature at the main post office, they were targeted for west Stockton but landed up undelivered and were still in sacks at a remote post office east of Highway 99. The election date had passed as did the filing date to be reimbursed for mailing cost. I received an apologetic letter from the post office that recognized their blunder however late. Machado went on to become a state senior and, from all indications distinguished himself in the annals of California legislative bodies. He was well versed with water issues affecting farmers and the San Joaquin delta. Personally, I did not feel any remorse about the election; everything was a learning experience.

Mickey Rooney and Department of Aging

In early 1997, because I was a faithful constituent, the governor appointed me to the Department of Aging. My post was the Assistant Director for External Affairs and it included being in the Director's internal staff. Officially I was the Public Information Officer (PIO) for the department.

The office was at 16th and K Street in a red brick building and my office on the fourth floor overlooked liquidamber trees with birds flitting between the branches. This was a gorgeous view in the Fall. Aging was such an improvement over working for Parks and Recreation. Total staff numbered 110 compared to the thousands at Parks. The Director, Dixon Arnett, was enthusiastic and quite a crack-up. He often paddled around in his stocking feet and a very large "NO WHINING" sign hung in back of his office door as a reminder to staff when he met with them privately. Josephine Raysbrook on my staff was from England. When she visited assisted living and senior center facilities she charmed them with her British accent. Arnett gave her the unofficial title of "Madame Ambassador." Next door to my office was the department's legislative guru. Like me, Mel Kaukin was also an assistant director, a warm but strange dude who took to keeping his door closed. I accused him of either avoiding his secretary or taking afternoon naps on his couch.

External affairs meant maintaining contacts with the media, newspapers, senior magazines, and the counties' local aging departments. I was surprised Aging never used a newsletter to reach its various constituencies. I rolled out the first edition with a message from the director and deputy director and encouraged each of the counties' aging departments to submit news or bragging rights in their area; of course, a 'Minnick's Musing" section was included. Quickly and easily staff took the responsibility for all the quarterly issues.

In 1998 the United Nations launched the International Year of the Older Person and the federal counterpart suggested that the states develop innovative programs to include some type of celebratory event. We needed an official spokesperson and found Stuart Greenbaum, a young, wiry, soft-spoken public relations person. His firm, CAUSE-CELEB, connected television and movie celebrities to non-profit organizations causes. After tossing around a few celebrity names, we decided that Mickey Rooney would be ideal. He was well known, energetic, and still active. Rooney was in San Francisco playing the wizard in a Wizard of Oz production. Dixon, Stuart and I met him between shows. We agreed that on October 14, 1998 Rooney was to appear in front of an audience of aging advocates in the governor's conference room. Greenbaum and I were to shepherd him around. When Rooney stepped off Southwest Airlines at the Sacramento Airport, there was no mistake he was going to be a handful. He was dressed in a rather rumpled herringbone jacket, and both his pockets were stuffed with a racing newspaper and racing forms.

We were to give Rooney a quick tour around the capitol, a luncheon at Sutter's Club, present him with a plaque, have him say a few words, a quick television interview, and then send him home. As soon as he walked in the conference room cameras were clicking away; of all people, Donna Gail of Stockton, stood up and beckoned to him. Rooney walked down a few rows to see what she wanted and she planted him with a big kiss. Somewhat surprised but quick on his feet he said: "Were we married before?" The laughter was resounding. In his speech he said he deplored the word "aging" and preferred that the department be renamed the Department of Experience, how true. He was the consummate actor and charmed everyone.

During my tenure External Affairs created a statewide directory of senior centers listing location, activities and, most importantly, information on their lunch programs. Because of Arnett's inexhaustible energy, I felt good giving one thousand percent. By late 1998 both Arnett and Fred Miller, the deputy director, chose to retire. This was a significant loss but they wisely forecasted changes in the political wind.

A Chicken Little Story

My government career ended when Gray Davis became California's new governor in 1999. Appointees from previous administrations expect termination letters. When they actually vacate their positions depend on a bit of hide-and-seek. The appointee might keep a low profile and wait until the governor or his appointment secretary decide when to dole out rewards to campaign contributors or those who had influence with legislators. Influence and financial support weigh heavily on where to appoint newcomers.

A "Y2K" (Year 2000) issue hung cataclysmically over all the state agencies from divisions down to departments. Many "what ifs" existed regarding the computers' clock - would they turn over automatically in the incoming year 2000 and the new millennium? Many of the machines' digits were not set for the next century. Would all the state computers programs run smoothly and simultaneously or would they just crash? Or, what if there was a power malfunction, could it really stop State government? The uncertainties and embellishment of doomsday forecasting created a "Chicken Little" mentality. There were meetings upon meetings from top down. Finally, a directive required every agency to submit an emergency plan to the Governor's Office by Fall 1999. As the public information officer for Aging, my job was to prepare such a plan. I kidded with a cohort one day saying as soon as all the pages are in the binder I probably would see my exit papers. Sure enough, the very next day after I submitted my report the new director came to my office and said I was terminated and had 24 hours to vacate my office. It was quick and cold. My public relations staff quickly pulled together a luncheon, a good-bye afternoon reception and at 5:00pm on September 19, 1999 I walked out of the four-story, red brick building at 16th and K Street. I was lucky. A few other appointees were given even shorter notice.

Department of Aging staff at a farewell luncheon on my behalf – 1999

The many connections and friendship ties remain strong even after I left state service. The senior staff members at Aging disbursed: Dixon Arnett relocated to San Diego, Mel Kaulkin resides in Pennsylvania, Jo Raysbrook passed away and Fred Miller is the closest to me in proximity. Former state ombudsman Phyllis Arcuni became an ex-Pat and now lives in Panama. Phyllis is the glue that keeps all us connected. When she returns to her large Atascadero house for short visits she organizes reunions and we look forward to laughter and libation.

I realize that, at times, my footprints while in state service were seen as fleeting, but then the opportunity to travel throughout the state, meet challenges, and associate with some of the nicest people were personal rewards. My professional career came to an end as a new century dawned.

Quan Ying / Hall of Heroes

Closer to home, I left the City Council at the end of 1995 and was still employed with the state when I began to move up the chairs at the Stockton Chinese Benevolent Association (CBA) in 1997, serving initially as the English Secretary. Historically the organization was an all-male bastion. The Chinese name for the organization is "Chung Wah", literally translated as the "Center of Chinese."

The zenith of Chung Wah and the Chinese community occurred between the 1920s to the 1950s. During this period its leaders built the current headquarters, established a Chinese language school for the young, organized a drum and bugle youth corps, purchased sufficient land for a cemetery; and, more importantly, raised funds for the China Relief Effort of World War II. The Chinese leadership waned in the ensuing decades and their landholdings deteriorated.

In 1999 I became its first female president. While I am not totally fluent in the Cantonese language and do not speak Mandarin, I got by. The board preferred to conduct everything in Chinese so I managed to develop my own Chinese-English style of presiding. A Chinese phrase, "*faan tung*" translates to "rice container". This literally described some members of the board, people who attended and were interested only in the meal that was served at the meeting. They came to fill their stomachs. This negative connotation suggests that nothing got done and everything was status quo. As president I felt I was the ox that was pulling a cart filled with *faan tungs*.

CBA bought a four-story, Beaux-Art/Italian Renaissance, terracotta building at the corner of San Joaquin and Lafayette Streets in the 1970s. It was built by the Salvation Army in 1911. The Chinese renamed it the Confucius Building. Several individuals leased the building over the years operating it as a hotel with some rooms rented out on hourly basis. It became a haven for prostitutes, drug addicts, and occasional dead bodies. The homeless shelter signed a contract to house their clients and when the contract expired, even the homeless did not want to return. By 1998 this dilapidated building incurred 76 code violations. The city prohibited entry unless repaired. In plain English, the building faced demolition. It seemed many board members were not aware of this dire situation. And those who did also knew the treasury was bare.

I approached the city's redevelopment department for suggestions. This led me to Cyrus Youssefi, an Iranian American developer, seasoned in building low and median housing in Sacramento and Stockton. His track record of crunching the numbers with tax credits and redevelopment monies was incredible. He had already completed three projects in Stockton. I had met him earlier while on the City Council and he remembered that I was the only person on the dais that voted against one of his projects. Nevertheless, all was forgiven as he guided me.

First, I was to ask for city block grant funds to pay for a feasibility study focusing on the building's location and possible usage. Coincidentally, a piece of land on Weber Point, home of the defunct Castaway Restaurant, was just sold and its proceeds earmarked for a charity by the owner, the Bank of Canton in San Francisco. The value approximated $800,000; the bank was letting the city decide the eventual beneficiary. I was furious when I learned the head of redevelopment earmarked all the monies to Mercy Charities. This organization was only testing the waters and showed only a slight interest in developing low income housing in Stockton. Here, we just completed a feasibility study intending to do something about the Confucius Building. Oh yes, I banged the table but was told the Chinese community did not have a track record of building anything. It was almost déjà vu from my SBA experience. The City Council and staff have never really helped nor given funds to the Chinese or Japanese communities; nearly all went to "minorities" or more specifically squeaky wheels. I took a delegation of Chinese board members to San Francisco and met with the Bank of Canton board. I reminded them that my father was one of the founders of the bank, I had sold Girl Scout cookies there, AND I had just gotten off the city council; why didn't any one of them contact me. They were very apologetic and said city staff never mentioned that the local Chinese were looking for funds. Since they were now out of the picture there was nothing they could do.

The completed feasibility study showed a housing project was doable; we were ready for Step 2. Youssefi suggested with tax credit dollars we could convert the building into a low-income senior housing project at a cost of $2.1 million dollars. I took on the redevelopment department again with a "you owe us" tone. Almost mockingly they agreed to help if I found the rest of the money.

Tax credit awards are given to nonprofit organizations, but CBA did not qualify under the Internal Revenue criteria since the organization leaders claim the institution as religious and under the guise of Confucius Church they were religiously tax exempted but not qualified to get federal dollars. With the help of Don Geiger and his office, we developed a 501.c.3 tax exempt foundation with by-laws structured so that four members of CBA will always be part of the foundation's nine member board (but will never have majority vote).We became a bonafide non-profit.

A plot survey of the Confucius Building carved out its boundary from the overall CBA properties and the building's name officially changed to *Quan Ying*. The new foundation and the building's name have several meanings in the Chinese language, all quite similar. The most common are: "A Gathering of Good People" or "Hall of Heroes." Subliminally, I thought: "Oh great, if this project fails people will say I created my own Hall of Martyr." But, we completed three important steps and now the fourth.

Youssefi and Patrick Sabelhaus, a very astute Sacramento tax-credit lawyer, began to craft an application for tax credit dollars. The first filing to the State Treasurer's Office fell short and did not quite qualify. There was a second and finally a third try. With the encouragement of State Treasurer Matt Fong and his office, this time we struck gold. It was a $1.2 million dollar tax credit contract with Alliant, a Los Angeles-based investment company. Assistant Treasurer Walter Liang ushered us into his office and asked if I wanted to make the call to Stockton's redevelopment and inform them of the good news. I asked for Steve Pinkerton, who headed the office and said: "We are in Sacramento and we got it, now where is the city's share of the money?" His response was, "You must be mistaken. You folks weren't even on the screen." He thought I must have been attending some type of workshop getting an orientation of some sort. Even then it told me how little faith city staff had, but I felt so good! Since Pinkerton made the promise his staff had to scramble pulling monies from various pots to come up with $880,000 for start up money we needed to begin construction. Meanwhile our contract with Alliant took much longer because of federal and state involvement.

Cyrus Youssefi's company began demolition work immediately. Every floor, room, and alcove was demolished leaving the outside walls as a shell. We did retain some of the historic elements such as the original back stairs and the wainscoting. The corners tied and seismically retrofitted conformed to earthquake requirements and handrails and lights adhered to the American Disability Act standards. An elevator addition was affixed to the west side of the building and under a scalloped-shape, green awning stood a bright red, double door entrance. To eliminate any and all evil spirits that may have dwelled there at one time I asked for blessings from two St. Mary's priests, one was Hispanic and the other Filipino. This was just in case the spirits were linguistically challenged.

Quan Ying ground breaking:
L to R: Sylvia, Cyrus Youssefi, Walter Liang, Asst. State Treasurer, Mayor Gary Podesto, Don Geiger and Conrad Mar

The grand opening of this 20-unit, low income, senior apartment took place in the spring of 2001 replete with firecrackers, lion dance, and the offering of a roast pig to the Chinese spirits. This particular event made the Chinese community proud. April 2001 the first tenant moved it and within five months the building was totally occupied. The tenant mix was a warm study in race relationships – Hispanics, Native American, Filipino, White, and Chinese. The language barrier was not a social deterrent. There were many touching examples of tenants caring for each other and they were fastidious in not allowing social disruptions. The rent is modest and is charged below market rates in accordance with federal guidelines. Almost from the very beginning, Judy Hong with her husband Bevin, oversees the everyday operation. The Hongs are truly God's gift to the Chinese community and to Quan Ying. If not for Cyrus Youssefi's business acumen and our friendship, Quan Ying would have been only a fleeting footprint.

Quan Ying Low Income Senior Apartments
301 South San Joaquin Street, Stockton, CA.

Chapter 16

A Mother's Day Tragedy

The weather was beautiful on Mother's Day 1999. Temperature was mild, the trees showed promise of buds and flowers. That day showed wonderful promise, although I had not heard from Donna and Darcy, but I knew they would call eventually. The sisters were having a reunion. Working for Hawaiian Airlines as the cargo director, Darcy invited Donna and her husband, Mike Forsch, to spend a few days in Hawaii to celebrate their tenth wedding anniversary. It was such a generous offer. Donna took great effort packing for romantic days ahead from clothing to negligee and even got herself manicured and pedicured. I was amused by her selection of nail polish. They needed a vacation from their hectic schedule - she in merchandising and he a pharmaceutical representative for Warner Chilcott. Donna was especially excited because she was scheduled for an invitro-fertilization (IVF) procedure when they returned home. She suffered two miscarriages a few years earlier and thought it was time to try again, this time with a little medical help.

For their gift we gave them one night at the El Rancho Inn in Millbrae before they flew off the next morning. Darcy surprised them with an anniversary card and keys to a green Mustang convertible, an additional something from us. They were ecstatic. The happy couple loaded the car with golf clubs, suitcases, and numerous tote bags and headed for the Turtle Bay Resort at North Shore in Oahu. Lapping up the waves, palm trees, and several rounds of golf, accompanied by champagne at Darcy's house. These were the ideal plans. There was nothing structured except the two girls planned to meet sometime on Mother's Day to share a call to me.

Our day in Stockton went along pleasantly. We caught a Mother Day's event at the Scottish Rite Temple on Alpine Avenue. The Mills Brothers put on a wonderful show. They sang all the familiar oldies affirming they and we were getting up there in years. Traditionally, Mother's Day was at Mike and Donna's home in West Laguna, just south of Sacramento. On major holidays she made elaborate dinners for us and Mike's parents, Jim and Sheila. Mother's Day was no different. However, since it was a special year for the youngsters we wanted them to enjoy themselves. Richard and I were at Donna's three weeks earlier for lunch to celebrate my birthday. She gave me a gift certificate for Nordstrom apologizing that she didn't have time to buy me anything. She was ever thoughtful. The day passed and on this Mother's Day 1999 the girls' call never came.

Mother Nature Stricks A Blow

Sounds often get incorporated into my dreams. Half conscious I heard the phone ring in the distance but dismissed it thinking who would call so late except a prankster. The answering machine in the study was on for messages. The phone rang again and again. And finally I heard a little voice crying, "Mom, mom pick up the phone." Stumbling into my office, I grabbed it and turned on the light. It was Darcy speaking in a quick, trembling voice, something about a terrible accident and Donna was missing. My heart dropped and I snapped to attention. It was 4:00 AM, May 10, 1999. Many people injured, some killed and others missing at a place called Sacred Falls. An earthquake, rockslide – what? Heck with the specifics, we quickly made plans: call the Forsch family, throw some clothes into a bag, Richard stays home and mans the phone while I drive to the Sacramento airport to meet up with Jim and Sheila. Darcy arranged for us to fly to Los Angeles to catch the next Hawaiian Airline flight to Honolulu International. We already missed the direct flight from Sacramento. The wait time at LAX seemed an eternity.

We finally boarded. My mind remained numb to comments of sympathy by flight attendants. I didn't want to hear sympathy as if it was a death wish. I was distracted by questions running through my mind as to what to do, how bad was everything? The continuous "how come" rolled into just random thoughts of Donna, the last time I saw her, our mother-daughter bonding times on her various birthdays, images of both girls in school, their antics, their squabbling, the proud moment when Donna drove the little Honda up and down Commerce Street when she finally mastered the stick shift. I could still see her dragging herself home after late nights working security at the Stockton Macys store. She was a company faithful having worked in Sacramento, San Francisco and, of course, she had begun her corporate career in Stockton. Only recently she sought a change and started a job at Julius, the Polo Ralph Lauren store in the Pavilions in Sacramento.

Thinking back, Donna met Mike in her junior year at California State University-Sacramento. Of German-American descent, Mike was a local Sacramento boy and seemed okay except it appeared he was less ambitious and more interested in sports and sporting events; whereas Donna was ever conscientious, dutiful. Mike called her a work-alcoholic. To me she was a typical American Chinese. They both graduated in 1984; he in Business and she in Social Studies with a minor in Art History. After a fairly long courtship, or rather, when they finally got their act together they married on May 6, 1989. Donna, being the take-charge person, planned her wedding without asking for help or finances. She felt it would be a hardship for us. After their wedding they honeymooned in Hawaii. Richard and I went along with some cousins from Tennessee.

Donna and Mike Forsch – 1998

What was I going to do without Donna? She was not just a daughter but, oftentimes, a companion and confidant. She took pride in being my personal shopper, believing my taste in clothes was not up to her standard. Whatever style of clothing and even hairdo she always looked gorgeous turning many a head. She had flair and was quite domestic at times. Many of their social activities involved his fraternity brothers in Sigma Phi Epsilon. This was my Donna, a real good girl. I was so proud of her.

I had never been close to Sheila and Jim Forsch. On the flight to Hawaii the Forsches left me to my world of silence except I recalled Sheila saying very directly: "You take care of your daughter; we will take care of our son."

We landed around 10:00 PM. Darcy was there with an elderly Japanese couple, Jim and Yoshi Tanabe, volunteers from the Red Cross. They were assigned to help in whatever way possible. Very kind and gentle, many years later our friendship blossomed into the true feeling of Ohana, the Hawaiian word for family. Darcy's face intoned an awful fact, they found Donna's body and she was identified by her motor vehicle license thumb print. Gone was any element of hope and there was no possibility for denial. I couldn't break down, couldn't give into personal grief. I will feel the pain and loss, but not now. Pummeled by a personal tragedy that was gaining worldwide attention, I needed to "buck up," and be strong to handle the many duties ahead. I went home with Darcy to Wailua and the Forsches left with the Tanabes to a respite hotel set aside by the Red Cross.

It was late but I called Richard and told all I knew and promised to tell more when additional details unfolded. Meanwhile I needed Diane Barth's phone number at the *Stockton Record*, the local newspaper. She was one of the better reporters and would be sensitive to our situation.

A Painful Reality for Many

Sacred Falls is at the end of a lush, green, narrow canyon between Hauula and Punaluu, on the northeast side of Oahu and not far from the North Shore. The park sits on 1.3 plus acres and is considered one of the Oahu's most popular and picturesque spots on the island. Travel guides list it as a "must" for mainlanders. Approximately 50,000 visitors visit the state parks annually. The trail into the actual fall is at least 2.2 miles long, peppered with boulders, rocks and its elevation is uneven. But upon reaching Sacred Falls the scenery is breathtaking with water gently cascading down from high above.

At approximately 2:30 PM, May 9, 1999, countless witnesses visiting the area heard a loud rumble; some described it as a freight train passing through. Others waited to see if there was a rush of water but saw none. Still others looked around not expecting the worst. As an article indicated "scores of people were in the pool at the base of the falls or sitting on nearby rocks." An estimated 30 cubic yards of boulders, rocks, and debris plunged to the valley floor. Geologists described the avalanche's debris as entering through a dry waterfall chute "…that funneled the material from 500 feet above to the crowd below at about 70 to 100 miles per hour. Some of the rocks shot across the canyon and ricocheted off the opposite wall before falling." "The entire area was a potential kill zone with death and injury a random event." Gerald Weber, a geologic consultant, wrote in his findings after assessing the damages. [11]

The high rock walls prevented the use of cell phones. Rescue proved difficult in the rough terrain. Ambulances could not reach the area. Two helicopters were deployed, but the instability of more falling debris and the high narrow walls of the canyon prevented any chance of landing. Hovering, the vibration of the chopper blades added to the tenuous situation. Taking turns, the pilots lowered basket stretchers to the ground, loaded the wounded and flew off to the next staging area. One chopper belonged to the Honolulu Fire Department and the other, a Blackhawk helicopter, was based at Wheeler Air Field. The pilot of the latter flew eleven of the injured from the park's parking lot to Queens Medical in downtown Honolulu. All the hospitals stood on alert as this was soon recognized as the worst natural disaster in Hawaii in recent times.

Quickly the able-bodied near the waterfall took part in the rescue mission using T-shirts, towels and whatever available to carry out the injured with a school bus waiting in the parking lot. The less injured stumbled out on their own. Witnesses recalled body parts scattered between the boulders that were colored with blood. It was a race against time to save lives and park rescuers also realized everyone needed to clear out before darkness fell.

In total there were eight dead and at least fifty injured in various stages from critical to fair condition. It was three days before the body of 24-year old Sara Johnson of California was found. Among the other fatalities were two Canadians, a Master Sergeant stationed at Hickam Air Force Base, a brother and sister in their twenties, a seven year old girl, and Donna.

I gave Diane Barth a summation of what I knew the morning after my arrival. Barth did a yeoman's job of piecing the story together and giving it a local slant. I had two concerns. Thinking that if they took Donna's thumbprint to make identification the media might use the picture off of her driver's license. It was not a flattering picture somewhat analogous to a wanted poster. We had a much better picture of both Mike and her taken six months earlier. Richard quickly found it in the album and took it down to the newspaper office for Barth's use. A second request of Barth was to screen media contact. It was bad enough that our home phone was ringing off the hook; many friends and relatives were concerned. Richard kept a log which included three calls from a Stockton psychic, Helen Wong, who was desperate to contact me. A hungry press was the last thing Richard needed. Barth capably handled the media and we were sheltered from the onslaught of Sacramento television stations and even CNN.

Heroes in the Midst

Just prior to the rocks cascading a few sunbathers recalled seeing Mike and Donna. He was in the water just joking around while she sat on the rock nearby. As soon as they heard the first rumble he jumped out and she stood by waiting for him to put on his shoes. Quickly the boulders came and they both were hit - he on the head with rocks and debris penetrating his skull. Mike was knocked unconscious temporarily. As for Donna, both her legs were severed and her abdominal cavity exposed.

Jason Hill, a 21-year old pianist and member of the Pacific Marine Band, and Jay Long, a gunner mate 2nd class in the Navy decided to take in a little sun and check out Sacred Falls. Their walk turned into running down the trail as the injured streamed by running towards them shouting that they should turn around as rocks were falling. Instead the two, thinking young and invincible, ran down the trail to see if they could help. Jason Hill provided a first-person account of the tragedy he witnessed. The following is an excerpt from an email he sent. [12]

"As all these nameless, scared, crying people, some of whom were severely injured, passed us they kept saying 'HELP THE CHILDREN!' Soon I came upon a young couple…honeymooning from Salt Lake City…he was desperately trying to carry her but was exhausted, frightened, and injured himself. I…put this woman with blood soaked, makeshift bandages wrapped around her ankles, on my back. I didn't pay much attention to what either of them was saying, she was deaf but could speak. I was just trying to figure out how I was going to make it through whatever I would experience in the next few hours. I completed the one and a half mile trail of rocks and dropped her off with one of the few rescue crews that had shown up…and I took off running back to the trail. Along the way I passed people with various injuries, most of which were severe.

"I came upon an older couple holding a man covered in bloody rags. They introduced themselves as Matty and Dave. Then she said "This is Mike." I could not believe this woman was laughing and joking around while this man was laying there bleeding to death, then it hit me. She was keeping Mike's mind occupied while they waited for help. Matty said that Mike was hurt so bad that he could not be moved. Eventually the helicopters and rescue crew penetrated deep in the trail to the worse of the victim."

Jason and Jay along with a few others were able to carry Mike to a small clearing where the injured were loaded into basket stretchers and flown to the next staging area. As Jason continues:

"I ended up on a small ledge riddled with bodies and body parts and a few people desperately trying to help save them. Someone told me these were the last five, and that I should not go back there because there was a man who had been decapitated. Two men leaned over a woman who had been crushed by rocks. They were giving CPR to this woman, Donna Forsch. One of the men working on Donna turned out to be Geoff Scott, a neck and spine surgeon connected to University of California-Irvine medical center. Dr. Scott guided us as we needed help with medical situations. He was clearly agitated that the EMTs who finally arrived did not carry basic supplies such as oxygen and intubation tubes. He could not understand why professional EMTs were not equipped with basic trauma response equipment. Exhausting all reason with the crew, Dr. Scott went back to working on Donna.

"…Danielle Williams, the seven year old, was one of the last to be evacuated but her condition so severe Dr. Scott recommended that we not air lift her but to carry her out. There were enough people by now to help carrying the stretcher and others taking turns giving her CPR. However, along the way, her little heart gave out before she reached the head of the trail.

"...I looked around and realized that it was the same few people who had been giving everything they had since the beginning of the whole ordeal. There was Jay, my hiking partner, Dr. Scott and the other man who had been working on Donna, Dave and Matty; sure, there were some fresh faces, but these precious few had done so much already were here at the very end...."

Phil Preen, stationed at Hickam Air Base and working on a graduate degree, happened to hike to the falls with his school advisor. Here is his account written on May 13 and September 29, 1999:

"As we kept going [towards the falls] more injured folks were making their way down the hill.... I ran ahead to see if anyone needed help...when I got there people who were still there were badly hurt and couldn't be moved. People still near the slide needed to be moved from the area because rocks were still falling ... a corpsman, myself and two other people moved Donna and one other lady away from the rocks to under the trees...we laid her on her back so she could breathe easier and I held a t-shirt up so that she could not see her injured legs. I put my shirt under her head so that she would be comfortable and started talking to her. When I asked her if she lived in Hawaii she said, no, she was there visiting her sister and was up at the falls site[sic]-seeing. She said she was from California but it was hard to understand which city she said. I thought she said Elk Grove, but since I was born in Elk Grove Village, Illinois, I wasn't sure if that was right or what it sounded like.

"... I kept telling her to squeeze my hand to give her something to concentrate on. I thought she said she did not have any pets so I asked her if she at least had a bird or a fish or some sort of pet. I think she thought that was funny. She did say she did not have any kids and that she was married. She told me to tell her husband, Mike, that she loved him. At one point she asked that we let her die; but, I kept telling her to hang on until help got there. She said she was having trouble breathing so I would tell her she was breathing fine and to help her relax I would tell her to listen to the water fall and the leaves blowing on the trees. That seemed to relax her and she could breathe deeper breaths. After a while, which now I don't know how long, she stopped talking. I would ask her questions and she would tighten her grip on my hand and let me know she was still listening. I asked her if she had any brothers and she signaled with her left hand, no. When I asked her about sisters, she raised one finger. Someone asked me to help hold/ support another woman who had severe head trauma. ...I told Donna I would be right back and asked another man who was there to hold her hand while I was gone. I kept talking to Donna while I was helping this other woman trying to calm her down. I looked over at one point and two people were performing CPR on Donna but I do not remember who it was. I do remember

thinking though that Donna was gone by that time and felt bad I was not there with her. I hoped she didn't think I left her….

"…when help did arrive I asked for blankets to help the injured folks get warm. I helped put people on stretchers and then transferred them to the helicopters. I put a coat on Mike to warm him up and then I noticed he was bleeding real bad from his ankle I asked for gauze and tape. I replaced the strip of shirt someone had used as a tie and the bleeding seemed to stop. Someone said he looked ok and I said yes, except he could use a shave. I helped carry him down the hill to where the helicopter came down to pick him up and helped load him into the basket. I did not put it together until I was walking back down the hill that he might have been Donna's husband…time for me literally stood still. I had stared my watch when we started our walk and turned it off when I walked out of the park. Five hours had passed but it sure didn't feel like it. I broke down when I walked over to the Red Cross table and stayed there for awhile. The Red Cross rep asked me about what I went through….

"…I could not sleep that night. Every time I turned off the lights it felt like there was someone in the room … I called the Red Cross number the next day and left a message there for them to find a Mike and pass along Donna's message."

Nathan McCotter, and David Pahk, two volunteers from the Sacred Falls Assistance Progam were operating the information and care stand some 2.2 miles from the falls. Pahk used his cell phone to call for help and within an hour both he and McCotter were in the thick of the wounded and dead brought out to the head of the trail by various means. Pahk recalled: *"there was an attractive woman...her face was perfect. And then I looked I could see further down…part of her waist…from there on…it was just all spaghetti…*[13]

The heroic efforts of those who tried to help are beyond words. Both Preen and Hill's emotions and exhaustion caught up to them that night and lasted most probably a lifetime.

Darcy heard about the accident when she turned on the television in the late afternoon. Fearing the worse she drove to the site and recognized the green Mustang and the beach towel she had lent her sister. For the next several hours she franticly searched for both of them and located Mike at the Kuakini Hospital. She described him as bloodied, black and blue, his face swollen and he was incoherent. But no word of Donna yet until the following morning.

Ticking Off Necessary Chores

My stay in Hawaii was filled with appointments: the coroner's office to pick up Donna's jewelry (wedding ring and earrings); gather their clothing and belongings at the Turtle Bay Resort, run to Honolulu's downtown to Borthwick Mortuary to pick out a casket, and make arrangements to fly her body home. Although her extremities were severed the rescuers matched the color of her fingernail polish to that of her toenails. I thought about her getting a manicure and pedicure before her trip. At least all of her came home. Finally, I went to visit Mike at the hospital. Sheila warned me before I entered Mike's room that I was not allowed to tell him that his wife died. How could they possibly hide this from him? What had they been telling Mike for the past four days? Wouldn't it be better that his parents break the news to him? I could not understand their rationale and I felt such anger. Mike was conscious, recognized me and asked, "How's Donna?" I was exhausted and my eyes fairly swollen from tears, I must have looked like heck. My reply was, "Read my face can you tell my mood? Try and get well, I'll expect to see you in Stockton in ten days." I was not in the mood to speak words of comfort.

I did reach Helen Wong by phone and she was insistent that I go to Sacred Falls, call out Donna's name and tell her to "go towards the light." As the last chore before heading home Darcy and I went to the Sacred Falls gated entrance. We couched our visit as curiosity seekers to avoid the press who were still lingering around. We hoped our telepathic message reached Donna. Even though our words were only muttered the intent was there.

Back in Stockton the list of chores grew exponentially: Funeral arrangements set for May 22nd at De Young Mortuary Shoreline Chapel, a PA system and additional chairs ordered for the walkway surrounding the mortuary, and arranged for the reception at the Lincoln Clubhouse. Friends organized the refreshments, Uncle Judge Frank Kim who married Donna and Mike to officiate. I created a pamphlet in lieu of the traditional program and selected the music – *Tears In Heaven* by Eric Clapton, *Wind Beneath My Wings* and *I Remember You* as sung by the late Don Ho. Donna loved that song for it always reminded her of Hawaii. Calls continued, visitors came, and Darcy arrived a few days later bringing many floral arrangements from Hawaii sent by friends and her company. A beautiful *hale lei* rested on top of the casket, flower wreaths and potted azaleas lined the sanctuary and even out to the front door. I was pleasantly surprised that Jim Soares, owner of the Chapel of the Palms, was the first person to sign the memorial book at the De Young Chapel. Back in 1978 Soares came to Donna's aid when Richard's father passed away and we were on vacation. He had great respect then thinking she was so young but acted so mature and his remembrance showed after all these years.

At Donna's burial at Stockton Rural Cemetery, Stockton

On the day of the funeral Mike and his parents arrived about half an hour before the service. He was in a wheelchair and looked quiet and absolutely grief-stricken. We placed him in the front row of the family section between Darcy and me. It was quite noticeable that he had a metal plate on his head with pus leaking out around the edges. About a week later they removed the plate and cleaned the wound further and decided not to replace the covering. Donna's classmates, a cousin, Mike's father, and nephew spoke. Then fraternity brothers of Sigma Phi Epsilon filed up separately and laid a red rose near her casket. My tears swelled further when they closed the casket and locked it with a key, just this act made everything feel so final.

Since grave diggers do not work on weekends we buried Donna at Stockton Rural Cemetery on Monday. She had with her a small makeup bag, a fashion magazine, and coins for use in the afterlife. Her headstone reads:

FORSCH
Donna Kim Chan
June 9, 1960 – May 9, 1999
"*loving, kind and forever beautiful*"

Constructive Grieving

I believe active people do not stop and become inactive, allowing themselves time to grieve; well, maybe, some may. But there are people who look for ways or take up a cause to release their emotions. Darcy, back in Hawaii, hurt terribly and missed her sister with despair. By Memorial Weekend she was in her backyard building eight crosses, painted them white and planted them outside the gate of Sacred Falls, one for each of the victims. Soon pictures of the crosses appeared in the press and strangers dropped off offerings of flowers and leis. The Department of Land and Natural Resources removed the crosses after a month. The state officials closed Sacred Falls indefinitely but began to set up a community advisory task force to decide the fate of the park. Naturalists and environmental organizations wanted to keep the park open. This was a natural thought for those who were not there to witness the devastation. Governor Ben Cayetano quickly denied any state responsibility. He claimed signs were posted as to the danger in the park. The park is still closed today.

Darcy became the key figure in helping family members connect with one another through a website she created. It was dedicated to the victims. As she told the *Honolulu Advertiser*, *"There were a lot of unanswered questions among us,"* she said, *"and in a way we've formed our own support group." There were so many prior accidents at Sacred Falls. Why didn't the State do anything before? I just want to make sure the next tourist who visits here is ensured a safe visit." "Denial, frustration, anger - it's like a huge emotional rollercoaster that sometimes you wish you could get off."* [14]

The next day Phil Preen contacted the Red Cross looking for Mike so he could deliver Donna's message that she loved him. Preen as well as Jason Hill, independently, found Darcy's website and contacted her, each emailing their individual experience. Both men never knew the other's name even to this day but, each spoke of the heroic effort by the other. They knew themselves as severely traumatized. A number of years later Jason Hill was diagnosed with Post Traumatic Stress Syndrome.

Several victims' family members also contacted Darcy and she began seeking legal help for them knowing that the State had already declined any responsibility. She researched the archives and learned of at least five previous rock falls, flash floods, and hiking incidents at the park that resulted in nine other deaths. In 1982 a four-year old died when rocks came tumbling down and hit her head; her stepfather was knocked unconscious and broke his collarbone; in 1995 a Navy man snorkeling at Sacred Falls was found floating face down in the pool. A 1988 internal land department memo required park caretakers to wear hard hats when working near the falls. She turned her evidence over to the law firm of Park, Park and Remillard who agreed to represent a total of 32 victims and families. Four years later a circuit judge found the state negligent in warning visitors of the hazards of this Oahu tourist attraction. Darcy's grieving process constructively benefitted many.

Mike's healing took longer. Although he went to physical therapy, his head injury caused *Grand Mal* seizures. He will take epileptic medication for the rest of his life. The pharmaceutical company promised to keep his job open for four months; by the second month he found himself unemployed. He has difficulty searching for words and he process thoughts slower than the normal person. Because of mounting financial problems Mike lost their beautiful house in Laguna and went to live with his parents for a while. I did see him while he was in therapy to assess his progress. We both compared our dosages of Prozac and counselors.

There were many sympathy cards and they all needed responses as well as the donations in her memory. The monies were all earmarked for the Quan Ying Foundation, my low-income senior housing project. I wrote to each person a personal note rather than just using the note card provided by the mortuary. It took several weeks to finish answering over five hundred plus and it did occupy my time. I mostly internalized my grief but once in a while it surfaced such as the time I learned that Mike and his mother, Sheila, got rid of Donna's things without even contacting Darcy or me. It was inconsiderate and unconscionable. I would have cherished some sentimental items and gifts I gave her. Mike did return the Chinese jewelry I gave Donna in her youth and when she got married. My anger and disappointment did not dissipate until I sought help from Patricia Bettinger, a counselor with innovative therapy. There were times my tears involuntarily rolled down my cheeks or I found myself subconsciously taking gasping breaths and yearning to turn back the clock, wishing all this was not real.

The Unexplained

Is there a connection between death and the supernatural? Some of our Chinese Hawaiian friends remembered being warned as youngsters not to go to Sacred Falls and the word "sacred" must have some type of connotation but they couldn't remember specifics. One Hawaiian interpretation was that the waterfall's pool was a direct route to the underworld where spirits reside. One question in the mind of many was what provoked the boulders to tumble; some thought it might have been earthquakes or some other scientific explanation. However, we heard that one of the visitors that fatal day admitted her young daughter had peed into the pool just before the avalanche. Did this innocent little girl anger the gods?

While Darcy was able to achieve results in her grieving process, I, on the other hand, faced some unanswered thoughts that swirled in my mind, some going back to my own family history and others involving Donna's father side of the family. I have a habit of looking for connections rather than dismissing thoughts as disconnects. For instance, there is in the American Cantonese tradition that pregnant women should not attend funerals; supposedly the spirits may harm the unborn. Decades previous in the mid-1930s Donna's grandfather, Wahso D. Chan, was hit by a car while walking home from work in San Francisco. His wife, Mary (my mother-in-law/Don's mother) was pregnant with her second son, and went to the funeral. She had a right since it was her husband who died. But the deceased's mother (Don's grandmother) cursed Mary out loudly and publicly said that her attendance had put a curse upon the family.

Years later when Don and I decided to marry, his mother (Mary) offered her old wedding ring which I took gladly thinking I would pass it along as a wonderful tradition. Then when Donna and Mike got married Donna used the ring as her wedding band. I divorced Don after ten years of marriage. Donna and Mike's marriage also ended after ten years. Her grandfather died in an accident and so did she. My question – was the ring cursed? I gave the ring back to Don and asked that he not pass it on to other family members. Eventually he drove to Marysville and buried it at his father's grave.

On my mother's side of the family it was curious that three women from three succeeding generations all died at the age of 38. My grandmother lost her second daughter, Taidy, in 1950. In my mother's generation, her sister, Auntie E, lost a daughter, Clarissa in 1997 also at age 38. And now in my generation I lost Donna who died also at the age of 38. Was this a fluke or will it strike the next generation?

Upon Donna's death my beliefs about death changed. I never felt this way when my parents, other relatives or even Ah Pau (grandma) died. Some Chinese believe a person has two souls - one goes to heaven and the other remains on earth in an afterlife. The dead just step over a threshold into an invisible realm but still remain around or close to us. If we pay attention the departed leaves signs that they are nearby. People have told me they talk to their departed and it is perfectly normal. I agree. I associated Donna with jewelry or anything that sparkles such as diamonds or rhinestones. Often times I see a sparkle in the most unusual places, on the carpet, a droplet in the early morning dew or even a quick reflection in a semi-darkened room – I know Donna is nearby.

A shaman friend assured me that Donna found the light and she waited at Sacred Falls until we got there before she left this world. I talk to her often and ask advice or share some funny thoughts. Once I was frustrated when leaving a cruise ship and couldn't find my luggage, I said: "Okay Donna, where are they?" I looked up and there they were five rows away. I have even bargained with her. I promised to change my attitude and work on improving my relationship with Mike and his parents if she will find a good husband for Darcy. It took about two or three years before Darcy met Mike Markley. They married in 2004 at Heron Island, Australia. I was there. It took travelling on three airplane and one helicopter. It was a beautiful wedding on the far side of our world. Yes, Donna came through and I wouldn't trade Mike Markley for the world. I'm now at peace knowing Donna is still with me.

Chapter 17

A Door Closes

The year 1999 was a year of losses great and small – daughter Donna, my position as Assistant Director in the State Department of Aging, my gall bladder, and facing the closure of Heritage West Books. The 1990s were watershed years and my state of California career was coming to an end. I did not look forward to the new century. I was physically, mentally and emotionally drained. I was 58 years old and Richard 80.

Physical and Mind Challenges

People react differently when faced with trauma. I consulted a counselor and took Prozac. Richard, being a typical male, was not interested in seeking help. Yet, Donna's death affected his health which began to deteriorate slowly initially, but pervasively. There was no immediate sign, he did not break down but would tear up and remain quiet. When people internalize deep anger, hate, or even frustration it eats into the body; it affects the heart, creates cancer or even causes death. Richard had more than his fair share of disappointments in life; yet he projected a stoic persona. Even after we married he never was capable of releasing past hurts that weighed heavily on him.

Richard had a number of health issues - a continuing asthma problem, a hip replacement in the late 1980s and, by 1986, his heart began to give him trouble. One weekday, when our friend Dean De Carli dropped by for a quick chat, Richard started to slouch in his easy chair. Normally he sat upright and listened attentively. But on this occasion he just leaned back almost sliding off his chair. After our visitor left I asked if something was bothering him. He said last night's lamb dinner did not set well and he thought he had indigestion.

He was never fond of lamb; was he hinting for me to never cook it again? His discomfort lasted quite a while. Finally, he agreed to go to emergency. X-rays and other tests showed a myocardial infarction, his lower left heart muscle had atrophied. In addition he experienced a number of atrial fibrillation often called "A Fib" where the heart chamber values did not synchronize the pumping of blood through the heart chambers.

For Christmas 1999 Darcy found us a beach house on the North Shore in Hawaii. Although she was busy working we managed lots of visits. In addition, Richard's youngest son, Thor and his grandson, Evan, lived in Honolulu. Their relationship had not been close but it afforded Richard an opportunity to see more of that side of the family. We enjoyed the tropical climate, made new friends, and tried different foods. It was a complete change of pace. For a short period we invested in a condominium in Oahu and spent every three months there but within two years travelling became increasingly difficult.

Richard's posture began to change and he often leaned against a door frame or sought support of a post, a table or some thing stationary when he stood. He did not enjoy walking, claiming his back ached. I thought he might have strained it or perhaps had a sciatica problem. His condition continued to deteriorate and x-rays showed the beginnings of osteoarthritis. I blamed it on the Albuterol asthma inhaler. Rather than a prescribed temporary use Richard became addicted to the medication which, among other side effects, included osteoarthritis.

At the beginning of 2000 other symptoms appeared including Transient Ischemic attacks also known as "TIA" or mini strokes. A prostate test showed he had two tumors in his prostate and the doctor suggested hormone therapy. The first dose, Luprene, did bring the PSA (prostate specific antigen) count down but with the second dose he developed a blood clot in his leg, further damaging his walking ability. Richard's immobility moved rather quickly as he went from a cane, to a walker and, by 2002, Darcy gave him a lightweight wheelchair for Christmas. It was still very heavy and difficult to put into the car. The trunk's well was deep and I had to balance it on my knee before hoisting it high enough to slip it in. By 2004 we bought another car with a flatter trunk.

Together we toughed out Richard's heart problems, sudden TIAs, A Fibs, and dealt with the tumors in the prostate, asthma, scoliosis, hearing loss, and incontinence. Infections became puzzles, what part of the body was it affecting? How serious was it? Serious enough to warrant going to Emergency? Our many trips via ambulance or car took its toll. Often we waited five to six hours in the emergency lobby and the longest wait was a long fourteen hours before the doctor even looked at him and decided he had to be hospitalized. I have learned to hate the emergency facilities at all hospitals. The idea of taking patients on a first-come, first-serve basis rather than prioritizing the type of emergency tells of inadequate administrative procedures. Once during a long wait period, I saw a body bag brought into the emergency area for someone who died while waiting for care.

I developed my own encyclopedia of medical terms and prescriptions. The heart required Coumadin, and dosage depended on weekly to monthly blood tests: Dioxgin to keep his heart rate from running away with an A Fib, Oxycodone for pain and osteoarthritis, Zithromax, an antibiotic, for upper respiratory infection, Bactrim, Levoquin for other infections, Amiodarone for blood clots and to control the A Fib (the side effect of this drug was that the skin will turn green from sun exposure) and Richard did develop a green cast on his skin for a while. We had tanks of oxygen delivered to the house.

After one particular hospitalization he needed Heparin shots to be delivered through the skin of his abdomen. I did not know the first thing about giving injections, but I did what I had to do. Twice a day for ten days I took aim. I was told not to shoot in the same place but to mark the previous aim. By the tenth day my "x" formation on Richard's stomach looked like a running game plan of John Madden, the Oakland Raider's coach. Some of the injection sites had yellow streaks, suggesting the muscle was bruised. These were morning injections after my morning coffee; whereas there were no streaks in the evening as my martinis really helped me relax before I shot him. The spreadsheet of medication and dosages changed almost monthly; they were tacked on the refrigerator and other rooms in the house. When we travelled even for doctors' visits, we armed ourselves with the wheelchair, and a small, portable M-6 oxygen tank, as well as a tote bag for other necessities. The doctors and I formed a team with one goal – to sustain Richard at a comfortable level.

The Diminishing Mind

Aging is a sad process. At the age of 80 Richard's CT scans and MRIs began to show a gray shadow enlarging in the cranial cavity. Could an increase in gray matter numb the mind? We laugh at "senior moments" a momentary lapse which gets passed off as inconsequential. Yet, I saw signs and no matter what, we could not arrest this mental enemy. It was evident his spatial perception no longer existed. Once I brought Richard some tulip bulbs from Amsterdam. He was quite pleased thinking of his German Dutch heritage. The planting instructions called for planting the bulbs down about six inches. I watched in silence when I saw that he had dug a trench one and a half feet deep. Needless to say, those tulip sprouts never saw the light of day. Taking away his driver's license took some negotiation. He thought he could still drive but was convinced otherwise when the agent, with my quiet pleading, suggested that our insurance rate would drop if I became the sole driver and he the navigator. Once in a while he would quietly reach over and rest his hand on the gear shift to get the same pleasure drivers feel with the motions of a motorized vehicle. As a treat I took him to the local Home Depot or Lowes and put him into their motorized wheelchairs; he was in his element speeding down the aisles, backing up or making U-turns in the aisle. I walked slowly behind confident that he wouldn't run into any merchandise. He felt pleased that he still retained some driving skills.

Richard had always been an avid reader. He was particularly fond of military history and ordinance magazines. Our collections of both were extensive. Slowly he abandoned the books and just flipped through the magazines. Then he would pick up the same magazine several times and worried that we were getting charged with repeated copies of the same magazine. In time he no longer read but just looked at the pictures and turned to spending time with the Sunday comics. This same abandonment of television shows also occurred. He loved detective movies and serials but later found it difficult to relate to the plot line and cast of characters. Eventually, he resorted to holding the remote control like a six shooter clicking through the channels.

Alzheimer's disease seems to be the most familiar among the various types of dementia. Richard did not have Alzheimer's but did exhibit other forms of dementia. It was hard to judge if his synapses were connecting. His executive skills such as abstract thinking or reasoning no longer existed; however, he still could do simple things such as opening the door with a key. Richard recognized people or if he did not, he never let on and was gracious in conversation. Like others with dementia his talking lessened over time; yet, his mannerisms continued to be gentlemanly.

Pairing Loving and Caring

The words, I love you, are almost meaningless unless one becomes committed to give one's all. No chore is base or disgusting if it helps a loved one. I felt a real emotional sadness to see Richard being robbed of his body and mind. I was willing to do anything and everything, fearing of worsening conditions and dreading the thought of losing him. Much like when I was a young mother, I stayed alert to all his needs and slept ever so lightly especially in the middle of the night when I heard him moving about. Did he need me, would he fall out of bed or, worse yet, was he having a medical issue? I was basically alone caring for Richard. Lifting him when he fell became difficult as was bathing and caring for bodily functions.

By late 2003 I decided to seek part-time help; just couple hours a day, three days a week. Even then I needed to be around during his waking hours. He feared that when there were new people in the house they would rob us. He did not like strangers' cooking and got upset if the caregiver did things that he thought might displease me. Richard was quite a watchdog even though he was dependant.

Medical supplies, ointments, adult diapers, pads, hospital bed, equipment and, of course, the caregivers' pay took a financial toll. I wanted to be sure that he still had enough of a sound mind to realize we needed to sell his gun collection and some of our stocks to make ends meet. These were investments and it was the appropriate time to cash them in. He understood but, I remembered him saying in frustration, "Why am I like this? What is wrong with me?" At those times it was gut wrenching.

I filed for social security at age 62, taking the early payout not only to help with our retirement income but also to insure that Richard gets hospice care through Medicare. Since he never paid into social security while working at Caltrans, his Medicare services came through my benefits. Even though I received a lesser amount than I would have at age 65, it was a personal choice, one of many.

Ever Vigilant

After a few more falls and rehabilitation therapy in various assisted living facilities, his doctor convinced me that Richard needed more care. I suspected that the doctor was also thinking of my health. The local facilities were a mixed bag; some adequate but not all. Our first experience at assisted living was at Hampton Rehabilitation near St. Joseph's Hospital. He was sent there for rehab after a fall. The day he was admitted his roommate, while sitting in a motorized wheelchair, charged at him and hit Richard's head so hard it broke his left hearing aid. Richard also suffered cuts and bruises on his legs from the wheelchair. Poor Richard was so scared he trembled for hours and did not want me to leave him alone. He had an immediate room change but, interestingly, there was no apology. Staff did not admit to any wrong doing and feared such an admission might lead to a lawsuit. I was furious. I needed to make sure this type of room assignment would never happen to others, particularly when confronted by a patient with a propensity for violence. I am not the type to sue over negligence but I guaranteed they would not hear the last of it. A carefully documented packet complete with photos and a narrative went to the State Licensing Department, the Chief of Staff at Kaiser Hospital where we had our medical plan, and to my State Assemblyman. I noted the incident and other deficiencies in the facilities, mostly unsanitary conditions. I heard from all three. Both Kaiser and the Licensing Department sent their own investigative teams. As a result, months later, the facility was cited and fined for several infractions. Kaiser indicated that they would think twice before sending other patients there.

Valley Gardens on Knickerbocker Street waxed and waned in my judgment. One day while Richard was there, an elderly lady friend went to visit him. When she left he escorted her to the parking lot to make sure that she got into her car safely. However, the staff immediately panicked and thought he was leaving the premises. They put a monitor on him in case he should walk out the front door again. As much as I tried to explain that it was his courteous habit to walk visitors to their car, the staff wouldn't have any of it. Also in this same facility there was a house cat, a resident pet that roamed throughout. One day it scratched at the exit door so Richard helped open the door to let the cat out; the alarms blared and staff came running thinking Richard was taking off again. Not surprisingly, Richard's stay at Valley Garden was short lived.

In 2005 Richard became a resident of Ambassador Gardens on Swain Road. The majority of the nursing staff was Filipinas and these workers have a reputation for being excellent caregivers. The facility was also only a mile from our home making visitation easy. No nursing home is perfect, but the main criteria were staffing, cleanliness and maintenance, decent food, and attention to the patients. Richard had a rather large private room with bath, plenty of storage space, his own television, easy chair, and enough room for visitors.

Since I visited often I saw the dynamics among the residents. There was an elderly lady who used to make me smile, her name was Roxie. She developed a relationship with a Mexican man, also a patient, and they decided they were going to get married or so went the local gossip. Once in a while they had lovers' spats. On one of those occasions, Roxie, whose room was next to Richard's, dragged her comforter to Richard's doorway and asked if she could climb into his bed. He was sitting in his easy chair looking at the television. He said, "Okay, but you better leave before Sylvia comes." And he continued to watch his program not the least interested in Roxie. The staff had a difficult time removing Roxie for she swore Richard had given his permission. It was rather late at night but the staff called to explain the situation so I drove there and cheerfully announced when I went to the room, "I'm here."

Richard actually had the best care at Ambassador. The staff liked him and he received lots of personal attention. He never lost that gentleness and good manners. During one of my daily visits, while cutting his nails, as a matter of conversation, I asked, "Richard, when you are on the other side, would you watch out for me?" I think he knew what I meant and he said without hesitation, "Of course."

Richard enjoying a visit with his youngest son, Thor

A Door Closed

I was at a friend's house for dinner and then drove her mother home. As I entered the house the answering machine showed multiple messages. It was St. Joseph's Hospital asking that I call immediately. The last message said that Richard had passed away. What a shock. I had been at Ambassador for the better part of the day and before I left I wheeled him into the dining room for dinner. We had spent most of the afternoon looking at a Cracker Barrel map listing all their locations on the East Coast. He was so interested; one could tell his eyes brightened when trying to recollect some of the places he had visited. Staff indicated they thought he fell asleep at the dinner table. Quickly paramedics came but it was too late.

By the time I was allowed to see him it was close to midnight. Richard was covered with a white sheet but not his head and his eyes were wide open. The nurse said they tried to close his eyes but could not. I touched his hair and his skin felt very soft, then I slowly lifted my hands to his eyes and gently closed them all the while thinking, it's time to sleep, Richard. And, I thanked him. Later, the same nurse told me sometimes the person waits and assured me Richard was waiting for me to do this final act. I believed him. It was the most tender feeling I've ever experience. The date was May 6, 2006 and Richard had reached the age of 86.

We had Richard's funeral at the Chapel of the Palms in Stockton with our old friend Jim Soares taking care of the details. Richard used to talk lovingly of his days when he worked on a Arizona-Mexico ranch. Instead of flowers we graced the casket with two serapes, his 1936 boots, cowboy belt and hat.

For a proper send off Darcy placed three small bottles in his hand - one scotch and two gins. We included a copy of SAMFOW for him to read in the afterlife and pictures of his boys and our family. An old friend, Reverend Larry Thomas officiated. I chose songs that reflected his life: *Country Road* sang by John Denver, a throwback to his early West Virginia-Tennessee childhood; Frank Sinatra's *I Did It My Way*, and Roy Roger's *Happy Trails to You.*

The chapel was full and Richard would have been happy as his three boys came for the farewell, Rich Jr., the oldest, from Portland; Lance from Mallorca, Spain and Thor from Hawaii.

I, too, was happy and grateful knowing that I had shared thirty-six years with this wonderful man.

Epilogue

Things do change with time. In 2006, a door closed in my life. As the old saying continues – "and another opened." I had a chance meeting with Wellman Chin at the fiftieth reunion of Francisco Junior High. I earlier described him as the quiet but "pachuco-looking dude" in our old 114 homeroom. Fifty-two years had passed without any contact between us; in reality, there never was any contact while we were in school. We found we had similar life experiences and interests although he lived his, for the most part, in the Los Angeles Area, and I in the Central Valley. It was delightfully refreshing to hear and speak Chinglish (a mixture of Cantonese and English), and share the memories of the 50s and 60s pop lyrics. A bigger bonus was that Wellman cooks Chinese food - the old comfort soul food of salted-fish steamed with pork, lotus root soup, and black bean spareribs.

Wellman moved to Stockton in 2007. Our wedding, in 2009, was local and simple. Darcy served as my matron of honor and cousin Frank Kim performed the service.

There is something to be said about marriage at this time in my life – patience, tolerance, and a feeling of contentment. I am amazed at the changes occurring in Wellman – he has taken on some of Richard's traits. For instance he saves used or non-functioning parts hoping that one day he could re-use that one particular bolt or screw. Who knows - a friend might find the need for an old dot matrix printer. It is almost déjà vu, our garage is beginning to be filled with questionable items. And like Richard, Wellman's answer to unusual purchases is: "It was on sale."

I know I am blessed and I am grateful. How many men would accompany their wives to the cemetery to lay flowers on a former husband's grave? He does. We have a togetherness routine – he fills the canisters with water as I cut and arrange the flowers. Both Richard and Donna must be watching over us.

I am not as active as before. It must be one of the side effects of aging. My body is slow and it frustrates my brain. Senior moments are embarrassing when places and old friends' names don't roll off my tongue as quickly. I am no longer interested in the sales at Macy's or Target; I don't need any more new sheets, towels, toaster, electrical appliances, or even new cars. My "stuff" should last my lifetime (I hope). I now am beginning to wonder where will I be ten years from now – in this house, in an assisted living facility or will I be dead?

Wellman and I enjoy simple pleasures – cruising, watching Korean dramas on the television, visiting with old friends, or sharing quiet time. Once in a while I have things on my plate and I get a little active, but they are nothing I can't handle.

My parents lived a life of luxury and hobnobbed with world leaders; but, they missed milestones in their children and grandchildren's lives. I am happy for my siblings. Eldest sister Patricia and hubby, Larry, are well into 55-plus years of marriage and juggling the comings and goings of 14 grandchildren who frequent their San Francisco home. Sister Gloria and Peter also have an active household in Palo Alto with three married daughters and five grandchildren. I, on the other hand, have grand-dogs and grand-cats. Brother Phil and wife Chen travel extensively because of his work. While their lives are rather frantic I believe they will settle down one day.

L to R: Philip, Sylvia, Gloria, Auntie E, Uncle Tim and Patricia
At the dedication of the Thomas Foon Chew Way, San Jose

My daughter Darcy and her husband, Mike, are happy. They have no desire to get off the island of Oahu.

Darcy and Mike Markley

How do I assess my life? Sure, I underwent some trauma in my early life; but, I got over it. Experiencing those moments of physical pain, feelings of loss, and even periods of loneliness actually made me a more sympathetic person. I am as passionate about America as when I first arrived in 1951. I appreciate Stockton. I was able to plant roots that eluded me in my younger years and it was the perfect place to raise my children. I am grateful for many people who have touched my life and were there for me. We have shared laughter, we've shared tears. We've connected, we've stayed in touch and all the while I believed in the philosophy of never burning bridges.

My choices in life made me the person I am. I have no regret.

Enjoyment in our senior years – 2012

Appendices

ENDNOTES

Chapter 1

[1] Sun, Patrick Pichi, *Recollections of a Floating Life*, Phoenix Press, Quezon City, Philippines, 1972.

Chapter 4

[2] In the 1980s Ruth Chew, Jimmy Chew's widow brought me to meet Mr. Ito. He was living in the Curtis Park area of Sacramento. He was in his 90s.

[3] At the time of his death, Tom Foon Chew's estate was estimated at $150,000 in 1931. Today's value according to GDP is $12,200,000.00.

Chapter 5

[4] A true heroine, American Airlines flight attendant Betty Ong was working the Boston to Los Angeles flight on September 11, 2000. She was the first to alert officials of terrorists' attack. The plane hit the North Tower of the World Trade Center. Ong was born and raised in San Francisco. The renovated Recreation Center was dedicated in her name on July 14, 2012.

Chapter 14

The many Stockton Record citations are clumped together based on subject matter:

[5] *Quality of Life* (5/15/1990, 6/28/1990, and 7/2/1990);

[6] *SCUM/SMAC activities* (10/3/1991, 12/12/1991, and 1/31/1992);

[7] *Gold Rush* (10/24/1990 and 10/31/1990);

[8] *Council Survey* (3/4/1991 and 6/23/1991);

[9] Darrah, Joan, *GETTING POLITICAL: Stories of a Woman Mayor*, Quill Driver Books, 2003. (Pages52,126, 129,131-134).

Chapter 16

[11] *Honolulu Advertiser* (5/4/2009 and 4/5/2009)

[12] Email from Jason Hill to Darcelle Chan (11/11/1999)

[13] *Star Bulletin* (5/17/1999)

[14] *Honolulu Advertiser* (5/9/2000)

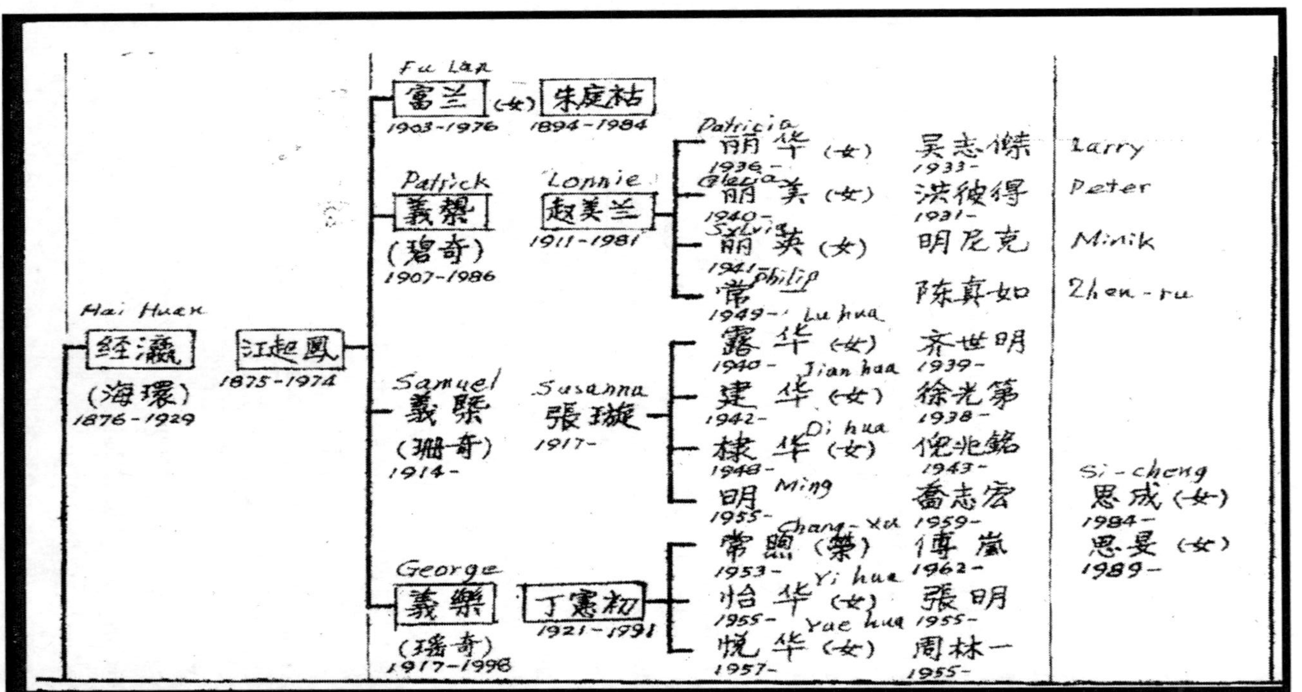

Chapter 2 - Uncle Sam Sun handdrew this Sun Family Tree listing three generations including our Chinese names

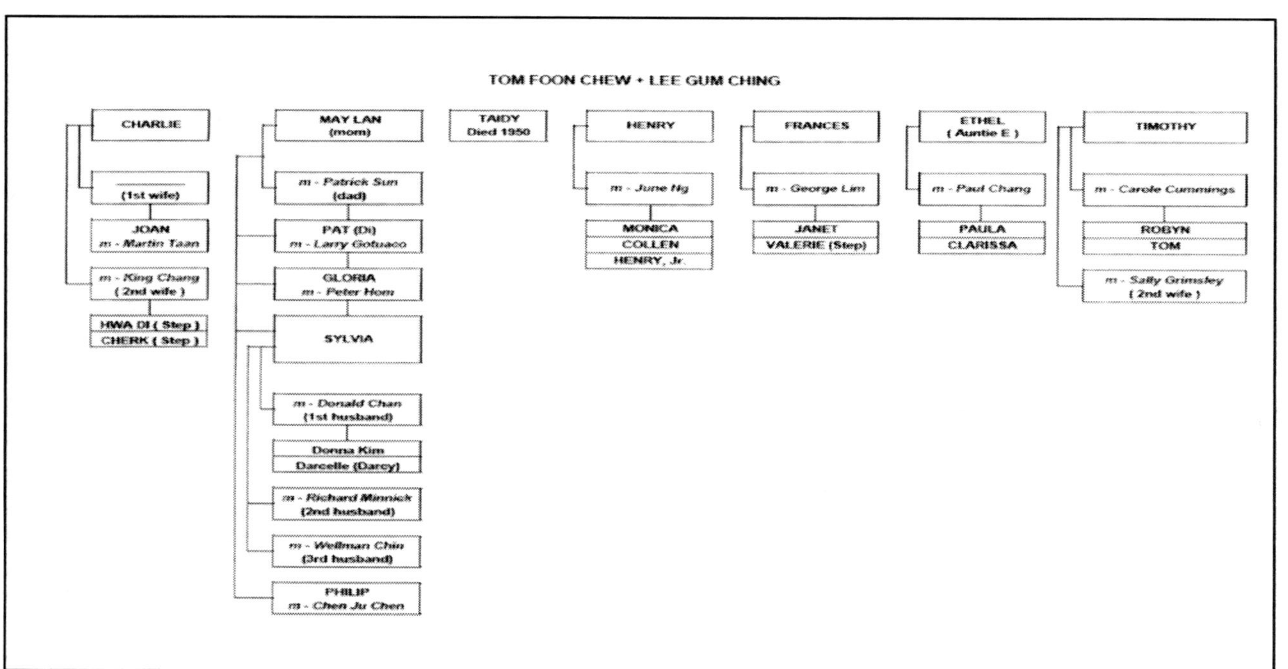

Chapter 4 - Tom Foon Chew family tree showing three generations created by Wellman Chin

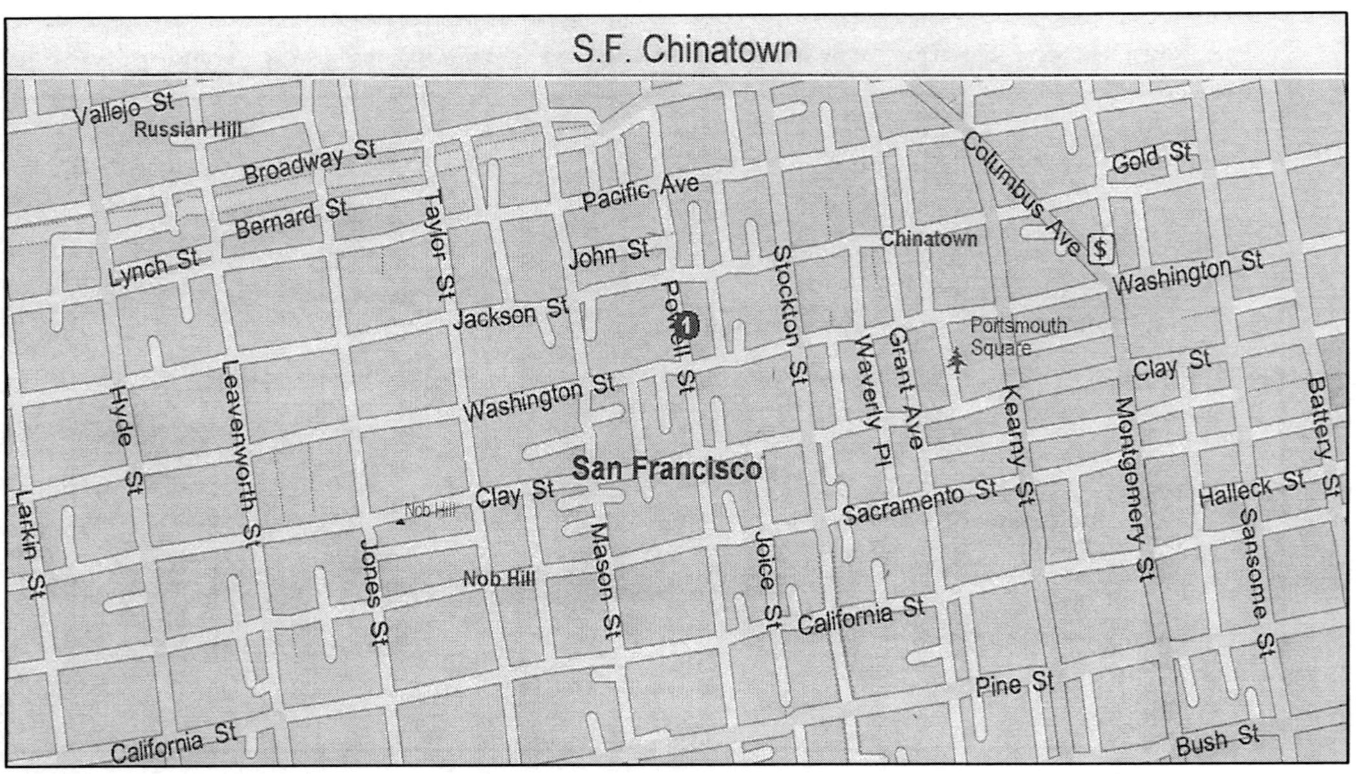

Chapter 5 - Grandma Chew's Building [1] at 1122 Powell Street between Washington and Jackson Street, S.F.

Court orders hotel owners to pay

LETTERS

Stop politicking on drugs, crime

MAC attack works

INSIDE: Bus drivers for food—B-2

The Stockton Record

METRO

Wilson picks Sylvia Minnick to fill state recreation post

City Hall gets action

Stockton councilwoman accuses Darrah of racism

Stockton Voters Retain Asian Councilmember

Still playing those games in City Hall

City Council owes public the full story

Cleaning up

Harvey felt like a victim

Council demanded

Look at all the positive people, man

one bright light

Stockton Record

LOCAL

Minnick pushes world-class

Chapter 14 - Assorted news clippings from the S*tockton Record*

NOTES

CPSIA information can be obtained at www.ICGtesting.com
Printed in the USA
LVOW07s2141100615

442027LV00011B/243/P

9 780615 827483